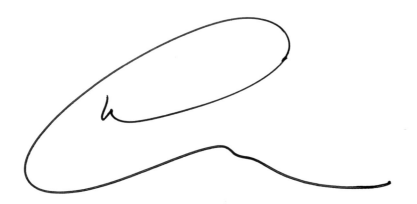

**DANIEL HUMM &
WILL GUIDARA**

THE NOMAD
COOKBOOK

Photography by Francesco Tonelli

Desserts by Mark Welker

TEN SPEED PRESS
Berkeley

5-1   85 Bros.
Ribes   floridum
Wild black Currant.
May.   Moist

CONTENTS

WELCOME, dear reader, to The NoMad, or rather to its cookbook.

In the following pages we will welcome you as fully as we possibly can into our little world. We are going to tell you about our food, our cocktails, the wonderful people on our team, and some of the bumps in the road we encountered as we opened our hotel on the corner of Twenty-Eighth and Broadway.

It all started in early 2011, when Daniel and I were at DBGB debating whether or not we would order a second burger, and out of nowhere he said: "I think it should be the Rolling Stones."

Sorry, I need to back up a bit.

———

This all *really* started the first time we heard that Eleven Madison Park needed "a little more Miles Davis." If you've read anything about our restaurants, you've probably heard this story before, but it's important to tell it here again as it has had everything to do with everything that's happened since.

A few years earlier, in 2006, we were taking our first steps to evolve Eleven Madison Park (EMP) into the fine dining restaurant it is today. The "Miles" line came in our first review, during a very formative time—we were trying to find exactly what our new identity would be, craving language to help articulate the direction which we wanted to go. With this one line, a reviewer telling us she wished we had a little more Miles—we were given a gift.

In the months that followed, we researched Miles obsessively and drafted a list of eleven words that were most commonly used to describe him, among them "fresh," "cool," "collaborative," and "endless reinvention." These became our mission statement, and guided us as we made the hundreds of changes over the course of our restaurant's continuing evolution.

See, some of our favorite restaurants are those that, once opened, are fully realized and will live forever without change. But EMP is not like that. It's a project that we will never be done with, a concept that is always in motion. Still, in 2010, after four years of *very* focused attention, we realized it was time for us to begin the process of building our second restaurant.

The prospect of another restaurant is so exciting, but scary as hell. Your second act can determine if you're the next Rolling Stones or the next Vanilla Ice. We knew we wanted the new place to be more casual than EMP—its louder and looser sibling—but that was really all.

So we started looking for a space, figuring where we decided to build it would help identify what it was going to be. We looked all over the island of Manhattan, from Battery Park City to the Upper East Side. But nothing felt right, and everywhere we went, EMP felt so far away. We knew that we needed to maintain a significant presence at EMP, so our next restaurant needed to be close enough to allow for that.

The last project we looked at before we discovered The NoMad was another hotel on Madison Avenue, and of everything we'd seen or considered, it was the one we were most excited about. We'd met with the ownership, we'd started to design the space, and we'd even spent quite a bit of time with a kitchen designer figuring out how we could tweak the existing kitchen to fulfill Daniel's needs as a chef. But as it we came closer and closer to finalizing the deal, we realized that something just didn't feel right—even today I can't articulate what it was. So at the eleventh hour we walked away. It was a hard decision, though we felt confident it was the right one. Still, frustrating to be back at the drawing board.

Thankfully, that frustration was short-lived. The next day, the kitchen designer we had been working with let us know that there was a project in the works practically around the corner from EMP. He asked if we would like to schedule a meeting with the owners to check it out.

So, a week and a half later, Daniel and I did something we had never done before: we walked out of EMP and we headed north. We walked across Madison Square Park, took a left on Twenty-Sixth Street and a right on Broadway, and walked to the corner of Twenty-Eighth Street.

———

New York City is an amazing place; within one block or two, your surroundings can completely change. Here we were, after a five-minute stroll from where we had spent nearly every waking hour of our lives for the past few years, and we were someplace we had never been.

Here, there were no more fountains and art installations and majestic trees. The mothers and their strollers were gone, as were the bankers on benches eating Shake Shack. The world had shifted to hawkers selling fake designer bags and imposter perfumes, endless rows of wig shops, and the ever-present smell of weed (something that continues to be a distraction every day as we walk back and forth between the two restaurants).

Daniel looked at me, confused, and asked, "Will, what are we doing here?" I wasn't so sure myself. Already we were both regretting having scheduled the meeting, thinking our next few hours would be a waste of time.

Then we looked up.

They say you only become a real New Yorker once you stop looking up, and I can say with confidence that we both, a long time ago, became hardened New Yorkers. So, I'm not sure why we broke character, but once we did, it was as if the neighborhood had transitioned from black and white into color.

We could see beyond the gated storefronts and gum-littered sidewalks to the grand neighborhood this had once been. Our pessimism dissolved, and we walked into the building that would become The NoMad Hotel to meet with the guy who would be our partner in the venture, Andrew Zobler.

Andrew was behind the Ace Hotel a block north of here, and he is definitely the person we credit with having had the vision to realize what this bizarre little tangle of streets north of Madison Square Park could become. We made our way through the debris-strewn construction site of what would one day be the dining room, and met Andrew standing where table 53 would one day be.

We stood together for hours, intensely discussing everything from the building and the history of the neighborhood to our collective ideas about what we wanted to build here. Literally thousands of details needed to be worked on, but by the time we parted ways, a shared vision had come into focus. This wasn't about creating something new, but about reinventing something that once was. At EMP, the goal had been to create the four-star restaurant for the next generation—*our* generation. At The NoMad, we'd try to do the same—this time, for the grand hotel.

————

You see, back in the day, the grand hotels were the center of all things social in New York City. People would flock to The Waldorf, The Plaza, The Palace, or The Carlyle when they sought a place to sleep, to dine, to drink, to commiserate. They were places where native New Yorkers and travelers alike would come to form community. When you were at The

Waldorf Astoria, it didn't matter if you were lounging about enjoying a feast or a cognac—or if you were even conscious—you were doing it at The Waldorf.

But at some point, it stopped being cool to hang out at hotels. Even restaurants in hotels fought fiercely for their brand independence, coming up with their own names and often adding separate entrances. New York City's great halls of community faded from local popularity, becoming places for tourists to visit. We wanted The NoMad to change that—to be beautiful, rich, and luxurious, but fun, cool, and accessible. We wanted it to be a place where the people who greet you at the front door and check you into your room are the same as those who take your order at lunch, or serve you a cocktail at 1 a.m.

With that as the goal, it felt like there was no better neighborhood in which to do it than here, arguably the center of Manhattan. Ours is truly a city that is constantly changing, sometimes for better and sometimes for worse, and this neighborhood had definitely fallen on hard times. The idea that we could have an opportunity to play a role in reviving it was exhilarating.

These streets were once home to Tin Pan Alley, the original "Broadway" theater district, and to Jerry Thomas's bar. New York's elite once strolled its streets. But the city grew and people's attention turned elsewhere, as it tends to, and the beautiful Beaux Arts buildings were left to wither. Gorgeous building lobbies were cut up into stalls and populated by vendors of cheap goods; beautiful hotels were degraded into boarding houses. It, sadly, devolved from a neighborhood people dreamed of being part of to one they crossed at night quickly and with trepidation. It was time for its renaissance.

Both of these lofty ideas—reinventing the grand hotel and playing a role in rebuilding a neighborhood—were wonderful, but they were chiefly about looking back into the past. As our second restaurant, this new venture needed a unique voice, its own point of view; it couldn't be derivative of what we had already done. Like EMP years earlier, it needed language—an identity, a voice—to help guide it. It needed its muse.

————

So, yes, back to that second burger at DBGB, and Daniel's suggestion that we should look to the Rolling Stones. I laughed at first because the Stones are Daniel's favorite band, so it seemed like a pretty lazy suggestion. But he seemed convicted in it. Apparently he had been reading a lot about them recently and encouraged me to do the same. While I have always loved their music, reading about them taught me to understand and appreciate them on a whole different level.

When the Stones were really young, living in the UK, just establishing themselves as musicians, they bought every blues album that came out of the Southern United States. They studied that music exhaustively, learning every song note for note. They immersed themselves in American blues and R&B, and then they imbued it with their own style, creating their unique approach to rock-and-roll.

In that sense, they were as deliberate and focused as any organization we had ever learned about. But they were also the crazy, out-of-control, drug-addled madmen we've all heard the stories about. It was in their ability to find and keep a balance between these two extremes that allowed them to change music as we know it. Nothing they did was unintentional. Everything was well conceived, carefully planned, and perfectly executed.

Of course it was—innovation like that doesn't happen by accident.

And so we did what we had done at EMP years before and put together a list of eleven words: Loose, Alive, Universal, Enduring, Deliberate, Glamorous, Original, Genuine, Eclectic, Thoughtful, and Satisfaction. It was inspiring to us—the idea that something could be vibrantly energetic and chaotic while also being purposeful and refined. It was exactly what we wanted for The NoMad. EMP was attempting to be fine dining that was less stuffy. The NoMad would be a casual restaurant that was more composed. We envisioned a room with trappings as luxurious as any, where a guest, whether dressed in a designer suit or a pair of jeans, could peruse an extensive wine list and thoughtfully conceived menu and experience refined service in an unpretentious environment.

We pictured a restaurant where you could have a three-hour meal or a few too many cocktails and some tasty snacks; a place where you could eat fried chicken and drink champagne or feast on foie gras and savor Sauternes. All this while listening to the Rolling Stones and remembering that the whole point of this dining out thing is to connect with other human beings around a table, sharing good food, good drink, and good conversation.

———

Any grand project needs a grand designer, and ours was the famed Parisian, Jacques Garcia. I felt so cool when I called my father and told him, "Dad, I'm going to Paris to work on the design of our new hotel." Meeting Jacques quickly reminded me that I was indeed *not* cool. At one point, we were discussing the back bar—grand and tall, awash in mahogany. There was something strange in the plans: five wooden elephants, each six feet tall, among the bottles of wine and booze. The pragmatist in me recognized the elephants as being completely nonfunctional. Not to mention that they were utterly ridiculous.

"I love the design," I said, "but let's get rid of all of the elephants." Jacques stared at me, his expression very clearly saying, "You stupid American. *Je suis Jacques Garcia.*" But, being a classy sort of guy, he simply said, "The elephants will stay." Three hours of elephant-focused debate ensued and, with both parties exhausted, we were able to settle on two elephants only. It was a good thing Jacques didn't fully relent, because he was seeing what we couldn't. Those giant wooden elephants have become a prominent feature of the hotel, and that bar is now lovingly referred to as "the Elephant Bar."

———

Once the design was complete, it was time to put our team together—arguably the most challenging part of the entire opening process.

In our company, Daniel and I look at welcoming someone onto our team like welcoming them into our family. At EMP, we would agonize over each hire, observing candidates for days before deciding one way or the other. In opening The NoMad, we would have no such luxury: we needed to hire 150 people, most of whom we had never met; train them as best we could; and put them in a position to represent us to the world—all this at a time when the dining public would be watching our every move more than ever. It was intense, to say the least. We made a few mistakes, some of which had us scrambling weeks before our opening. But we made many more good choices, and through luck or fate, some of the best people in the industry chose to join our team. It also helped quite a bit that some of our key people who had already spent years working alongside us at EMP came north to help in the endeavor.

Some grand ideas worked out beautifully, such as the last-minute addition of a giant hearth oven on the ground floor: the weight of which required us to reinforce the entire building's foundation, but without it our now-famous roast chicken would be impossible. Others were less successful: our idea for a family-style tasting menu that featured a two-compartment lazy Susan that housed a hidden course, and cured meats served tableside as if from the delicatessen. We served this menu until we realized that serving a tasting menu alongside our à la carte menu showed both a lack of confidence and an inability to cut the cord from EMP.

In the world of beverage, there were highs and lows as well. Our good friend Garrett Oliver, brewmaster of Brooklyn Brewery, crafted a beer, "Le Poulet," to accompany our roast chicken. It was, in a word, a triumph—together they taste unbelievable. But the specially designed carts that we had built for our "modern take on luxury bottle service" in The Library were a complete and utter flop. To this day, we still believe there could be something cool there, but it may be the case that Leo, Daniel, and I are the only ones who do.

You see, by virtue of being in this business, you have decided that your goal in life is to make people happy, but you've accepted the fact that those same people will be forever judging your work.

Building something like this from the ground up—a first for most of us on the opening team—proved to be an immensely emotional experience. This place was a reflection of all of us. We were putting everything we had into it, hoping that on the first day, the people who walked through our doors would connect with it in some small way.

One night, two months after our opening, our general manager, Jeffrey, and I were standing together in the dining room, comparing notes on the evening's service. Suddenly, a feeling of satisfaction and pride washed over me. So many of the things we had imagined, planned, and dreamed were materializing around us.

Surveying the room, I saw we *were* in the grand hotel that we had envisioned. The neighborhood *was* changing around us, and quickly. And here we were, standing inside this place that, in some way, helped bring about the change.

Uptown and downtown were colliding here, as we had hoped they would. The cool kids from downtown and Brooklyn were sitting next to the Upper East Siders and the bankers. Famous chefs guzzled cocktails and movie stars grazed salads. Gastronomes constructed multi-course dinners while jet-setters had a snack and a glass of wine.

Incredibly, The NoMad had come to be what we had discussed that afternoon in the debris-strewn construction site.

———

It's a few years later as I sit here writing these last lines. Dinner service is in full swing downstairs. And I'm happy to report that a great majority of the team that was here on that opening day is still here, albeit a little older and a little wiser. Funny how, as I write this, and as the team works on getting this cookbook in order, we find ourselves feeling all the same things we did on that first day we opened our doors to the world. We're proud. We're nervous. Mostly, as always, we're excited to share this with you.

We hope you enjoy.

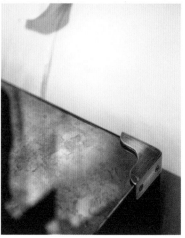

NAMING A NEIGHBORHOOD

by Andrew Zobler

I'm not sure when I first realized that there was something remarkable about this neighborhood. I'd been here plenty of times, but it was always somewhere I walked through on my way to different, more beautiful parts of the city. I always thought of it as the place with the dilapidated buildings, the unusual concentration of wholesale shops, and the graffiti covered scaffolding.

But somewhere along the line, something happened as I was passing through its streets. I guess you could say that I started to fall in love. Perhaps it was its proximity to my favorite park in the city. Or perhaps it was the fact that it was so rough around the edges; that opportunity, that chance to help turn it around, caught my attention and compelled me to go all in on the neighborhood that is now widely known as NoMad.

It all started when my intensely talented partners and I developed and opened the Ace Hotel on Twenty-Ninth Street off Broadway. With its gorgeous structure and distinctive atmosphere, the city welcomed the Ace with open arms. But from the moment the massive lobby began welcoming its thousands of visitors, I could not help but to begin dreaming of another hotel project: one that would bring a whimsical yet luxurious tip of the hat to another era of this long-forgotten stretch of Broadway.

I had begun to notice 1170 Broadway—every detail of it, including its cupola, undeniably a crown jewel of the neighborhood. The whole structure stood out from its surroundings—its potential for elegance and refinement shone so brightly in my eyes. Could we bring it to life? It was one thing to get hipsters to walk down these questionable streets to hang at the Ace. It was another thing entirely to expect the beau monde to make the same trip. But we knew we had to try. We had created an outpost in the neighborhood; the creation of a second, more elegant hotel would solidify the birth of a new district.

And so it did. When word got out about the new hotel, the *New York Times* ran a story attempting to name the district SoMa, for South of Macys. But that name—tying us to a retail store rather than to the whole of this wonderful neighborhood and the beautiful park to the south—did not do our aspirations justice. So NoMad was born: North of Madison Square Park.

I wanted this hotel to be in the great European tradition, and among other things that meant dining was to be front and center. So it was essential that I find the perfect restaurant partners. I talked to many talented people, but nothing felt right. It was frustrating and exhausting—until the day I first met with Daniel and Will, this fiercely gifted young duo, full of ideas, inspiring at every turn, and with an intense magnetism. There was no doubt we had hit the mark—it was an instant understanding, as if we were brothers reuniting. We spent hours talking about culture and family, and about the experience we wanted for our future guests. We wanted uptown luxury with a downtown sensibility. We wanted permanent and not "of the moment." We wanted old-school service with an edge. We wanted romance.

I will forever feel grateful for the two years I got to spend building this hotel with Daniel and Will. And watching what they have created in the kitchens and dining rooms of The NoMad has been nothing short of extraordinary. Each time I sit down in one of the great dining rooms and prepare myself for another memorable meal served by a phenomenal team, I realize anew how special this place is and how blessed I am for this one-of-a-kind partnership. I can't wait to see where it goes from here.

A DAY
IN OUR
LIFE

by Jeffrey Tascarella

JUNE

One week before I was to be married, Will Guidara asked me if I'd like to go for a walk.

We would not be dodging the roller-bladers and horse-drawn carriages in Central Park. There was to be no leisurely, leafy, townhouse-coveting stroll through the West Village. Navigating the human traffic jam that was the pedestrian walkway of the Brooklyn Bridge was not in our plans. Instead, Will picked a very random place to go on a golden-sunny Saturday—a neighborhood that didn't really have a name.

At the time, I was running my own restaurant in Midtown. Business was decent, and I was wearing jeans to work and playing Flaming Lips in the dining room. After years of opening and operating restaurants in New York, Will and I had become friends through the community with which we surrounded ourselves. We spent the occasional weekend afternoon over a few pints, sharing and dreaming. I told stories of renegade busboys and irate guests, while Will shared tales of Relais & Chateaux ceremonies and Christmas at the Boulud household. I'd watched the team at Eleven Madison Park riding rocket ships to something beyond simply "a place to get dinner." I was proud of them and felt honored to call them friends—and even allies—in the craziness that is the New York City restaurant biz.

I was, admittedly, a bit envious of EMP. There was the custom china, the airplane hangar they used for a wine cellar, and the stately custom-made gueridons on which they carved and plated and frothed and foamed tableside. They had won nearly everything a restaurant can win—their James Beard medals alone were enough to sink a man to the bottom of the ocean.

All that was great, but there was something even more extraordinary about the place: at EMP, they could—somehow—simultaneously shock, inspire, and delight. They pushed the envelope in both cuisine and service, but they could make you laugh. The food was avant-garde, yes, but it was always delicious. Everything was meticulous and everything was perfect, but it was always *fun*.

From afar, it all seemed incredible, but I was the general manager at my restaurant and Will was the general manager at his, and that was that.

We continued walking down the street darting between leaky piles of sun-warmed garbage and those selling impostor fragrances. On a hot day in New York City, neighborhoods have their signature smells—Times Square has the charming aroma of burnt pretzels, and Wall Street is tempered by blasts of salty sea air. But here? Nothing postcard-worthy.

Will took a phone call: it was Daniel Humm, the tall, jovial chef who had been responsible for introducing me to carrot marshmallows and lavender ducks and many, many other delights. Daniel was coming to meet us, making his way through the park.

"So—what are we doing?" I asked. "Are we going to Koreatown?" It was a few blocks north.

"Nah, too early for kimchi," Will said.

The Empire State Building loomed above us, as it does.

"What do you think of this neighborhood?" Will asked.

"Here?" I asked. "I went to Macy's once, a long time ago. I'm still a bit traumatized from the experience."

"Think about it though," he said. "We're pretty much dead-center in the greatest city in the world. Madison Square Park is a few blocks downtown. Midtown, Gramercy, Chelsea: a few blocks that way, that way, and that way," he said, turning and pointing down desolate streets.

"Now, forget where we are standing, and look up at these buildings."

We did look up, and he was right: the buildings were gorgeous, almost Parisian. Soaring high above the discount stores and barren metal gates at street level were seemingly ancient sculptures of gargoyles and gods perched above beautiful arched windows; forgotten balustrades worthy of palaces; and columns that begged for a coat of ivy.

Daniel was on the corner; he waved excitedly to us as we crossed the street to meet him.

"Hey Jeff, what do you think?" he asked.

"What's up, Chef? Think of what?"

Will pointed across the street at a building with a decorative rounded bay facing onto Broadway. It rose twelve or thirteen stories, and perched on its roof was a bronze dome that looked more Florence than New York.

"What if, right here, we took the idea of the grand New York hotel and built a new one, from scratch?" he said. "A place where people could come to stay in a beautiful room, to have an amazing meal, to have drinks, to socialize, to rest, to party . . . a hotel that could define a neighborhood."

"I think it sounds incredible," I said.

"Well, Daniel and I have met and partnered with some phenomenal people, people who share that vision, and that's what we're going to do," Will explained.

"And Jeff, we hope that you will run it," Daniel said.

10 A.M.

(Eh . . . maybe 10:15, depending on how last night went) I arrive at the restaurant. As I enter, the hotel doormen are wheeling luggage and flagging down cabs; the housekeepers are scrubbing and detailing the black awnings outside and the intricate mosaic lobby floor.

Nora, our morning manager, is here and smiling—even though she's been awake for a very long time already. More than one hundred guests have come and gone before I walk in the door. Breakfast guests, I've found, are creatures of habit, and we prepare for that: having noted their preferences last time they visited, we're ready with their coffees, granolas, and omelets just the way they like them. We take someone's morning coffee and croissant as seriously as we do a tasting menu at our sister restaurant across the park.

Now, the last few diners are lingering over their newspapers, listening to Thelonious Monk and Nellie McKay. Many of the cooks have been here since four in the morning, preparing for lunch service: baking breads; monitoring bubbling cauldrons of stock on the stove; turning artichokes and shaving the woody ends off asparagus; dipping radishes in butter; stuffing chickens with foie gras and black truffles.

Usually when I arrive, everyone is eating family meal together in The Parlour. Dishwashers sit with sommeliers, line cooks with servers, pastry cooks with dining room managers. Family meal is *important*. We're fortunate to have a team that hails from all over the world. Often, a young line cook is given a chance to prepare a feast from "back home" and share it with all of us. This means that breakfast probably isn't going to be bacon and eggs. We might have homemade fermented Thai sausages with fiery som tum and sautéed morning glory, or saag paneer and chicken makani with fresh roti.

I pass through the kitchen on the way to my office and greet the morning sous chefs and chef de cuisine Lockwood, a soft-spoken gent who bristles with intensity. He's busy tasting every component of every single dish that will be served this afternoon, tweaking the seasoning here and there, questioning his cooks if he detects a mistake. The chefs are always pushing; they demand perfection. It's inspiring to watch.

Chef Lockwood tells me that the kitchen servers were a little sluggish last night, and that the new trainee might need to review his food descriptions a bit more; I make a note to address these issues with Alex and Nicolas, my dining room managers. They will find a way to rally the staff tonight and to spend some extra time training the new kitchen server.

I've got roughly 150 emails by now. It looks like the hotel engineering team may be planning to polish the wood floors in our event spaces, but we have an inquiry for a party that evening. That party is also probably going to want us to make them a cake, and a majority of the guests are gluten free. The nice Norwegian family staying in the hotel who had dinner with us last night wrote a very lovely thank you note, which is always a pleasure to see, but the older couple staying here for their anniversary thought our drinks were too strong and our lobster too salty; I'll write them a note and send something nice to their room. I'll consult with Benjy, our surprisingly young and almost comically British maître d'—he'll know just what to send.

A lot can happen in an operation that truly never closes, so there's lots to read about. I review the reports from the late night team at the bar next door, as well as the overnight room service summaries. There are the financials—how is the business doing? How is the staff doing? Many other emails, I'm fortunate to say, are guests looking to join us for dinner or to book a party. I try to accommodate as many as possible until I feel like I may be pushing my luck with the evening maître d's—if I make a reservation for someone on a table that doesn't exist in the physical world, they're going to be the ones stuck in a very bad situation.

Every minute or so, a different guy with a hand truck pops his head into our office and shouts "Delivery!" Deliveries are seemingly nonstop at this point. Our purchasing manager, Mark, works alongside our receiving team and ensures our shipments are to our order and of the highest quality; less-than-perfect seafood, vegetables, and meat are promptly sent away. Mark has already spent his morning at the farmers' market in Union Square to purchase chef-requested items or to grab anything that looks particularly delicious or inspiring. Maintaining relationships with the many farmers we work with is also an essential part of his role.

The deliveries continue: fruits and vegetables come first, then meat and fish. Later in the day, supplies will arrive: things like hundreds of pounds of linens and paper goods. Finally: endless cases of booze, wine, and beer, all of which have to be compared to our purchase order for accuracy, organized by our beverage team, entered into our inventory system, and cleanly stowed in the wine cellar. This is the calm before the storm.

SEPTEMBER

I'd been spending my mornings at a makeshift office in the construction site chaos that was slowly becoming The NoMad. By day, I'd wear my canary yellow hardhat while comparing the styling of various hand-etched water glasses for the dining room, or the thickness and finish of leather swatches that I hope will one day bind our wine lists. I'm trying to ensure that the elements of the opening in my charge are kept within budget, but that rare linen from Milan would make the perfect napkin. . . .

That was my day job. Since I had joined the company in a very high position from completely outside the ranks, Will thought it would be a good idea for me to work my way up through the dining room at Eleven Madison Park in my spare time.

So at 4 p.m., I would don my company-issued vest and tie and walk through Madison Square Park to my night job, as a kitchen server at EMP.

A kitchen server's job is to bring the food from the kitchen to the guests, study the cuisine, and act as ambassador for the chefs while in the dining room. These entry-level employees (most of whom have incredible educational backgrounds and hospitality résumés) spend their time as kitchen servers mastering the steps of service, including wine, spirits, beer, and coffee, and the restaurant's culture. Eventually, they take their next step, to assistant server, where they are more involved in the maintenance of the table (clearing, crumbing, water). Then, after some time, they may be promoted to server, where they become responsible for coordinating the table's order, as well as the setting of silverware and glassware for the following courses. After a long while and a demonstration of mastery in all aspects of the restaurant, a server could be promoted to captain, that person who guides the guests' experience from their arrival to their departure.

And here I was, from out of the ether, the newly appointed general manager, and I had done *none* of these things. I thought of the captains at EMP who had worked for years to attain their position in the restaurant: their will to study more after a fourteen-hour day at work, through wine tastings and service classes; their grace under pressure; their successes and their setbacks. And then I show up. A nobody. An interloper who doesn't even know what those four leaves in the EMP logo are.

If I were one of these hospitality Jedi, I'd have told me to take a hike. But no one ever did. There were no whispers as I walked by, no strange looks from across the room. No one showed the least desire to tell me I had no business being there and that I should leave, and quickly. Instead, I was genuinely welcomed with open arms. The staff would save me a seat at family meal. They would gently help me with my pronunciation of *umeboshi*, which garnished the foie gras dish, and the *beerenauslese* wine that was intended to accompany it—and yes, that wine was served in a light green stemmed Riesling glass and was the fourth course—or was it fifth?—and if the guest had an aversion to stone fruit, we could prepare the dish with a granola garnish. I forgot exactly what comprised the granola and prayed I didn't have to eventually *spiel* it.

That was some higher level knowledge, to be fair. My job at first was seemingly simple: to respond with a hearty "Oui!" along with the rest of the team when, after the click-clack of the expeditor's printer, the chef would shout, "Order in, four-top, tasting menu!" Then, I would wait my turn in line, silent, back straight, until I was called upon. The kitchen could not execute a menu of such precision for so many guests without order, so we waited, stoic and steely with focus.

Over and over in my head, I recited the dishes and their components, praying I would succeed in presenting them at each table; all the time my early-morning meeting scheduled for tomorrow—and the hotel's opening date—loomed.

12 P.M.

Lunch service begins with a bang: unlike dinner, the guests arrive all at once. The kitchen will have to produce approximately four hundred plates of food in two hours. The dining room will be seated with more frequency, and most guests will be in a bit of a rush. Lunch is truly a challenge.

The kitchen is chugging along and my colleagues are working the floor, freeing me to attend meetings and work on projects. One of the benefits of having a restaurant in a big, beautiful hotel is that you have access to a big, beautiful boardroom. We have one and we use it—a lot: meetings coordinating with the hotel staff for engineering and maintenance; educational classes on food, beverage, and service; financial meetings with our controllers, Toni (quiet and kind until you mess up your paperwork) and Marcia (who doesn't let me get away with anything). If I need a breather, I bother Laura, our special events director, who, aside from absolutely crushing her job overseeing the plethora of private

events we host, is Really That Nice. I semi-jokingly refer to her as my spiritual advisor; she keeps the fabric of our culture kind and strong.

Lunch is rocking. The p.m. sous chef team—Rowdy, Reilly, Joe, Zach, Brad, Sean, John: guys you'd want next to you if you suddenly found yourself in a World War II movie—are arriving for the start of their thirteen-hour day. They will immediately formulate their battle plan for the next four hours, then divide and conquer. Not only are they the ones charged with preparing the most complicated, expensive, and technically difficult items in the kitchen (cleaning tuna loins, portioning foie gras, making black truffle puree), they are each also responsible for seeing that their respective teams' stations are completely set up and ready for tasting with Chef Daniel and Chef James, the executive chef. (James, who joined us from Eleven Madison Park, may love Notorious B.I.G. just as much as haute cuisine. We share an office: he tries me out on Jay-Z songs, I attempt to open his ears to the beauty of improvisational rock; neither of us has been successful as of this writing.)

At 2 p.m., the evening line cooks and dining room managers arrive. The sous chefs will give the line cooks their goals for the next two hours. It's fast and furious at this point. The dining room managers are preparing the floor plan, plotting which servers will be working where and with whom; the maître d's will have notes for them if there are any regulars coming in who have preferences for certain servers and tables so they can be paired accordingly.

At 3 p.m., the entire kitchen has their premeal team meeting with Chef James and Chef Daniel. They talk about goals for the night ahead, what went right and what went wrong yesterday, and any other special circumstances for the evening. Meanwhile, the pastry team is blazing through their production of ice cream, portioning chocolates and cheeses, building macaroons, dusting truffles, shaving financier chips, whipping mousselines, and, of course, baking.

Starting at 4 p.m., things start to happen fast. The hourly dining room staff arrives, ready to work and in uniform. They immediately get to their assigned sections in the dining room and begin setting up, cleaning, and detailing their stations. At 4:15 p.m., the kitchen puts up the evening family meal. (My personal favorite has always been rigatoni Bolognese with lots of grated Parmesan and red pepper flakes.) Chef Mark makes a ridiculously good giardiniera, so muffuletta day is pretty great as well.

At 4:45 p.m., the dining room and kitchen management meet with the maître d' for the evening. We discuss nearly every party coming in to dine: Is this their first time? Is it their birthday? Are they in the restaurant business? Are they allergic to shellfish? What was their last experience like with us? Do they like wine? What kind? Is there anything else special we can do for them?

At 5 p.m., the dining room team heads up to The Parlour to have line-up: an all-dining room meeting that covers not only particulars of our food, beverage, and service, but also broader, more abstract philosophical topics (empathy and kindness), all in the interest of increasing the quality of our service and taking better care of our guests. All staff members are encouraged to participate—be it in a "blind" wine tasting, a discussion of other important restaurants past and present, or suggestions about how we can get better, through the minutiae or in broad strokes.

Meanwhile, in the kitchen, Chef Daniel and Chef James are tasting through the entire menu, every component of every dish, as Chef Brian did before. This is critical: if a sauce is improperly made, it's going to be a very difficult thirty minutes for the kitchen to be prepared for service.

Doors open at 5:30 p.m. Guests are literally lining up outside to join us for dinner, so I end line-up the same way every day, the way they do at EMP: "Have a good service!" I shout, and the staff responds with a resounding *"Oui!"*

NOVEMBER

We were about five months away from opening, and due to the bureaucratic nightmare that is opening not only a business, but a *hotel*, in New York City, the building's fire alarm test had been sounding for the past two days, complete with flash-bang strobes. *Woooooooot. Wooooooot.*

We sat at the boardroom table on the third floor of the hotel: Will, Chef Daniel, and I; Meredith, the managing director of the hotel and her team; and representatives from be-pôles, the amazing Parisian design firm that we worked with on the hotel's identity and graphic design.

We had been there for an hour or two, having a heated discussion about the "Do Not Disturb" signs that guests would hang on their doorknobs.

"It should read, 'Make up my room' on one side and 'Don't Disturb' on the other, and that's it," someone said.

"No, it feels like we're disrespecting the housekeeping staff: 'Do this. Do that.' It should say 'Make Up My Room, Please' and 'Do Not Disturb, Please,'" someone else said.

"Those 'pleases' sound forced and fake. 'Please Enter' or 'Please Do Not Disturb.'"

"'Please Enter'? That's ridiculous."

"How about, 'Please, My Room Needs Attention' and 'Please Don't Enter.'"

Every detail in the hotel was decided upon this way; a group of passionate people unwilling to let things fall to chance. Our umbrellas, notebooks, and pens; our bellmen's boots and ties; the way the herbs were framed and hung on the walls; the exact font of our menus and our emails down to the kerning of the text within. Choosing items for the minibar was especially fun.

Opening was drawing near. I was blessed with an incredible management team, both dining room and kitchen—truly greater that any general manager could ever hope for—culled not only from Eleven Madison Park, but from other great restaurants around the country. I was beginning to realize very quickly that my job was primarily going to be getting out of the way and letting these people, as we say here, *crush it.*

They got to work. Billy, our service director, gentlemanly as a nineteenth-century aristocrat, began working on the training schedules and planning the "friends and family" breakfasts, lunches, and dinners. Camilla, our assistant general manager, who lives to connect with her guests (and is prone to hyperbole on the greatness of everything around her), wrote our service manual, all seventy-plus pages of it. Assisting her was Julian, our resident joker from Los Angeles, whose humor brought us up whenever we needed it most. Brandon, the Southern gentleman who I was determined to turn into a jaded New Yorker (to no avail) worked on designing our menus and our IT structure.

Thomas, the former medical student and classical pianist–cum–wine director was charged with building a world-class wine list in only a matter of weeks, and Leo, who moves at a speed that you *cannot* keep up with, created a bar program that would go on to be an award-winning behemoth. Our guest relations manager, Kristen, would help design our reservation book and train our staff in their language and poise; sometimes we wondered if our guests were coming for the chicken or for the pleasure of seeing her.

Chef Daniel and his team were fortunate enough to have a good amount of time in their new and beautiful kitchen. They practiced their craft: refining dishes, simulating crushingly busy services, creating new dishes, and throwing others out the window. If your timing was right, and you could steal away from some of your afternoon meetings and pop downstairs, you could eat *very* well for lunch.

There was so much more we had to do! We had to choose our linens and finalize our glassware and silverware. We had to work out details with the potter Jono Pandolfi on the line of china we were designing with him; design our beautiful copper service trays and our wine buckets with the Brooklyn metalworker Aleksey Kravchuk; construct elegant liquor and pastry carts

with the wonderful people of Regency in Park Slope. What about our napkins, our flowers, our candles? Our music? What kind of lightbulbs fit in this fancy Parisian sconce that Jacques Garcia selected for us?

5:30 P.M.

It happens so fast: the many bars and dining rooms fill up—quickly. My colleagues and I divide and conquer, straightening the wall sconces, checking that the tables, napkins, and candles are aligned. The music and the lights are programmed to change with the start of service, but they still need a human touch and some tweaking.

The kitchen is still racing to set up their stations, getting everything perfect, organized, ready to go. Though the doors have opened upstairs, it will still be a bit of time before guests are settled, have had a cocktail, and have perused the menu and ordered something. At roughly 5:45 p.m. the expeditor's printer starts up: it will not stop for another six hours or so.

The expo tears the first ticket off his machine and calls it out to the kitchen: "Ordering, two fruits de mer, followed by one foie gras and one egg, followed by a chicken!" And since this is the first order of the evening, he adds: "Let's have a good service!"

The kitchen's *"OUI!"* has an intensity that William Wallace or General Patton would be very happy with.

And with that, it starts. For the next few hours, nearly three hundred guests will join us for dinner. Another two hundred will join us in the Elephant Bar and library; two hundred more will join us at the NoMad Bar next door. Stacy, our events manager, will oversee the private functions on our rooftop, which could be an intimate dinner in the cupola or a cocktail party for two hundred. Chef James has his hands in it all, orchestrating the whole show, jumping behind the line to cook when needed—whatever it takes to ensure that all three kitchens (main, rooftop, and bar) are functioning well.

Our team will be tested, but they will persevere. They truly enjoy finding novel ways to connect with guests and to provide a special experience for them, and when the entire team works together, it is magical.

At 11 p.m., the dining room is still humming and the bar is busier than it has been all evening. But behind the scenes, the sous-chefs are starting to take an inventory of the entire kitchen. Mindful of the reservation count for tomorrow, they begin their calls to their butchers, their fishmongers, their farmers: we need to do this all again tomorrow.

At midnight, the expo shouts "All in!" The last order has come through the printer. This is the signal to start breaking down the kitchen around these final orders. As the last of the appetizers hit the floor, the garde-manger is emptied and cleaned; the same continues for the rest of the line. Chef Ashley, who is responsible for The NoMad Bar kitchen, still has a few hours to go. Her team works a fast and furious service late into the evening.

At 1:30 a.m., the evening sous chefs are compiling their reports to communicate to the a.m. team: What happened tonight? What went right? What went wrong? Where do we need assistance?

By 2 a.m., the main kitchen is nearly broken down. Now the overnight cooks arrive: they will man the room service menu and assist in setting up for breakfast service.

At 2:30 a.m., the p.m. kitchen crew is done—changed into their street clothes and off to bed or, for those with the energy, off for a pint with the crew to exchange war stories.

APRIL

The restaurant and hotel finally opened on March 26, 2012.

We all worked very hard from early morning until late at night. Weekends, wives, friends, family—they all had to be placed on the back burner as we geared up. Yes, we were tired and we were stressed. After so much time massaging this idea through endless hours of debate, creation, and inception, to then present it to the world, to give it to people, to have it be an actual, real thing, was daunting. Yet to have it all come together was incredible.

The people came, and they loved it, and they came back again and again.

One night, when it felt like everything wasn't about to spiral out of control, Will, Chef Daniel, Leo, and I went for a walk around the block. Spring was in the air and the sun was hanging on a bit longer in the evening, so it was dusk. We walked past the wig shops and the silly perfume stores for a bit, and then rounded the corner, and looked up.

Tall above us was a beautiful building, enormous black flags cantilevered from the façade blowing mightily in the wind. A scatter of lit and darkened windows dotted the brick, and, at the hotel's peak was our bronze cupola, illuminating from above, a beautiful beacon in its namesake neighborhood.

And that felt pretty damn good.

HOW TO USE
THIS BOOK

Ever since we decided to write this cookbook, our entire team has had an ongoing debate about accessibility. With our first book, Eleven Madison Park, we were so scared that people would feel intimidated by its recipes that we did everything we could to make them less imposing. Chief among our efforts was the decision to use imperial units (cups, tablespoons, etc.) instead of the metric system, which is what we use in our kitchen.

But we underestimated the people buying our books. People weren't craving convenience, they were craving precision. It wasn't complaints about accessibility that we received, it was complaints that we weren't presenting our recipes in the way we used them in the restaurant. So here, we decided that you, the reader, who shelled out your hard-earned money for a look behind the curtain, should learn to do things exactly as we do.

With that as a foundation, we've tried to make this book as accessible, easy to follow, and intuitively organized as possible.

If it happens that measuring ingredients by weight is a departure from the way you are used to cooking, please don't be deterred or overwhelmed: all you need is a simple metric kitchen scale to get started. We're pretty sure you will find it makes things easier in the end.

All of the recipes are organized just as we organize our menu, with sections for Snacks, Appetizers, Mains, and Desserts. Following those sections are our Basics, the building blocks of our food, which are referenced in nearly every recipe. These are the recipes for our dressings, pickles, stocks, crumbles, dough, butters, ice creams, and sorbets. Some treat these as individual recipes to be used in dishes of their own.

And nested at the back of this book, you will find another, with the recipes for our cocktails by our extremely talented colleague Leo Robitschek.

Unless otherwise stated, rely on the following rules:

Butter is unsalted
Cream is heavy
Eggs are extra large
Flour is all-purpose
Foie gras is grade A duck
Gelatin is gold-strength sheets
Herbs are fresh
Juice is fresh and double-strained
Milk is whole
Olive oil is extra virgin
Pepper is ground fresh
Salt is kosher
Sugar is granulated

All recipes are intended to be made from start to finish without storing ingredients for extended periods of time unless otherwise noted.

It's also important that we emphasize our understanding that seasoning is a personal preference. As a result there are instances when we list salt as a general ingredient without a specific quantity. Be sure to taste and adjust based on your palate.

And, if at any point you get stuck, have a question about a recipe or an ingredient, or just want to say hello, please feel free to email us at cookbook@thenomadhotel.com. We are here to help.

SNACKS

RADISHES
Butter-Dipped with Fleur de Sel

Makes 16 radishes

115 g butter, softened
16 Easter egg radishes
3 g salt
Fleur de sel

Line a baking sheet with acetate and set aside. Place the butter in a bowl over a double boiler and gently warm through while whisking continuously. Be careful not to get the butter so hot that it breaks. Season the butter with the salt. When the butter is fully tempered, it should look like melted chocolate. Dip each radish halfway into the butter and transfer to the prepared tray. Each dipped radish should have an opaque glaze that is not too thick. Immediately refrigerate the dipped radishes to fully set the butter, about 30 minutes. Serve with fleur de sel.

CRUDITÉ
with Chive Cream

Serves 4

————

CHIVE CREAM

> 150 g crème fraîche
> 50 g Chive Oil (page 284)
> Grated zest of 1 lemon
> 15 g lemon juice
> Pinch of cayenne
> Salt

Chill the bowl of a stand mixer. Place the crème fraîche in the chilled bowl and whip to medium-stiff peaks at medium speed. Remove the bowl from the mixer. Using a rubber spatula, gently fold the chive oil, lemon zest, lemon juice, and cayenne into the whipped cream until fully incorporated. Season with salt and keep refrigerated.

————

TO FINISH

> 1 fennel bulb
> 16 peeled baby carrots
> 16 sugar snap peas
> 12 Cherry Bomb radishes
> 8 baby corn ears
> 8 Sun Gold tomatoes
> 12 cherry tomatoes
> 8 pencil asparagus tips
> 8 romanesco florets
> 8 haricots verts
> 4 yellow wax beans
> 4 yellow cauliflower florets
> 4 white cauliflower florets
> Pea tendrils

Cut the fennel bulb in half and then into 6-mm (¼-inch) thick slices. Trim and discard the core. Fill four bowls with crushed ice and divide and arrange the vegetables evenly among the bowls. Garnish with the pea tendrils. Serve cold with the chive cream.

TOMATO
*Variations on Toast
with Basil*

Serves 4

—————

MARINATED TOMATOES

*8 small heirloom tomatoes, sliced 6 mm (¼ inch) thick
12 basil leaves, torn in half
45 g White Balsamic Vinaigrette (page 285)*

Combine the tomatoes with the basil in a mixing bowl and dress with the vinaigrette. Toss to coat. Let the tomatoes marinate for at least 30 minutes, but no more than 4 hours. Remove and discard the basil before serving.

TO FINISH

*Tomato Relish (page 300)
4 slices miche, toasted
Roasted Tomatoes (page 299)
Demi-Dehydrated Tomatoes (page 297)
Fleur de sel
Freshly cracked black pepper
Basil tops
Basil buds*

Spread tomato relish over each piece of toast. Arrange the marinated tomatoes, roasted tomatoes, and demi-dehydrated tomatoes on each toast. Season the tomatoes with fleur de sel and black pepper and garnish each toast with basil tops and basil buds.

SALMON
Rillettes with Fines Herbes Bavarois

Serves 4

SALMON RILLETTES

1 salmon fillet, skin, bloodline, and pin bones removed,
about 455 g
Salt
2 lemons, sliced 6 mm (¼ inch) thick
Olive oil
40 g Mayonnaise (page 304)
115 g crème fraîche
Grated zest of 1 lemon
½ shallot, finely chopped
5 g finely chopped dill
5 g finely chopped tarragon
3 g finely chopped chervil
5 g sliced chives
20 g lemon juice

Cut the salmon into four pieces of equal thickness. Season the salmon liberally with salt on all sides. Line the bottom of a large saucepan with enough lemon slices to fully cover. Place the salmon pieces in the pan and cover with olive oil. Heat the pan over very low heat and cook until tender and flaky, about 18 minutes. Let cool to room temperature in the confit oil. Drain the salmon from the oil, pat dry, and transfer to a mixing bowl. Gently flake the fish apart without shredding and fold in the mayonnaise, crème fraîche, lemon zest, shallot, herbs, and lemon juice until fully incorporated; do not overmix. Reserve the salmon rillettes, refrigerated, in an airtight container until ready to serve.

FINES HERBES PUREE

50 g baby spinach leaves
50 g chives, coarsely chopped
40 g flat-leaf parsley leaves
15 g tarragon leaves
25 g chervil leaves
Ice water

Heat a pot of salted water to a boil over high heat and prepare an ice bath. Blanch the spinach and herbs each separately for about 5 minutes, until they are completely tender—when you rub them between your fingers,

they should fall apart. As they emerge from the boiling water, immediately shock each batch of greens in the ice bath and, once cold, remove and squeeze out any excess water. Place the blanched greens in a blender with a splash of ice water and blend on high speed until completely smooth. Pass the puree through a fine-mesh tamis and reserve in an airtight container, refrigerated, for up to 24 hours.

FINES HERBES BAVAROIS

3 sheets gelatin
150 g cream
2 egg yolks
80 g Fines Herbes Puree
10 g lemon juice
6 g salt
45 g water

Bloom the gelatin sheets in ice water. Using a stand mixer, whip the cream to medium peaks. Set aside and keep cold. Whisk the egg yolks, fines herbes puree, lemon juice, and salt in a separate bowl until fully incorporated. Heat the water in a saucepan over low heat until warm. Squeeze the bloomed gelatin to drain any excess water and combine with the warm water. Stir until fully melted. Remove the pan from the heat and temper the gelatin into the fines herbes mixture. Whisk together until incorporated. Fold the whipped cream into the thickened mixture in three additions. Once fully incorporated, place a layer of plastic wrap directly on top of the bavarois and refrigerate until set, about 3 hours. When ready to serve, whip the bavarois with a wire whisk until completely smooth.

TO FINISH

Fennel fronds
Fennel blossoms
Chervil
4 slices miche, toasted

Divide the rillettes among four glass jars. Top each with a quenelle of the fines herbs bavarois. Garnish each jar with fennel fronds, fennel blossoms, and chervil. Serve with miche toast.

CLAMS
Baked with Bacon and Garlic

Makes 24 clams

––––

STEAMED CLAMS

24 littleneck clams, about 900 g
1 shallot, sliced
3 cloves garlic, crushed
2 sprigs thyme
1 bay leaf
230 g dry white wine

Heat a large saucepan over high heat and prepare an ice bath. When the pan is very hot, add the clams, shallot, garlic, thyme, and bay leaf. Immediately pour the white wine into the pan and cover with a lid. Steam for about 4 minutes, shaking the pan occasionally to evenly cook the clams, until they all open. Remove the clams from the pan, place in a bowl along with any liquid released, and chill over the ice bath. Discard any unopened clams. Remove the clams from the shells, reserving the shells, and strain the cooking liquid through cheesecloth. Trim and discard the mantles from the clams. Store the cleaned clams in the strained cooking liquid and keep refrigerated. Scrub the shells clean and set aside.

––––

SURF CLAM PANADE

2 surf clams
28 g bacon, finely chopped
1 shallot, finely chopped
3 cloves garlic, finely chopped
115 g dry white wine
115 g Chicken Stock (page 303)
45 g butter
65 g Brioche Bread Crumbs (page 287)
15 g lemon juice
2 g salt

Shuck the surf clams and discard the shells. Trim and discard the mantles. Finely chop the cleaned flesh and keep cold. Heat the bacon in a large saucepan over medium heat, stirring occasionally, until the bacon is crispy. Remove the bacon from the pan and set aside, leaving the rendered fat in the pan. Add the shallot and garlic to the pan and cook, stirring occasionally, sweating the vegetables until tender, about 4 minutes. Add the

wine and deglaze the pan, then simmer and reduce the wine until almost dry. Add the chicken stock and bring to a simmer. Add the butter and stir to incorporate. Bring the liquid to a simmer and reduce until thickened to a glaze consistency. Remove the pan from the heat. Add the cooked bacon, clams, and bread crumbs to the pan. Using a rubber spatula, fold the mixture together until incorporated. Add the lemon juice and season with the salt.

––––

BRIOCHE TOPPING

30 g Brioche Bread Crumbs (page 287)
5 g flat-leaf parsley leaves, finely chopped
Grated zest of 1 lemon
3 g Parmesan, grated
Salt

Combine the bread crumbs, parsley, zest, and cheese in a bowl and mix well; season with salt. Reserve the topping in an airtight container, refrigerated, for up to 2 days.

––––

TO FINISH

1 lemon, cut into 8 wedges

Preheat the oven to 175°C/350°F. Arrange the scrubbed clamshells in a single layer on a baking dish, insides facing up. Place a steamed clam in each shell and fill with the panade. Top each shell with brioche topping and place the tray in the oven. Bake the clams until warmed through, golden brown, and crispy, about 15 minutes. Serve warm with the lemon wedges.

FRUITS DE MER

Serves 4

TOMATO BAVAROIS

2 sheets gelatin
100 g cream
115 g Tomato Water (page 301)
2 g salt

Bloom the gelatin in ice water. Pour one quarter of the cream into a mixing bowl and combine with the tomato water. Mix in the salt. Heat half of the tomato water mixture in a saucepan over low heat until warmed through. Drain the gelatin and squeeze to get rid of any excess water. Stir the gelatin into the warm tomato cream until fully melted. Remove the pan from the heat and stir the gelatin mixture into the remaining tomato cream until incorporated. Let cool to room temperature. Whip the remaining cream to soft peaks and fold into the tomato cream in three additions. Place a layer of plastic wrap directly on top of the bavarois and refrigerate until set, about 3 hours. Whip the bavarois smooth and transfer to a piping bag.

CRAB SALAD

1 king crab leg
1 roma tomato
10 g zucchini, diced 3 mm (1/8 inch)
3 basil leaves, finely chopped
30 g Lemon Mayonnaise (page 304)
15 g crème fraîche
Salt

Carefully remove the crabmeat from the shell, keeping the shell as intact as possible. Reserve the shell for the presentation. Pick through the crabmeat to ensure there are no stray pieces of shell or cartilage. Bring a pot of salted water to a boil and prepare an ice bath. Blanch the tomato until the skin just starts to loosen, about 10 seconds. Shock the tomato in the ice bath until cold. Peel and discard the skin, and halve the tomato. Remove and discard the seeds and cut the tomato into 3-mm (1/8-inch) dice. Blanch the zucchini dice in the boiling water until just tender, about 1 minute. Shock in the ice bath until cold. Drain the zucchini well and pat dry with a paper towel. Combine the crabmeat, tomato dice, zucchini dice, basil, mayonnaise, and crème fraîche in a mixing bowl and gently mix until incorporated. Season with salt. Keep refrigerated until ready to assemble.

KING CRAB AND TOMATO

Crab Salad
Tomato Bavarois

Cut the king crab leg shell into four 3.8-cm (1 1/2-inch) long pieces. Line a baking sheet with acetate. Lightly coat the acetate with nonstick cooking spray and wipe off any excess with a paper towel. Place the shells on the prepared baking sheet upright. Pipe a thin but complete layer of bavarois into the bottom of each shell segment. Refrigerate the shells for 30 minutes to let the bavarois set. Divide the crab salad among the shells, smoothing the top of the salad so that there is room for more bavarois to cap the shell, but being careful not to press the salad through the bavarois layer on the bottom: you want the layer of salad to remain concealed between the two layers of bavarois. Fill the shells with more bavarois, heaping it up over the tops of the shell lengths. Carefully twist the shells off the acetate and, using an offset spatula, smooth the bavarois on both sides of the shells, scraping away any excess and filling in any gaps as necessary. Place the shell lengths on their sides on the baking sheet and refrigerate until completely set, about 1 hour. Reserve in the refrigerator until ready to serve.

APPLE GELÉE

1/2 sheet gelatin
110 g Granny Smith apple juice (from about 2 apples)
1 g ascorbic acid
0.5 g salt

Bloom the gelatin in ice water. Heat the juice in a saucepan over low heat until warmed through. Remove the pan from the heat. Season the juice with the ascorbic acid and salt. Squeeze the gelatin of any excess water and stir it into the warm juice until fully melted. Let cool to room temperature. Divide the gelée among four ramekins and refrigerate until set, about 4 hours.

SEA URCHIN AND GREEN APPLE

4 sea urchin tongues
Apple Gelée
5 g Granny Smith apple, peeled and
*   diced 3 mm (1/8 inch)*
Chervil tops
Chive tips
Onion blossoms

Place one sea urchin tongue on each apple gelée. Garnish with the apple, chervil, chives, and onion blossoms.

CHAMPAGNE MIGNONETTE SNOW

3 shallots, thinly sliced
10 g black peppercorns
100 g champagne
150 g champagne vinegar
50 g water
5 g salt

Prepare an ice bath. Combine all the mignonette ingredients in a saucepan over medium heat. Bring to a simmer and remove the pan from the heat. Chill over the ice bath until cold. Refrigerate for 24 hours in an airtight container. Strain the mignonette through a chinois and discard the drained solids. Transfer the liquid to a baking dish and place in the freezer. Whisk the mixture to break up any large pieces. Continue to freeze, whisking every 20 minutes, until the mignonette is frozen with a fluffed texture, about 2 hours total. Reserve in an airtight container in the freezer.

OYSTER AND MIGNONETTE

4 oysters
Champagne Mignonette Snow
Puffed Buckwheat (page 288)
Wood sorrel
Sorrel blossoms

Just before serving, shuck the oysters, making sure to cut the muscle attaching the oyster to the shell before returning the oyster to the half shell. Spoon a generous amount of snow over each oyster. Sprinkle the puffed buckwheat over the snow and garnish with wood sorrel and sorrel blossoms.

LOBSTER SALAD

1 lobster, 575 g
11 g Lemon Mayonnaise (page 304)
2 g Sriracha
Splash of Worcestershire sauce
Splash of brandy
8 g lemon juice
2 g tarragon, finely chopped
Pinch of cayenne
Salt

Bring a large pot of water to a rolling boil and prepare an ice bath. Cook the lobster whole in the boiling water for 2 minutes. Using a spider, remove the lobster from the water. Wrap your hand with a kitchen towel and twist the knuckles and claws from the body. Shock the lobster tail and body in the ice bath. Return the knuckles and claws to the boiling water and cook for an additional 2 minutes. Shock the knuckles and claws in the ice bath. When cold,

drain the lobster and remove the lobster meat from the shells. Reserve the claw shells. Clean away any intestinal tract from the meat. Using a pair of sharp scissors, carefully trim each claw shell to shape the serving vessels for the salad as pictured. Clean the shells well in hot soapy water, rinse, and set aside.

Chop the cleaned lobster meat and place in a mixing bowl. Add the lemon mayonnaise, Sriracha, Worcestershire sauce, brandy, and lemon juice. Gently stir until incorporated. Fold in the tarragon and season with cayenne and salt.

LOBSTER AND TARRAGON

Lobster Salad
Grated lemon zest
Piment d'Espelette
Tarragon tops

Just before serving, divide the lobster salad among the reserved lobster claw shells. Garnish each salad with lemon zest, piment d'Espelette, and tarragon tops.

YUZU VINAIGRETTE

60 g yuzu juice
30 g olive oil
8 g salt

Combine the vinaigrette ingredients in a bowl and whisk until emulsified. Reserve the vinaigrette in an airtight container, refrigerated, for up to 3 days.

SCALLOP AND PISTACHIO

16 pistachios, coarsely chopped
2 U10 scallops, diced 6 mm (¼ inch)
5 g jalapeño, seeded, finely chopped
30 g Yuzu Vinaigrette
Salt
4 bay scallop shells
Chive blossom buds

Preheat the oven to 175°C/350°F. Place the pistachios on a baking sheet lined with parchment paper. Toast the pistachios until aromatic, about 8 minutes. Let cool to room temperature. In a bowl over ice, combine the diced scallops and jalapeño and dress with the yuzu vinaigrette. Season with salt and stir to combine. Divide the scallop mixture evenly among the four bay scallop shells. Garnish with the pistachios and chive blossom buds.

CONTINUED

HAMACHI AND HORSERADISH

40 g hamachi, diced 6 mm (¼ inch)
25 g olive oil
Fleur de sel
Peeled horseradish, for grating

Combine the hamachi and olive oil in a mixing bowl set
over ice and place in the fridge until ready to serve.
To finish, season with fleur de sel and gently stir to mix.
Divide the hamachi among four ramekins. Top each
with a fluffed mound of freshly grated horseradish and
a sprinkle of fleur de sel to finish.

TO FINISH

Fill a large bowl with crushed ice and arrange the
hamachi and horseradish, king crab and tomato, lobster
and tarragon, oyster and mignonette, scallop and
pistachio, and sea urchin and green apple over the ice.
Serve communally.

HUMM DOG
with Bacon, Black Truffle, and Celery

Serves 4

CELERY RELISH

70 g peeled celery root, diced 6 mm (¼ inch)
65 g celery, diced 6 mm (¼ inch)
40 g half-sour pickles, diced 6 mm (¼ inch)
15 g Pickled Mustard Seeds (page 294)
15 g white balsamic vinegar
5 g black truffle, diced 6 mm (¼ inch)

Bring a pot of salted water to a boil over high heat and prepare an ice bath. Blanch the celery root in the boiling water until tender, about 5 minutes, and shock in the ice bath. Blanch the celery in the boiling water until tender, about 3 minutes, and shock in the ice bath. When cold, drain the celery root and celery from the ice bath. Transfer the vegetables to paper towels to drain any excess water.

In a mixing bowl, combine the blanched vegetables with the pickles, pickled mustard seeds, and vinegar and mix well. When ready to plate, fold in the diced black truffle.

TRUFFLE MAYONNAISE

60 g Mayonnaise (page 304)
10 g black truffles, finely chopped

Combine the mayonnaise with the truffles in a mixing bowl and fold together with a rubber spatula. Reserve the mayonnaise in an airtight container, refrigerated, for up to 3 days.

TO FINISH

Canola oil, for frying
4 slices bacon
4 hot dogs
4 hot dog buns
4 slices Gruyère
Celery heart leaves

Preheat the oven to 175°C/350°F. Line a baking sheet with parchment paper. Heat 7.5 cm (3 inches) of canola oil in a heavy pot over medium heat to 175°C/350°F. Wrap a slice of bacon around each hot dog and use wooden toothpicks to secure it. Fry in the hot oil until the bacon is crisped and the hot dog is heated through, about 3 minutes. Transfer to paper towels to drain. Remove and discard the toothpicks. Spread each hot dog bun with truffle mayonnaise. Place a fried hot dog in each bun and top with a slice of Gruyère. Place the hot dogs on the prepared baking sheet and transfer to the oven. Heat the hot dogs just until the cheese is melted, about 2 minutes. Remove from the oven and top each with the celery relish. Garnish with celery heart leaves and serve immediately.

CHICKEN
Fried with Chile Lime Yogurt

Serves 4

BUTTERMILK MARINATED CHICKEN

920 g buttermilk
920 g milk
1 onion, sliced 1.3 cm (¹/₂ inch)
2 jalapeños, seeded and sliced 1.3 cm (¹/₂ inch)
25 g salt
1 kg boneless, skinless chicken thighs

Combine the buttermilk, milk, onion, and jalapeños in a large mixing bowl. Season with the salt and stir together until incorporated. Cut the chicken thighs into 7.5-cm (3-inch) pieces and place in the marinade. Stir to evenly coat and transfer to an airtight container, making sure the chicken thighs are completely submerged in the marinade. Seal and refrigerate for 24 hours.

YOGURT SAUCE

240 g Greek yogurt
15 g chipotle Tabasco sauce
15 g lime juice
5 g salt

Combine the yogurt, Tabasco sauce, lime juice, and salt in a mixing bowl. Whisk together until fully incorporated and smooth. Keep cold.

SEASONED FLOUR

840 g flour
30 g onion powder
25 g garlic powder
35 g salt
15 g smoked paprika
10 g dried thyme
5 g dried sage
2 g cayenne

Combine all the ingredients in a mixing bowl and stir to mix well. Transfer the seasoned flour to a shallow baking dish and set aside.

TO FINISH

Canola oil, for frying
1 lime, for zesting
Piment d'Espelette

Set a wire rack on a baking sheet. Drain the chicken thighs from the marinade. Strain the marinade through a chinois and transfer to a shallow baking dish; set aside. Remove and discard any pieces of onion and jalapeño from the thighs. Dredge each piece of chicken in the seasoned flour and dust off any excess flour so the pieces are evenly coated. Dip the chicken pieces in the reserved buttermilk marinade. Shake off any excess marinade and dredge each piece of chicken again in the seasoned flour. Dust off any excess flour and place the chicken pieces on the wire rack. Each piece of chicken should have an ample and even amount of breading. Place the chicken in the freezer until ready to fry.

Heat 7.5 cm (3 inches) of canola oil to 165°C/325°F in a heavy pot over medium heat. Working in batches to prevent overcrowding the pot, fry the chicken until golden brown, crispy, and cooked through, about 8 minutes. Transfer the fried chicken to paper towels to drain excess oil. Garnish the yogurt sauce with freshly grated lime zest and a pinch of piment d'Espelette and serve immediately alongside the fried chicken.

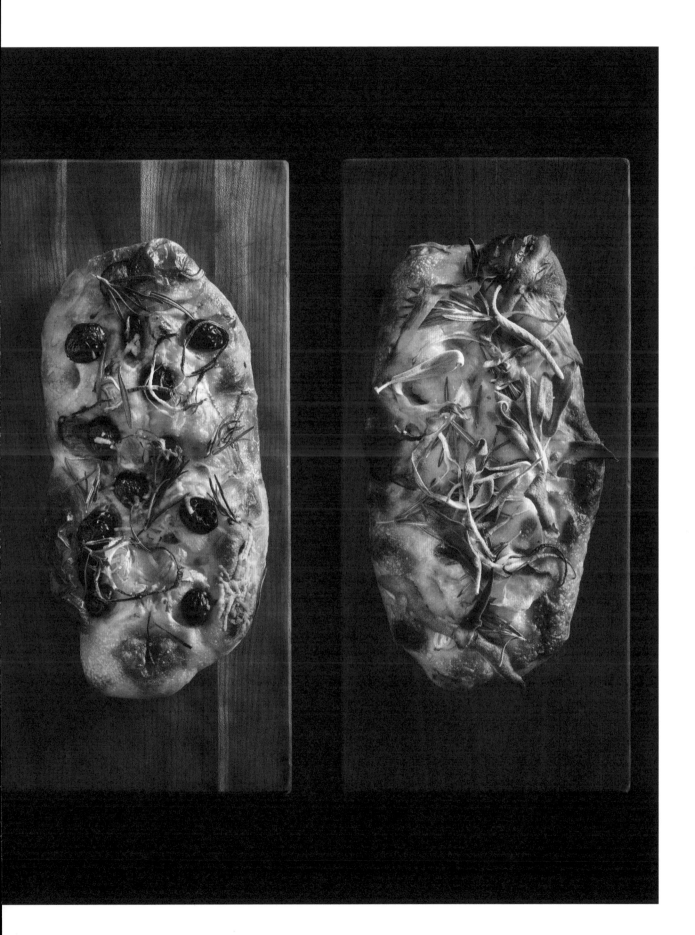

FLATBREAD
Spring Onion and Fingerling Potato

Makes 6

25 g olive oil, plus more for brushing
40 g onion, chopped
10 fingerling potatoes, 3 shaved crosswise
375 g water
5 g fresh yeast
12 g salt
500 g bread flour
15 g flat-leaf parsley leaves
2 g grated lemon zest
40 g spring onion tops, green parts only, thinly sliced
1 g coarsely ground black pepper
6 spring onion bulbs, shaved lengthwise
Fleur de sel

Heat the oil in a pan over medium heat. Add the onion to the pan and cook, stirring occasionally, until softened and lightly caramelized, about 8 minutes. Remove the pan from the heat and let cool to room temperature.

Place the seven whole fingerling potatoes in a large saucepan and cover generously with cold water. Bring the water to a boil over high heat. Season the water with salt and turn the heat to low; continue to cook at a gentle simmer until tender, about 35 minutes. Drain the potatoes and set aside.

Combine the water and yeast in the bowl of a stand mixer fitted with a dough hook. Add the salt and flour on top of the mixture at once and mix on low speed until all the flour is hydrated. Turn to medium speed and mix until the dough pulls away from the sides of the bowl and the gluten has developed, about 15 minutes. Add the cooked onions and oil, the cooked potatoes, parsley, lemon zest, spring onion tops, and black pepper to the dough. Mix until just incorporated.

Turn the dough out onto a clean and lightly floured surface. Fold the dough over in thirds. Rotate the dough 90 degrees and then fold in thirds again. Turn the dough over so that the seam side is facing down. Cover the dough with a damp towel and let rest for 20 minutes. Uncover the dough and repeat the folding and resting process two times. After the third folding, lightly coat the bottom of a bowl with nonstick cooking spray, transfer the dough to the prepared bowl, and cover with plastic wrap. Let the dough rest at room temperature to rise until doubled in size, about 2 hours.

Line a baking sheet with parchment paper and lightly spray with nonstick cooking spray. Uncover the bowl and divide the dough into six even portions. Shape the portions into balls and let sit on a lightly floured surface for 15 minutes to let the gluten relax.

Transfer the portions to the prepared baking sheet. Cover the portions with a damp towel and let proof at room temperature until nearly doubled in size, about 1 hour. Preheat the oven to 230°C/450°F. Using wet hands, flatten and shape the portions into elongated ovals. Press down with fingertips to form dimples across the dough.

Brush each portion with olive oil and top with the shaved spring onion bulb and fingerling potato slices. Season with fleur de sel. Bake until golden brown, rotating the baking sheet once, about 25 minutes. Remove from the oven and let cool on a wire rack.

FLATBREAD
Tomato and Basil

Makes 6

Garlic Confit (page 298)
Roasted Tomatoes (page 299)
375 g water
25 g olive oil
5 g fresh yeast
500 g bread flour
12 g salt
Fleur de sel
Parmesan, for grating
Basil leaves, torn in half

Drain the oil from the garlic confit into a bowl and submerge the roasted tomatoes in the oil to sit overnight. Drain the tomatoes and set both the tomatoes and oil aside.

Combine the water, oil, and yeast in the bowl of a stand mixer fitted with a dough hook. Add the flour and salt on top of the mixture at once and mix on low speed until all the flour is hydrated. Turn to medium speed and mix until the dough pulls away from the sides of the bowl and the gluten has developed, about 15 minutes.

Turn the dough out onto a clean and lightly floured surface. Fold the dough over in thirds. Rotate the dough 90 degrees and fold in thirds again. Turn the dough over so that the seam side is facing down. Cover with a damp towel and let rest for 20 minutes. Repeat the folding and resting process two times. After the third folding, lightly coat the bottom of a bowl with nonstick cooking spray, transfer the dough to the prepared bowl, and cover with plastic wrap. Let the dough rest at room temperature to rise until doubled in size, about 2 hours.

Line a baking sheet with parchment paper and lightly spray with nonstick cooking spray. Divide the dough into six even portions. Shape the portions into balls and let sit on a lightly floured surface for 15 minutes to let the gluten relax. Transfer the portions to the prepared baking sheet. Cover the portions with a damp towel and let proof at room temperature until nearly doubled in size, about 1 hour. Preheat the oven to 230°C/450°F. Using wet hands, flatten and shape the portions into elongated ovals. Press down with your fingertips to form dimples across the dough.

Brush the portions with garlic-tomato oil. Arrange the drained tomatoes, cut side up, and cloves of garlic confit, on each portion. Sprinkle with fleur de sel. Bake until golden brown, rotating the baking sheet once, about 25 minutes. Remove from the oven and let cool on a wire rack. Grate Parmesan over each portion and garnish with basil.

FLATBREAD
Grape and Pecorino

Makes about 6

375 g water
25 g olive oil
5 g fresh yeast
500 g bread flour
12 g salt
45 g pecorino, shredded, plus more for grating
30 g flat-leaf parsley leaves
25 g grated lemon zest
3 g coarsely ground black pepper
Garlic Confit oil (page 298), for brushing
Whole Thomcord grapes
Rosemary tops
1 shallot, sliced into thin rings
Fleur de sel

Combine the water, oil, and yeast in the bowl of a stand mixer fitted with a dough hook. Add the flour and salt on top of the mixture at once and mix on low speed until all the flour is hydrated. Turn to medium speed and mix until the dough pulls away from the sides of the bowl and the gluten has developed, about 15 minutes. Add the shredded pecorino, parsley, lemon zest, and pepper to the bowl and mix until just incorporated.

Turn the dough out onto a clean and lightly floured surface. Fold the dough over in thirds. Rotate the dough 90 degrees and fold in thirds again. Turn the dough over so that the seam side is facing down. Cover the dough with a damp towel and let rest for 20 minutes. Repeat the folding and resting process two times. After the third folding, lightly coat the bottom of a bowl with nonstick cooking spray, transfer the dough to the prepared bowl, and cover with plastic wrap. Let the dough rest at room temperature to rise until doubled in size, about 2 hours.

Line a baking sheet with parchment paper and lightly spray with nonstick cooking spray. Uncover the bowl and divide the dough into six even portions. Shape the portions into balls and let sit on a lightly floured surface for 15 minutes to let the gluten relax. Transfer the portions to the prepared baking sheet. Cover the portions with a damp towel and let proof at room temperature until nearly doubled in size, about 1 hour. Preheat the oven to 230°C/450°F. Using wet hands, flatten and shape the portions into elongated ovals. Press down with your fingertips to form dimples across the dough.

Brush the portions with oil from the garlic confit. Top each portion with the grapes, rosemary, shallot rings, and grated pecorino. Season with fleur de sel. Bake in the oven until golden brown, rotating the baking sheet once, about 25 minutes. Remove from the oven and let cool on a wire rack.

FLATBREAD
Sweet Potato and Sage

Makes about 6

50 g olive oil, plus more for brushing
125 g onion, chopped
100 g sweet potato, skin-on, diced 1.3 cm (½ inch)
375 g water
5 g fresh yeast
500 g bread flour
12 g salt
5 g dried onion flakes
1 g coarsely ground black pepper
1 sweet potato, for shaving
Sage leaves
Rosemary tops
Thyme leaves
1 shallot, sliced into thin rings
Fleur de sel

Preheat the oven to 230°C/450°F. Heat half of the oil in a pan over medium heat. Add the onion to the pan and cook, stirring occasionally, until softened and lightly caramelized, about 8 minutes. Remove the pan from the heat and let cool to room temperature. Combine the remaining 25 g of oil with the diced sweet potato in a mixing bowl, tossing to evenly coat. Transfer to a baking sheet lined with parchment paper, in a single layer. Roast the potatoes, stirring occasionally, until deeply caramelized, about 25 minutes. Remove from the oven and let cool to room temperature.

Combine the water and yeast in the bowl of a stand mixer fitted with a dough hook. Add the flour and salt on top of the mixture at once and mix on low speed until all the flour is hydrated. Turn to medium speed and mix until the dough pulls away from the sides of the bowl and the gluten has developed, about 15 minutes. Add the cooked onion and oil, the sweet potato, onion flakes, and black pepper to the dough. Mix until just incorporated.

Turn the dough out onto a clean and lightly floured surface. Fold the dough over in thirds. Rotate the dough 90 degrees and then fold in thirds again. Turn the dough over so that the seam side is facing down. Cover the dough with a damp towel and let rest for 20 minutes. Repeat the folding and resting process two times. After the third folding, lightly coat the bottom of a bowl with nonstick cooking spray. Transfer the dough to the prepared bowl and cover with plastic wrap. Let the dough rest at room temperature to rise until doubled in size, about 2 hours.

Line a baking sheet with parchment paper and lightly spray with nonstick cooking spray. Uncover the bowl and divide the dough into six even portions. Shape the portions into balls and let sit on a lightly floured surface for 15 minutes to let the gluten relax.

Transfer the portions to the prepared baking sheet. Cover the portions with a damp towel and let proof at room temperature until nearly doubled in size, about 1 hour. Preheat the oven to 230°C/450°F. Using wet hands, flatten and shape the portions into elongated ovals. Press down with fingertips to form dimples across the dough.

Brush the portions with olive oil. Using a vegetable peeler, shave the sweet potato lengthwise. Garnish each dough portion with shaved sweet potatoes, sage leaves, rosemary leaves, thyme, and shallot rings. Season with fleur de sel. Bake in the oven until golden brown, about 25 minutes, rotating the baking sheet once. Remove from the oven and let cool on a wire rack.

APPETIZERS

SNOW PEA
with Pancetta and Mint

Serves 4

SNOW PEAS

400 g snow peas

Using a paring knife, trim and discard both ends of the peas with the attached strings. Thinly slice the peas lengthwise. Keep in a container lined and covered with damp paper towels.

PANCETTA AND ONIONS

170 g pancetta, diced 6 mm (¼ inch)
1 white onion, diced 6 mm (¼ inch)

Heat the pancetta in a sauté pan over medium heat. Cook, stirring occasionally, until the fat is rendered, about 10 minutes. Using a slotted spoon, transfer the cooked pancetta onto a paper towel to drain. Add the onion to the same pan, using the rendered fat to sweat the onions. Continue to cook over low heat, sweating until tender but without any color, about 10 minutes. Remove the pan from the heat and transfer the cooked onion into a mixing bowl. Combine with the pancetta and mix well. Let cool to room temperature.

TO FINISH

20 mint leaves, thinly sliced
Pecorino, for shaving
White Balsamic Vinaigrette (page 285)
Cracked black pepper

Combine the snow peas, pancetta and onions, and mint in a large mixing bowl. Using a vegetable peeler, shave 30 g of the pecorino. Reserve twelve of the shaves for garnish and add the remaining shaves to the snow peas. Dress the salad with the white balsamic vinaigrette and toss to combine. Season with black pepper. Divide the mixture among four bowls. Garnish each salad with the remaining pecorino shaves. Finish each salad with additional black pepper.

WHITE ASPARAGUS
with Shad Roe and Quail Egg

Serves 4

––––

WHITE ASPARAGUS

8 jumbo white asparagus stalks
25 g olive oil
1 shallot, sliced
1 clove garlic, smashed
1 sprig thyme
Salt
120 g dry white wine
35 g lemon juice

Trim the woody end from each stalk, leaving the top 15 cm (6 inches). Using a vegetable peeler, peel the outer layer of each stalk from just below the tip to the bottom of the stalk. Set aside. Bring a large pot of water to a rolling boil over high heat and prepare an ice bath. Heat the olive oil in a saucepan over medium heat. Add the shallot and garlic and sweat until tender, about 5 minutes. Add the thyme and season with salt. Add the wine to the pan and bring to a simmer. Turn the heat to low and reduce by half. Add the lemon juice to the pan and remove from the heat. Chill over the ice bath until cold. Seal the peeled asparagus and cooking liquid airtight in a sous vide bag. Submerge the bag in the boiling water and cook until the asparagus is very tender, about 35 minutes. Shock the bagged asparagus in the ice bath until cold. When ready to serve, remove the asparagus from the bag and drain on a paper towel.

––––

SMOKED SHAD ROE

200 g salt
100 g sugar
1 pair shad roe, about 170 g

Combine the salt and sugar in a bowl and mix well. Bury the shad roe in the salt/sugar mixture. Refrigerate the shad roe and cure for 6 hours.

Preheat the broiler and soak 35 g of applewood chips in cold water for 10 minutes. Remove the roe from the cure and rinse well with cold water. Pat dry and place on a wire rack set over a baking sheet. Drain the chips and line a roasting pan with aluminum foil. Arrange ten charcoal briquettes in a single layer in the pan and place under the broiler until lit, about 15 minutes. Remove the pan from the broiler and sprinkle the wood chips on top—enough to put out any live flames, but not so much that the embers are smothered. Turn off the broiler and let the oven cool. Fill two roasting pans with ice. Place the roe, charcoal, and ice in the oven that is shut off and tightly close the oven door. Check after 6 minutes to make sure the ice has not completely melted. After 20 minutes, remove the roe from the oven and immediately cover with plastic wrap. Refrigerate until chilled and transfer to an airtight container to reserve for up to 3 days.

––––

SMOKED SHAD ROE MAYONNAISE

Smoked Shad Roe
250 g Mayonnaise (page 304)
20 g lime juice
Salt

Cut the membrane of the shad roe open and scrape out the eggs. Discard the membrane. Combine the eggs with the mayonnaise and lime juice in a mixing bowl. Season with salt and stir to combine. Reserve the mayonnaise in an airtight container, refrigerated, for up to 3 days.

––––

TO FINISH

8 Slow-Poached Quail Eggs (page 300)
Fleur de sel
Dried Shad Roe (page 297)
Rye Crisps (page 289)
Dandelion greens
Buttermilk Vinaigrette (page 284)

Place two asparagus spears on each of four plates. Spoon the smoked shad roe mayonnaise into two spots on each plate. Drain the eggs from the water and season them with fleur de sel. Arrange the eggs among the asparagus and mayonnaise. Grate the dried shad roe over the asparagus. Divide the rye crisps among the four plates. Garnish each plate with dandelion greens. Froth the buttermilk vinaigrette with an immersion blender and sauce each plate.

SNAP PEAS
with Buttermilk and Chive Blossoms

Serves 4

500 g whole sugar snap peas
100 g shelled sugar snap peas
Buttermilk Vinaigrette (page 284)
Cracked black pepper
Chive blossoms

Cut half of the whole snap peas in thirds. Place all of the snap peas in a mixing bowl and dress with buttermilk vinaigrette, tossing to evenly combine. Divide the dressed snap peas among four bowls. Garnish the salads with black pepper and chive blossoms.

STRAWBERRY
with Cucumbers and Parmesan

Serves 4

PICKLED CUCUMBER

2 Asian burpless cucumbers
240 g White Balsamic Pickling Liquid (page 295)

Prepare an ice bath. Trim the ends off the cucumbers, then cut them into 6.4-cm (2½-inch) long barrels. Cut the sides from each barrel, yielding planks. Discard the inner core. Place the cucumber planks in a heatproof container. Bring the pickling liquid to a simmer in a pot over medium heat. Pour the pickling liquid over the cucumbers and immediately chill over an ice bath. Store the cucumbers in the pickling liquid, refrigerated, for at least 24 hours but no more than 2 weeks.

STRAWBERRY CONSOMMÉ

225 g frozen strawberries

Bring a pot of water to a rolling boil over high heat and prepare an ice bath. Line a colander with several layers of cheesecloth and place over a large mixing bowl. Set aside. Seal the strawberries airtight in a sous vide bag. Submerge the bag in the boiling water and cook until the strawberries release all of their juices, about 45 minutes. Remove the bag from the water and carefully open the bag. Pour the strawberries into the prepared colander. Let drain in the refrigerator for at least 6 hours. Discard the solids and reserve the consommé, refrigerated in an airtight container, for up to 1 week.

POACHED STRAWBERRIES

190 g strawberries, hulled and halved
Strawberry Consommé

Place the strawberries in a heatproof container and prepare an ice bath. Heat the consommé to a simmer in a saucepan over medium heat. Pour over the strawberries and immediately chill over the ice bath. Keep the strawberries in the consommé until ready to serve.

PICKLED RED PEARL ONIONS

50 g red wine vinegar
20 g water
5 g salt
20 g sugar
4 red pearl onions, peeled

Bring a large pot of water to a boil and prepare an ice bath. Combine the vinegar, water, salt, and sugar in a mixing bowl and whisk well to combine. Seal the liquid and onions airtight in a sous vide bag. Submerge the bag in the boiling water and cook until tender, about 25 minutes. Shock the onions in the ice bath until cold. Remove the onions from the bag and cut in half. Separate the petals of half the onions. Keep the onion petals and halves in the pickling liquid until ready to use.

TO FINISH

24 pistachios, halved
190 g strawberries, hulled and halved
Lemon Vinaigrette (page 285)
½ Asian burpless cucumber, sliced into
*   3-mm (⅛-inch) thick rounds*
4 green strawberries, hulled and sliced
*   3 mm (⅛ inch) thick*
100 g Parmesan, broken into small pieces
35 g olive oil
35 g aged balsamic vinegar
Basil tops
Strawberry blossoms

Preheat the oven to 175°C/350°F. Spread the pistachios on a baking sheet lined with parchment paper. Toast the pistachios until golden brown and aromatic, about 8 minutes. Let cool to room temperature. Dress the fresh strawberries in a mixing bowl with the lemon vinaigrette. Divide the dressed fresh strawberries, poached strawberries, and pickled cucumbers among four plates. Dress the cucumber slices in a mixing bowl with additional lemon vinaigrette. Arrange the cucumber slices, green strawberry slices, and pickled red pearl onions on and around the strawberries on each plate. Divide the pistachios and Parmesan chunks among the plates. Spoon olive oil onto the center of each plate and break the olive oil with the balsamic vinegar. Garnish each salad with basil tops and strawberry blossoms.

CHERRY
with Fennel, Brown Bread, and Yogurt

Serves 4

DEMI-DEHYDRATED CHERRIES

8 sour cherries, stemmed, pitted, and halved
200 g Simple Syrup (page 300)

Preheat the oven to 95°C/200°F. Line a baking sheet with parchment paper. Place the cherries in a heatproof container. Heat the simple syrup to a simmer in a saucepan over medium heat. Remove from the heat and pour over the cherries to cover. Let sit at room temperature for 5 minutes. Drain and discard the syrup. Spread the cherries in a single layer on the baking sheet and dehydrate the cherries in the oven until they appear wrinkled but still retain some moisture, about 2 hours.

BROWN BREAD SAUCE

50 g olive oil
125 g pumpernickel bread, cut into
    2.5-cm (1-inch) cubes
2 cloves garlic
1 sprig thyme
20 g sherry vinegar
Salt

Heat the oil in a saucepan over high heat. When the oil is hot, arrange the bread in a single layer in the pan. When the bread begins to brown, turn the heat to medium and stir occasionally to evenly cook. Add the garlic and thyme to the pan. Cook, stirring, until the bread is completely browned and crispy, about 9 minutes. Remove and discard the thyme. Deglaze the hot pan with the vinegar and fill with just enough water to cover the bread. Bring to a boil and turn the heat to medium. Continue to boil the liquid until reduced by half. Strain the mixture through a chinois, reserving both the cooked mixture and the liquid. Transfer the liquid to a blender and begin to blend on low speed. Add the bread mixture in small increments until it reaches a consistency resembling yogurt (you'll need about 250 g of the mixture). After reaching the proper consistency, puree on high until smooth and let cool to room temperature. Season with salt.

FENNEL BARIGOULE

65 g dry white wine
1 star anise pod
0.5 g fennel seeds
Zest of 1 lemon, peeled in strips
1 g salt
15 g olive oil
4 baby fennel bulbs, halved lengthwise

Prepare an ice bath. Bring the wine, star anise, fennel seeds, and lemon zest to a simmer in a saucepan over medium heat. Continue to simmer until reduced by half. Season with the salt and remove the pan from the heat. Chill over the ice bath until cold. Seal the cooking liquid and the oil with the fennel in a sous vide bag. Bring a pot of water to a rolling boil. Submerge the bag in the boiling water and cook until the fennel is tender, about 40 minutes. Shock the bagged fennel in the ice bath until cold. When cold, remove the fennel from the bag and set aside until ready to serve.

TO FINISH

2 baby fennel bulbs
Sheep's Milk Yogurt Sauce (page 306)
24 Bing cherries, pitted and halved
12 Rainier cherries, pitted and halved
8 sour cherries, pitted and halved
Olive oil
Fleur de sel
Lemon Vinaigrette (page 285)
Pickled Red Onion Rings (page 294)
Pumpernickel Crisps (page 289)

Using a mandoline, slice the fennel lengthwise very thinly. Immediately submerge the shaves in ice water until ready to finish. Swirl the yogurt and bread sauces separately on each of four plates. Arrange the fennel barigoule on the sauces. Combine the fresh cherries in a bowl and dress them lightly with olive oil and season with fleur de sel. Toss to combine. Divide the dressed cherries and demi-dehydrated cherries among the plates. Drain the fennel shaves and transfer to a separate bowl. Lightly dress the fennel shaves with lemon vinaigrette and toss to combine. Arrange the fennel shaves and pickled red onion rings on and around the cherries. Finish each plate with the pumpernickel crisps.

TOMATO
Tart with Eggplant and Rosemary

Serves 4

ROSEMARY TART SHELLS

190 g butter, softened
55 g confectioners' sugar
4 g salt
4 g fleur de sel
2 eggs, plus 1 yolk
5 g rosemary leaves, chopped
190 g all-purpose flour
230 g cake flour
15 g ice water

Using a stand mixer, paddle the butter, confectioners' sugar, and salts together on medium speed until the mixture appears lighter in color and texture, about 5 minutes. Add the eggs and yolk and mix until incorporated, about 2 minutes. Add the rosemary and turn to low speed. Add the flours and ice water and mix until just combined. Roll the dough between 2 sheets of parchment paper to 2 mm (¹/₁₆ inch) thick. Keeping the dough sandwiched between parchment paper, transfer onto a baking sheet and cover with plastic wrap. Refrigerate overnight to chill. Preheat the oven to 160°C/325°F. Unwrap the baking sheet and remove the top layer of parchment paper. Using a fork, lightly prick the dough all over to help prevent bubbles from forming while baking. Cut the docked dough into quarters and, using the parchment paper as an aid, line four 9-cm (3¹/₂-inch) tart shells with the rosemary sablé. Place the tart shells in the freezer until firm, about 1 hour. Bake the tart shells in the oven until golden brown, about 20 minutes. Let cool to room temperature on a wire rack.

EGGPLANT PUREE

1 eggplant, about 550 g
25 g olive oil
Salt

Preheat the oven to 175°C/350°F. Line a baking sheet with parchment paper. Halve the eggplant lengthwise and transfer to a mixing bowl. Dress with the olive oil and season with salt. Toss to evenly coat. Place the eggplant on the baking sheet, skin side down. Roast until tender, about 45 minutes. Let cool at room temperature until warm enough to handle. Scoop out the eggplant flesh and transfer to a blender; discard the outer skin. Puree on high until smooth and season with salt. Keep warm.

BASIL GRANOLA

10 g canola oil, plus more for frying
40 basil leaves
Salt
26 g popcorn
30 g freeze-dried corn
50 g puffed rice cereal
20 g basil seeds
16 g Parmesan, grated
4 g garlic, minced
2 egg whites
90 g glucose syrup
2 g piment d'Espelette

Preheat the oven to 150°C/300°F. In a large, heavy pot, heat 7 cm (3 inches) of canola oil to 175°C/350°F. When the oil is hot, quickly fry the basil leaves until crispy, about 10 seconds. Immediately spread the leaves on a paper towel to drain. Season with salt. Separately, combine the popcorn and 10 g of canola oil in a large, heavy pan over medium heat. Cover the pan with a lid and shake constantly until all of the popcorn is popped. Turn the popcorn out onto a baking sheet lined with parchment paper and let cool to room temperature.

Combine the popcorn, freeze-dried corn, puffed rice cereal, basil seeds, Parmesan, and garlic in a large mixing bowl. In a separate mixing bowl, gently whisk the egg whites until foamy. Whisk in the glucose, 3 g of salt, and the piment d'Espelette until just combined. Pour the glucose mixture over the popcorn mixture and, using a rubber spatula, stir just to combine. Gently fold in the fried basil leaves just until evenly distributed. Spread the mixture in an even layer onto a baking sheet lined with a nonstick baking mat. Bake the granola until golden brown and crispy, about 20 minutes. Let cool to room temperature. Break half of the granola into 2.5-cm (1-inch) pieces and transfer the rest to a food processor. Pulse several times to a coarse consistency. Do not overprocess. Keep both granolas in separate dry, airtight containers.

CONTINUED

MARINATED TOMATOES

28 heirloom cherry tomatoes, halved
12 basil leaves, torn in half
White Balsamic Vinaigrette (page 285)

Combine the tomatoes with the basil in a mixing bowl and dress with the white balsamic vinaigrette. Toss to coat. Let the tomatoes marinate for at least 30 minutes, but no more than 4 hours. Remove and discard the basil before serving.

PEELED TOMATOES

16 cherry tomatoes, red and yellow
Olive oil
Fleur de sel

Bring a large pot of salted water to a rolling boil and prepare an ice bath. Blanch the tomatoes in the water for 10 seconds. Immediately remove the tomatoes from the water and shock in ice water. When cold, carefully peel the tomatoes using a paring knife and discard the skins. Dress the tomatoes with olive oil and season with fleur de sel.

TO FINISH

80 g Tomato Relish (page 300)
16 Roasted Tomatoes (page 299)
Petite basil leaves and tops
Basil blossoms
Arugula leaves
Olive oil
Aged balsamic vinegar

Divide the eggplant puree among the four tart shells. The puree should come about halfway up the tart shell sides. Place the coarse ground granola in an even layer over the eggplant puree. Spoon the tomato relish over the granola. Place one filled tart at the center of each plate. Arrange the marinated tomatoes, peeled tomatoes, and roasted tomatoes on and around each tart shell. Garnish each tart with the petite basil leaves and tops, basil blossoms, and arugula. Finish each plate with the granola pieces, olive oil, and aged balsamic vinegar.

Jan. 15. 1843

12-12   61 Ranu

Ranunculus- lacustris

water crowfoot

July. Stagnant water

Rens. C. N.Y.

TOMATO
with Peaches and Almonds

Serves 4

CONFIT OIL

600 g olive oil
5 cloves garlic, crushed
Peeled zest of 1 lemon
10 basil leaves
3 sprigs thyme
2 sprigs rosemary
1 bay leaf

Heat the oil and garlic in a saucepan over medium heat. When the oil reaches 60°C/140°F, remove the pan from the heat and add the lemon zest and herbs. Let steep for 1 hour at room temperature. Strain the oil through a chinois. Set aside 15 g of the oil for the roasted almonds and 20 g for plating. Use the remaining oil for the peach confit.

PEACH CONFIT

40 g sugar
10 g salt
4 peaches
Confit Oil

Preheat the oven to 105°C/225°F. Combine the sugar and salt in a mixing bowl. Mix well and set aside. Halve and pit each peach. Quarter each half and transfer to the sugar-salt mixture. Toss to combine. Arrange the seasoned peaches in a single layer in a roasting pan. In a pot over medium heat, heat the oil to 95°C/200°F and pour over the peaches. Cover the pan with aluminum foil and place in the oven. Bake the peaches until completely tender but not falling apart, about 2½ hours. Cool the peaches to room temperature in the confit oil.

ROASTED ALMONDS

50 g almonds, skin on
15 g Confit Oil
2 g salt

Preheat the oven to 150°C/300°F. Line a baking sheet with parchment paper. Combine the almonds, confit oil, and salt in a mixing bowl and toss to combine. Spread the almonds on the baking sheet. Toast the almonds in the oven until fragrant, about 10 minutes. Let cool to room temperature.

MARINATED TOMATOES

4 heirloom beefsteak tomatoes, quartered
8 heirloom cherry tomatoes, halved
12 basil leaves, torn in half
White Balsamic Vinaigrette (page 285)

Combine the tomatoes with the basil in a mixing bowl and dress with the white balsamic vinaigrette. Toss to evenly coat. Let the tomatoes marinate for at least 30 minutes, but no more than 4 hours. Remove and discard the basil before serving.

TO FINISH

Ricotta salata, for grating
Basil tops and buds
Marjoram tops
20 g aged balsamic vinegar
20 g Confit Oil

Divide the peaches, marinated tomatoes, and almonds among four bowls. Grate the cheese over each salad. Garnish each salad with the basil and marjoram. Finish each salad with aged balsamic vinegar and confit oil.

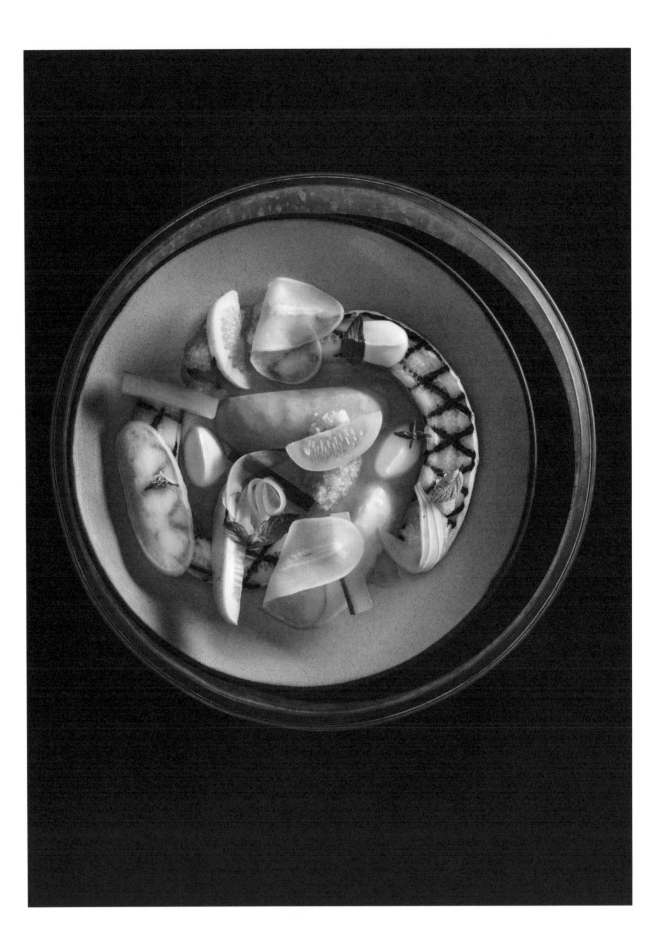

CUCUMBER
Variations with Yogurt and Mint

Serves 4

PRESSED SHEEP'S MILK YOGURT

170 g sheep's milk yogurt
Salt

Wrap the yogurt in cheesecloth and place in a colander over a bowl. Cover the wrapped yogurt with another bowl and place a heavy object in the bowl to act as a weight. Refrigerate the yogurt overnight as it presses. Unwrap the pressed yogurt and transfer to a bowl. Whisk the yogurt until completely smooth. Season with salt.

CUCUMBER CAVIAR

¹/₂ peeled, seeded, and finely diced English cucumber
Salt
25 g Pickled Mustard Seeds (page 294), drained

Line a colander with cheesecloth and set it over a mixing bowl. Season the diced cucumber with salt and place in the prepared colander. Let sit, refrigerated, to drain any excess water, about 2 hours. Just before serving, combine the cucumber dice with the pickled mustard seeds and stir to combine.

CUCUMBER SAUCE

10 basil leaves
10 mint leaves
1 peeled English cucumber
0.5 g xanthan gum
Salt

Line a colander with several layers of cheesecloth and set it over a large mixing bowl. Lightly bruise the basil and mint leaves and place on top of the cheesecloth. Set aside. Cut the cucumber into 2.5-cm (1-inch) pieces and place in a blender. Blend on high speed just until the cucumber is evenly crushed but not completely smooth, about 20 seconds. Pour the pureed mixture into the prepared colander over the bruised herbs. Refrigerate overnight to strain the cucumber water; do not force or squeeze the water out. Transfer the strained water to a blender, discarding the cucumber and herbs. Blend

on medium speed, slowly adding the xanthan gum and continuing to blend for 1 minute to fully hydrate the gum. Season the sauce with salt.

GARLIC PICKLES

2 Salt and Pepper cucumbers
660 g white distilled vinegar
600 g water
3 whole heads garlic, halved lengthwise
50 g salt
5 g whole coriander seeds
8 g mustard powder
2 g dried red pepper flakes
1 g ground turmeric

Place the cucumbers in a heatproof container. Combine all the remaining ingredients in a saucepan over high heat. Stir to incorporate and bring to a boil. Pour the hot pickling liquid over the cucumbers to cover and let cool to room temperature. Transfer to an airtight container, keeping the cucumbers submerged, and refrigerate for at least 1 week before using.

HOT PICKLES

4 lemon cucumbers
660 g white distilled vinegar
600 g water
50 g salt
10 g dried red pepper flakes
8 g black peppercorns
3 g whole coriander seeds
10 g sugar
4 g tomato paste
6 allspice berries
3 bay leaves
3 whole cloves

Place the cucumbers in a heatproof container. Combine all the remaining ingredients in a saucepan over high heat. Stir to incorporate and bring to a boil. Pour the hot pickling liquid over the cucumbers to cover and let cool to room temperature. Transfer to an airtight container, keeping the cucumbers submerged, and refrigerate for at least 1 week before using.

CONTINUED

CUCUMBER VARIATIONS WITH YOGURT AND MINT, CONTINUED

DILL PICKLES

2 white cucumbers
660 g white distilled vinegar
600 g water
100 g dill
50 g salt
15.5 g dill seeds
5 g dried red pepper flakes
3 g whole coriander seeds
3 cloves garlic

Place the cucumbers in a heatproof container. Combine all the remaining ingredients in a saucepan over high heat. Stir to incorporate and bring to a boil. Pour the hot pickling liquid over the cucumbers to cover and let cool to room temperature. Transfer to an airtight container, keeping the cucumbers submerged, and refrigerate for at least 1 week before using.

GRILLED CUCUMBERS

4 Asian burpless cucumbers
Fleur de sel

Preheat a grill pan over high heat. Cut the cucumbers into planks 6 mm (¼ inch) thick and pat dry with a paper towel. Place each plank, cut side facing down, on the hot grill pan and char well, about 4 minutes, rotating once in between to form grill marks. Remove the cucumbers from the grill pan and season with fleur de sel. Let cool to room temperature.

TO FINISH

½ English cucumber
1 lemon cucumber
Lemon Vinaigrette (page 285)
Petite basil
Petite mint
Olive oil

Cut the English cucumber into batons, with the skin but without any seeds, each about 6.4 cm (2½ inches) long. Thinly shave the lemon cucumber lengthwise and combine in a mixing bowl with the batons. Dress the cucumbers with lemon vinaigrette and toss to combine. Divide 2 garlic cucumbers, halved lengthwise; 2 dill pickles, halved lengthwise; 1 hot pickle, cut into wedges; the grilled cucumbers; and the dressed cucumber batons among four plates. Spoon the cucumber caviar and sheep's milk yogurt on and around the pickles on each plate. Garnish each plate with the dressed cucumber shaves, basil, and mint. Sauce each plate with the cucumber sauce. Break the sauce on the plate with several drops of olive oil.

SUMMER BEANS
with Tuna and a Soft-Boiled Egg

Serves 4

TONNATO SAUCE

9 cloves Garlic Confit (page 298)
40 g lemon juice
25 g caper brine
5 g Dijon mustard
1 egg yolk
75 g Lemon Oil (page 284)
75 g Garlic Confit oil (page 298)
150 g oil-packed tuna, drained
15 g capers, drained and coarsely chopped
Salt

Combine the garlic confit cloves, lemon juice, caper brine, and mustard in a blender. Start to blend on low speed. Add the egg yolk and blend until incorporated. Slowly add both oils and puree on high speed until fully emulsified. Transfer the sauce to a mixing bowl and gently fold in the tuna and chopped capers. Do not overmix the sauce. Season with salt and keep refrigerated until ready to serve.

SUMMER BEANS

36 haricots verts
36 yellow wax beans
8 golden sugar snap peas

Bring a large pot of salted water to a rolling boil over high heat and prepare an ice bath. Blanch each kind of beans separately, until they are just tender, about 3 minutes for the haricot verts and wax beans and about 1 minute for the snap peas. As they finish, shock the beans in the ice bath. When the beans are cold, drain them from the ice water. Trim and discard the stem ends from the beans. Halve half of the haricot verts and wax beans on a bias. Leave the remaining beans whole. Cut half of the snap peas into 1.3-cm (½-inch) pieces on a bias.

ROASTED RADISHES

12 Easter egg radishes, halved lengthwise
12 g grapeseed oil
60 g Lemon Vinaigrette (page 285)

Preheat the oven to 175°C/350°F. Heat the oil in a large sauté pan over high heat. Place the radishes in the pan, cut side facing down. Sear the radishes until caramelized and browned, about 2 minutes. Transfer the pan to the oven and roast until tender, about 7 minutes. Remove the pan from the oven and transfer the radishes to a paper towel to drain. Marinate the roasted radishes in a mixing bowl with the lemon vinaigrette for at least 30 minutes or up to 2 hours before serving.

BLISTERED TOMATOES

16 cherry tomatoes
60 g Lemon Vinaigrette (page 285)

Heat a large sauté pan over high heat. When the pan is very hot, place the tomatoes in it in a single layer. Cook, shaking occasionally, just until they begin to burst, about 2 minutes. Transfer the blistered tomatoes to a mixing bowl and marinate in the lemon vinaigrette for at least 30 minutes or up to 2 hours before serving.

TO FINISH

0.5 g xanthan gum
1 baby fennel bulb
Lemon Vinaigrette (page 285)
8 Taggiasca olives
Soft-Boiled Eggs (page 300)
Fleur de sel
24 Pickled Red Onion Rings (page 294)
Flat-leaf parsley leaves
Basil leaves

Remove the roasted radishes and blistered tomatoes from the lemon vinaigrette marinade. Combine the marinades from both in a blender. On medium speed, slowly add the xanthan gum and blend for 1 minute to fully hydrate. Set the vinaigrette aside. Spread the tonnato sauce onto four plates. Thinly slice the baby fennel lengthwise using a mandoline. Combine the fennel shaves with the summer beans and dress with lemon vinaigrette. Toss to combine. Arrange the dressed beans, fennel, roasted radishes, blistered tomatoes, and olives over the tonnato sauce. Cut the soft-boiled eggs in half, season the yolks with fleur de sel, and nestle the egg halves in among the beans. Garnish each plate with the pickled red onions, parsley leaves, and basil. Sauce each plate with the reserved radish and tomato vinaigrette.

KABOCHA SQUASH
with Red Pear and Pumpkin Seeds

Serves 4

ROASTED KABOCHA SQUASH

1 kabocha squash, halved
35 g olive oil
Salt
3 sprigs thyme

Preheat the oven to 245°C/475°F. Line a baking sheet with parchment paper. Remove and discard the seeds from the squash. Quarter each half and set aside one-quarter for the pickled squash. Cut the remaining quarters into 5-cm (2-inch) pieces. Combine the squash with the olive oil, salt, and thyme in a mixing bowl, tossing to combine. Transfer the seasoned squash to the prepared baking sheet. Roast the squash in the oven until thoroughly browned and tender, about 12 minutes. Discard the thyme. Keep the squash warm.

ROASTED PEAR

2 red pears
15 g olive oil
Salt
2 sprigs thyme

Preheat the oven to 245°C/475°F. Line a baking sheet with parchment paper. Quarter and core the pears. Cut each quarter pear in half lengthwise. Combine the pear wedges with the olive oil, salt, and thyme in a mixing bowl and toss to combine. Transfer the seasoned pears to the baking sheet and roast until thoroughly browned and tender, about 6 minutes. Discard the thyme. Keep the pears warm.

TOASTED PUMPKIN SEEDS

125 g pumpkin seeds
10 g olive oil
Salt

Preheat the oven to 175°C/350°F. Line a baking sheet with parchment paper. Combine the pumpkin seeds and olive oil in a mixing bowl, season with salt, and toss to combine. Spread the pumpkin seeds on the baking sheet and toast until fragrant, about 7 minutes. Let cool to room temperature.

PICKLED SQUASH

Reserved ¼ kabocha squash
200 g White Balsamic Pickling Liquid (page 295)

Using a mandoline, slice paper-thin arched shaves of squash and place in a heatproof container. Heat the pickling liquid to a simmer in a saucepan over high heat. Pour the liquid over the squash shaves to cover and let cool to room temperature.

SQUASH VINAIGRETTE

240 g butternut squash juice, from about 1 squash
0.75 g xanthan gum
10 g lime juice
Salt

Allow the squash juice to sit at room temperature for 1 hour to let the starch settle. Pour the juice off to separate from the starch. Discard the starch and transfer the decanted juice to a blender. Blend on medium speed, slowly adding the xanthan gum. Continue to blend for 1 minute to allow the gum to fully hydrate. Add the lime juice and season with salt.

TO FINISH

Parmesan, for grating
Lemon Vinaigrette (page 285)
1 red pear
Pumpkin seed oil

Grate the Parmesan over the warm roasted squash. Combine the squash with the pears and pumpkin seeds in a mixing bowl. Dress the squash and pears with the vinaigrette and toss to combine. Divide the dressed squash and pears among four bowls. Cut the cheeks off the pear and thinly shave the cheeks using a mandoline. Divide the pickled squash shaves and pear shaves over each salad. Sauce each salad with the squash vinaigrette and break the sauce with several drops of pumpkin seed oil.

BROCCOLI RABE
with Anchovy and Lemon

Serves 4

_____

CHARRED BROCCOLI RABE

20 broccoli rabe stalks
Lemon Oil (page 284)
Salt

Bring a large pot of salted water to a boil over high heat and prepare an ice bath. Trim and discard the bottom ends of the broccoli rabe stalks. Separate the leaves from the florets and set aside for garnish. Blanch the broccoli rabe tops in the boiling water until they are tender yet retain a little bite in the center, about 2 minutes. Shock the broccoli rabe in the ice bath. When cold, drain the broccoli and pat dry with a paper towel.

Heat a grill pan over high heat until very hot. Transfer the broccoli rabe to a mixing bowl and lightly dress with lemon oil. Season with salt and toss to combine. Char the dressed broccoli rabe on the grill, about 1 minute per side, and transfer to a paper towel to drain. Keep at room temperature until ready to serve.

_____

TO FINISH

Parmesan Sauce (page 305)
Lemon Oil (page 284)
Salt
Reserved broccoli rabe leaves
Lemon Vinaigrette (page 285)
8 anchovy fillets
8 lemon segments
Parmesan, for shaving
Broccoli flowers

Spoon the Parmesan sauce into the center of each of four plates. Lightly dress the charred broccoli rabe in a bowl with lemon oil and salt. Gently toss to combine. Divide the charred broccoli rabe among the plates. Dress the broccoli rabe leaves with the lemon vinaigrette in a separate bowl and toss to combine. Divide the dressed leaves, anchovy fillets, and lemon segments on and around the charred broccoli rabe on each plate. Using a vegetable peeler, shave Parmesan over each plate and garnish with broccoli flowers.

RADICCHIO
with Granny Smith Apples and Mozzarella

Serves 4

APPLE VINEGAR

1 Red Delicious apple, quartered and cored
1 Mutsu apple, quartered and cored
500 g apple cider vinegar

Cut the apple wedges into 2.5-cm (1-inch) pieces and place in a heatproof container. Heat the vinegar in a saucepan to a boil and pour over the apples to cover. Let cool to room temperature. Transfer to an airtight container and refrigerate for 3 days. Strain the infused vinegar and discard the apples. Reserve the apple vinegar in an airtight container, refrigerated for up to 1 week.

APPLE VINAIGRETTE

60 g Apple Vinegar
20 g olive oil
60 g grapeseed oil
8 g salt
8 g sugar

Combine all of the ingredients in a mixing bowl and whisk well to combine, making sure to dissolve the salt and sugar. Reserve the apple vinaigrette in an airtight container, refrigerated, for up to 1 week.

TO FINISH

1 Granny Smith apple, quartered and cored
1 Honeycrisp apple, quartered and cored
White Balsamic Vinaigrette (page 285)
6 mozzarella balls, halved
Olive oil
Fleur de sel
Cracked black pepper
1 head radicchio, quartered and cored,
  leaves separated
2 heads butter lettuce, leaves separated
Basil leaves

Cut each quarter apple lengthwise into four wedges. In a bowl, lightly dress the apple wedges with white balsamic vinaigrette. Brush the mozzarella balls with olive oil and season with fleur de sel and black pepper. In another bowl, combine the radicchio and butter lettuce leaves. Dress the lettuces with apple vinaigrette. Divide the dressed lettuces among four bowls. Divide the apple wedges, mozzarella pieces, and basil leaves among the salads and layer them among the lettuces.

FLUKE
with Sorrel and Royal Trumpet Mushrooms

Serves 4

BLACK ONION POWDER

2 Spanish onions, thinly sliced
230 g water
20 g squid ink

Heat the onions and half of the water in a large saucepan over medium heat. Cook, stirring frequently, until the onions begin to soften. Continue cooking and stirring, adding the remaining water in 20 g increments as needed to prevent burning until the onions are completely soft and slightly caramelized, about 45 minutes.

Preheat the oven to 95°C/200°F. Line a baking sheet with a nonstick baking mat. Add the squid ink to the onion and stir to incorporate. Cook for 2 minutes, just to cook the squid ink, and transfer onto the prepared baking sheet. Evenly spread the mixture as thinly as possible. Dry in the oven until completely dehydrated, about 6 hours. The onion sheet should feel brittle and very hard. Break the sheet into small pieces and grind in a spice grinder to a very fine powder. Pass the powder through a fine-mesh strainer. Reserve the powder in a dry, airtight container for up to 1 week.

AMARANTH CRUMBLE

95 g amaranth
70 g Black Onion Powder
Canola oil, for frying

Bring a large pot of salted water to a rolling boil over high heat. Add the amaranth and turn the heat to medium. Cook, stirring occasionally, until the amaranth is completely tender, about 35 minutes. Preheat the oven to 105°C/225°F. Drain the amaranth and spread evenly on a baking sheet lined with parchment paper. Dry the amaranth in the oven until completely dehydrated, about 2¹/₂ hours.

Heat 7.5 cm (3 inches) of oil in a heavy pot to 230°C/450°F. Quickly fry the dried amaranth in small batches until puffed and golden brown, no more than 5 seconds. Immediately spread each batch of fried amaranth on a paper towel in a single layer to prevent burning and

to drain. Let the amaranth cool to room temperature. Combine the fried amaranth with the black onion powder in a mixing bowl. Stir and mix well. Reserve the crumble in a dry, airtight container for up to 1 week.

SORREL SAUCE

35 g baby spinach leaves
100 g sorrel leaves, coarsely chopped
2 egg yolks
Ice water
95 g grapeseed oil
30 g Lemon Oil (page 284)
¹/₂ shallot, finely chopped
Grated zest of ¹/₂ lemon
Salt

Bring a pot of salted water to a boil and prepare an ice bath. Blanch the spinach in the boiling water until completely tender, about 5 minutes. When you rub the spinach between your fingers, it should fall apart. Immediately shock the spinach in the ice bath. When cold, drain the spinach and squeeze dry. Combine the blanched spinach with the sorrel, egg yolks, and a few drops of ice water in a blender. Puree on high speed until completely smooth, adding more ice water as necessary to achieve a smooth consistency. Turn the speed to medium and slowly pour in both oils to emulsify. Transfer the sauce to an airtight container and keep refrigerated. Just before serving, stir in the shallot and lemon zest and season with salt.

PICKLED TRUMPET MUSHROOMS

1 (5-cm/2-inch) square piece of kombu
470 g dry white wine
240 g White Balsamic Pickling Liquid (page 295)
15 g salt
12 small royal trumpet mushrooms

Rinse the kombu under cold running water until softened and pliable. Drain and set aside. Heat the wine in a saucepan over medium heat and bring to a simmer. Reduce the wine by three-quarters. Add the pickling liquid, softened kombu, and salt to the pan and stir to incorporate. Remove the pan from the heat and let steep at room temperature for 10 minutes. Add the mushrooms to the pan and return the heat to medium. Return the liquid to a simmer and cook the mushrooms until they are tender, about 3 minutes. Remove the pan from the heat and let cool to room temperature. Strain the mushrooms

CONTINUED

and reserve the liquid. Discard the kombu. Set aside 165 g of the strained liquid for the pickled mushroom vinaigrette. Place the mushrooms in the remaining liquid and keep refrigerated.

PICKLED MUSHROOM VINAIGRETTE

165 g reserved mushroom pickling liquid
0.5 g xanthan gum
70 g Lemon Oil (page 284)

Pour the pickling liquid into the blender. While blending on low speed, slowly add the xanthan gum. Continue to blend on medium speed for about 1 minute to fully hydrate the gum. Slowly pour in the lemon oil while continuing to blend to emulsify. Reserve the vinaigrette in an airtight container, refrigerated, for up to 1 week.

TO FINISH

1 fluke fillet, about 225 g
Fleur de sel
2 royal trumpet mushrooms
Olive oil
Sorrel leaves

Slice the fluke 3 mm (1/8 inch) thick on a bias. Divide the slices into four portions and brush generously with the pickled mushroom vinaigrette. Season with fleur de sel. Place each fluke portion in the center of each plate. Using a mandoline, slice the mushrooms lengthwise paper thin. Brush the mushroom slices with olive oil and season with fleur de sel. Divide the mushroom slices, pickled mushrooms, and 90 g of amaranth crumble among the plates, arranging them around the fluke. Sauce the plates with the sorrel sauce and garnish with sorrel leaves. Serve immediately.

PEEKYTOE CRAB
with Daikon and Granny Smith Apple

Serves 4

CRAB SALAD

200 g peekytoe crabmeat
50 g Mayonnaise (page 304)
40 g peeled daikon, diced 3 mm (⅛ inch)
40 g peeled Granny Smith apple, diced 3 mm (⅛ inch)
10 g sliced chives
10 g lime juice
Salt
Piment d'Espelette

Check the crabmeat for any shells. Place on a paper towel to drain any excess water. Combine the crab with the mayonnaise, daikon, apple, chives, and lime juice in a bowl and mix until incorporated. Season with salt and espelette and stir to combine. Keep refrigerated.

PICKLED DAIKON

1 daikon, about 350 g, peeled
400 g White Balsamic Pickling Liquid (page 295)

Using a turning slicer, julienne the daikon into long strands. Place the daikon in a heatproof container. Bring the pickling liquid to a boil in a saucepan over high heat. Pour the hot liquid over the daikon and allow to cool to room temperature. Strain off 60 g of the daikon pickling liquid through a chinois and set aside for the daikon vinaigrette. Reserve the pickled daikon in the pickling liquid and keep refrigerated.

DAIKON VINAIGRETTE

120 g Chicken Stock (page 303)
60 g reserved daikon pickling liquid
15 g honey
1 g xanthan gum
75 g canola oil
Salt

Heat the chicken stock in a saucepan over high heat. When the stock is at a simmer, turn the heat to low and continue to simmer until reduced by half. Add the pickling liquid and honey, stirring to combine. Remove the pan from the heat and transfer the mixture to a blender. While blending on medium speed, slowly add the xanthan gum and continue to blend for 1 minute to fully hydrate the gum. Slowly add the oil, blending to emulsify. Season the vinaigrette with salt and reserve in an airtight container, refrigerated, for up to 3 days.

TO FINISH

2 Granny Smith apples, peeled

Use a 9-cm (3½-inch) ring mold to divide the crab salad among four plates. Drain the pickled daikon from the pickling liquid and transfer to a mixing bowl. Dress the daikon with the vinaigrette and arrange over the crab salad rounds. Using a turning slicer, julienne the peeled apples into long strands. Divide the apple strands among the plates, placing them on top of the pickled daikon.

SMOKED TROUT
with Cucumber and Avocado

Serves 4

SMOKED TROUT

> 4 trout fillets, about 125 g each, skin on and
>   pin bones removed
> Salt

Gently pat the trout fillets dry with a paper towel. Pack the trout fillets in salt and refrigerate for 10 minutes. Remove the trout from the salt and rinse thoroughly in cold water. Pat the fillets dry with a paper towel and lay out skin side down on a wire rack set over a baking sheet. Refrigerate overnight, uncovered.

Preheat the broiler. Soak 35 g of applewood chips in cold water for 10 minutes. Drain. Place ten charcoal briquettes in a single layer in a roasting pan lined with aluminum foil. Place the charcoal in the broiler until lit, about 15 minutes. Remove the charcoal from the broiler and sprinkle enough wood chips over the charcoal to put out any live flames, but not so much that the embers are smothered. Turn off the broiler and set the oven to 135°C/275°F. Place the trout in the oven with the charcoal and tightly close the oven door. Hot-smoke until the trout is just cooked without drying out, about 8 minutes. The flesh should flake apart easily. Remove the trout from the oven, let it cool until the pan can be safely wrapped with plastic wrap. Wrap the pan tightly with plastic wrap and transfer to the refrigerator to cool completely.

When chilled, unwrap the trout, remove and discard the skin, trim the lower belly part of each fillet, and reserve for the rillettes. Portion the trimmed fillets by gently breaking into two large pieces by hand. Keep refrigerated.

YOGURT SAUCE

> 60 g cucumber juice (from about 1 unpeeled cucumber)
> 160 g Greek yogurt
> 1/2 clove garlic
> 25 g White Balsamic Vinaigrette (page 285)
> Salt

Combine the cucumber juice and yogurt in a mixing bowl. Using a Microplane, grate the garlic into the yogurt and whisk to combine. Slowly whisk in the vinaigrette to emulsify. Season with salt.

CHIVE CUCUMBER PLANKS

> 2 Asian burpless cucumbers
> 15 g Chive Oil (page 284)
> 1 g salt

Cut the cucumbers into planks 6 mm (1/4 inch) thick. Combine the planks with the chive oil and salt in a sous vide bag and seal airtight. Keep the cucumber planks refrigerated in the bag for at least 3 hours before serving.

PICKLED LEMON CUCUMBER

> 1 lemon cucumber
> White Balsamic Pickling Liquid (page 295)

Cut the cucumber into twelve wedges and place in an airtight sealable container. Cover the cucumber with the pickling liquid, seal, and refrigerate overnight.

DILL CREAM

> 60 g Mayonnaise (page 304)
> 100 g crème fraîche
> Grated zest of 1 lemon
> 1 shallot, finely chopped
> 2 sprigs dill, stems removed and finely chopped
> 10 g lemon juice
> 3 g salt

Combine all the ingredients in a mixing bowl and mix well. Reserve in an airtight container, refrigerated, for up to 2 days.

CONTINUED

TROUT RILLETTES

120 g reserved trim from the smoked trout
75 g Dill Cream

Gently mix the trout and dill cream in a mixing bowl with a rubber spatula. Keep refrigerated.

TO FINISH

4 Kirby cucumbers
½ avocado
Lemon Vinaigrette (page 285)
Fleur de sel
Olive oil
8 cucamelons, halved
Blooming cucumbers
Bronze fennel
Fennel pollen

Using a mandoline, shave one Kirby cucumber crosswise into 1.5-mm (¹⁄₁₆-inch) thick slices. Shave another Kirby cucumber lengthwise into 1.5-mm (¹⁄₁₆-inch) thick slices. Submerge the cucumber slices in ice water. Cut the remaining two Kirby cucumbers into planks 6 mm (¼ inch) thick. Cut the avocado into eight wedges. Dress the avocado wedges and cucumber planks with lemon vinaigrette and season with fleur de sel. Drain the pickled lemon cucumbers from their pickling liquid.

Swirl the yogurt sauce onto each of four plates. Brush the smoked trout pieces with olive oil and season with fleur de sel. Remove the chive cucumber planks from the bag and drain on a paper towel. Divide the chive cucumber planks, Kirby cucumber planks, smoked trout, avocado wedges, trout rillettes, and pickled lemon cucumbers over the yogurt sauce. Drain the cucumber slices, combine them with the cucamelons in a mixing bowl, dress with lemon vinaigrette, and season with fleur de sel. Arrange the cucumber slices and cucamelons over the trout on each plate. Garnish each plate with the blooming cucumbers and bronze fennel. Finish each plate with fennel pollen.

MACKEREL
with Beets and Wasabi

Serves 4

PICKLED GREEN STRAWBERRIES

8 green strawberries, hulled
White Balsamic Pickling Liquid (page 295)

Combine the strawberries in an airtight container with enough pickling liquid to cover and refrigerate for at least 1 week and up to 1 month.

BEET VINAIGRETTE

Reserved cooking liquid from Demi-Dehydrated Beets (page 297)
30 g beet juice (from about 1/4 large beet)
5 g red wine vinegar
Salt

Heat the reserved cooking liquid and beet juice in a saucepan over medium heat. Simmer, stirring occasionally to prevent burning, and reduce until it has a syruplike consistency. Remove the pan from the heat and strain through a chinois. Whisk in the vinegar and season with salt. Allow to cool to room temperature. Keep refrigerated until ready to serve.

KOMBU-CURED MACKEREL

1 (18-cm/7-inch) square piece of kombu
80 g salt
40 g sugar
1 mackerel fillet, about 340 g

Rinse the kombu under cold running water until softened and pliable. Cut the kombu into small pieces with scissors. Combine the kombu, salt, and sugar in a food processor. Blend together until the mixture resembles wet sand, about 3 minutes. Place the mackerel, skin side down, in a nonmetallic baking dish. Completely cover the flesh of the mackerel with the kombu-salt cure and cover with plastic wrap. Refrigerate for 40 minutes to cure. Rinse the cure off the mackerel under cold running water and pat dry with paper towels. Keep refrigerated until ready to serve.

YUZU ORANGE VINAIGRETTE

60 g yuzu juice
40 g orange juice
7 g sugar
0.5 g xanthan gum
25 g Lemon Oil (page 284)
Salt

Combine the yuzu juice, orange juice, and sugar in a blender and begin to blend on low speed. Slowly add the xanthan gum and blend on medium speed for 1 minute to fully hydrate the gum. Slowly add the lemon oil and blend to emulsify. Season with salt. Reserve the vinaigrette in an airtight container, refrigerated, until ready to serve.

TO FINISH

Fleur de sel
Wasabi, for grating
12 Demi-Dehydrated Beets (page 297)
2 baby red beets
2 baby yellow beets
2 baby chiogga beets
1 shallot, thinly sliced into rings
Wasabi leaves
Olive oil

Using a kitchen torch, lightly brown and blister the skin of the cured mackerel. The fillet will curl slightly. Slice the cured mackerel into 6-mm (1/4-inch) thick slices. Brush the slices generously with the yuzu orange vinaigrette and season with fleur de sel. Grate the wasabi over the fish and divide the slices among four plates. Brush the dehydrated beets with olive oil and arrange among the mackerel slices. Using a mandoline, slice the baby beets lengthwise into paper-thin shaves. In a small mixing bowl, dress the beet shaves with yuzu orange vinaigrette. Divide the dressed beet shaves among the four plates, dividing the colors evenly. Slice the pickled green strawberries and arrange among the beet shaves. Garnish each plate with shallot rings and wasabi leaves. Sauce each plate with the beet vinaigrette and break the vinaigrette with several drops of olive oil.

TUNA
Seared Tartare with Radishes and Capers

Serves 4

PICKLED BLACK RADISH RIBBONS

1 black radish
120 g White Balsamic Pickling Liquid (page 295)

Prepare an ice bath. Using a turning slicer, cut sheets from the black radish with the skin. Trim the sheets into ribbons 20 cm by 2.5 cm (8 inches by 1 inch) long. Place the ribbons into a heatproof container. Heat the pickling liquid to a simmer in a saucepan over high heat. Pour the liquid over the ribbons so they are covered completely. Chill over the ice bath.

PICKLED BLACK RADISH DICE

1/2 peeled black radish
60 g White Balsamic Pickling Liquid (page 295)

Cut the radish into 3-mm (1/8-inch) dice. Place the diced radish in a heatproof container. Heat the pickling liquid to a simmer in a saucepan over high heat. Pour the pickling liquid over the diced radish to cover. Allow to cool to room temperature.

FRIED CAPERS

Canola oil, for frying
20 capers, drained, rinsed, and patted dry

Heat 7.5 cm (3 inches) of oil in a large, heavy pot to 160°C/325°F. Fry the capers until crispy, about 3 minutes. Remove the capers from the oil and transfer to a paper towel to drain.

APPLE CAPER SAUCE

240 g apple juice (from about 6 Granny Smith apples)
15 g white soy sauce
10 g caper brine
1.5 g xanthan gum

Combine the apple juice, soy sauce, and caper brine in a blender and begin to blend on low speed. Slowly add the xanthan gum and continue to blend on medium speed for 1 minute to fully hydrate the gum. Transfer the sauce to an airtight container and keep refrigerated.

TO FINISH

300 g bigeye tuna, diced 3 mm (1/8 inch)
1/2 peeled Granny Smith apple, diced 3 mm (1/8 inch)
10 g capers, rinsed and chopped
40 g white soy sauce
5 g Chile Oil (page 284)
35 g Lemon Oil (page 284)
Grated zest of 1 lemon
3 g salt
Black radish, for grating
1 Granny Smith apple
Watercress sprigs
Olive oil

Heat a griddle to 260°C/500°F. Combine the tuna, pickled black radish dice, apple dice, chopped capers, white soy, chile oil, lemon oil, lemon zest, and salt in a mixing bowl and stir gently just to combine. Cut four 15-cm (6-inch) squares of parchment paper. Set four 8.5-cm (3 3/8-inch) ring molds on top of the parchment squares. Divide the tuna mixture evenly among the four molds and gently press to evenly fill the molds. Transfer the tartare rounds with the ring molds to the griddle and slide out the parchment papers. Sear the rounds of tuna tartare on the griddle until well browned, about 30 seconds. Using a wide offset spatula, transfer the rounds to a paper towel to drain. Carefully remove the molds from the tuna tartare rounds and invert each onto the center of a plate. Divide the fried capers among the tartare rounds. Grate the black radish over each round. Using a turning slicer, cut sheets, with the skin, from the apple. Cut the sheets into ribbons 20 cm by 2.5 cm (8 inches by 1 inch) long. Garnish each tartare with the apple ribbons, pickled black radish ribbons, and watercress sprigs. Sauce each plate with apple caper sauce and break the sauce with several drops of olive oil.

SCALLOP
with Sea Urchin and Fennel

Serves 4

SCALLOPS

8 U10 scallops, about 365 g

Remove and discard the side muscle from each scallop. Slice the scallops lengthwise into 6-mm (1/4-inch) thick rounds. Punch the scallop slices with a 4-cm (1 1/2-inch) ring cutter. Place the scallop rounds in a single layer on a baking sheet lined with acetate. Keep refrigerated until ready to serve.

GREEN APPLE SAUCE

180 g Granny Smith apple juice (from about 3 apples)
1 g ascorbic acid
Salt
2 g xanthan gum

Add the ascorbic acid to the apple juice immediately after juicing to preserve its green color. Strain the juice through a coffee filter to clarify. Season with salt and transfer to a blender. Begin to blend at low speed and slowly add the xanthan gum. Blend on medium speed for 1 minute to fully hydrate the gum. Strain the sauce through a chinois and keep refrigerated.

FENNEL SHAVES

1 fennel bulb

Thinly slice the fennel bulb crosswise, beginning at the top end, using a mandoline. Reserve the fennel shaves in ice water until ready to serve.

GRANNY SMITH APPLE ROUNDS

1 Granny Smith apple

Using a mandoline, slice the apple 1.5 mm (1/16 inch) thick. Punch the slices into rings without skin, using a 4-cm (1 1/2-inch) ring cutter.

TO FINISH

Olive oil
Fleur de sel
Fennel pollen
Cracked black pepper
Sliced chives
16 sea urchin tongues
White Balsamic Vinaigrette (page 285)
Fennel blossoms
Bronze fennel fronds

Brush the scallop slices with olive oil and season with fleur de sel, fennel pollen, and cracked black pepper. Garnish with sliced chives. Divide the scallop slices among four plates. Arrange the sea urchin tongues and apple punches on and around the scallops. Drain the fennel shaves and dress with the white balsamic vinaigrette in a bowl. Garnish each plate with the dressed fennel shaves, fennel blossoms, and fennel fronds. Sauce each plate with the green apple sauce. Break the sauce on each plate with several drops of olive oil.

FOIE GRAS
Torchon with Tête de Cochon, Radishes, and Nasturtium

Serves 4

TÊTE DE COCHON ROLL

*1 young pig's head, cut in half vertically,
    brain removed, about 2 kg*
Pork Brine (page 306)
Pig's Head Cooking Liquid (page 305)
8 g salt
20 g sherry vinegar

Submerge the pig's head in the pork brine and refrigerate for 24 hours. Preheat the oven to 120°C/250°F. Remove the pig's head from the brine and rinse thoroughly with cold running water. Pat dry. Place the brined head in a roasting pan and cover with the cooking liquid. Cover the pan with aluminum foil. Cook the head until the jawbone easily separates from the skull, about 4 hours. Remove from the oven and allow to cool just enough to handle. Carefully lift the head out of the cooking liquid. Strain the cooking liquid through a chinois and skim the fat from the surface. Set aside 65 g of the liquid to season the meat. Pick all of the meat from the bones, keeping the lean meat and fat separate. Discard the skin and bones. Small dice the fat and set aside. Chop the lean meat and weigh it. Weigh out one-quarter of the lean meat's total weight in diced fat and combine it with the lean meat in a mixing bowl. Season the meat/fat mixture with the reserved cooking liquid, salt, and sherry vinegar. The mixture should be moist but not soupy.

Portion the mixture into 100 g portions. Line a work surface with a double layer of plastic wrap. Spread one portion of the mixture along the bottom end of the plastic wrap in a line 15 cm (6 inches) long. Using the plastic wrap, tightly roll the mixture into a cylinder. Twist the ends of the plastic wrap around the cylinder to make the roll as tight as possible. The diameter of the cylinder should be 2.9 cm (1⅛ inches) wide. Tie off the ends. Use a small, sharp paring knife to pop any air bubbles. Repeat with the remaining mixture. Refrigerate until firm, about 6 hours, or overnight. Any remaining rolls may be kept, tightly wrapped and refrigerated, for up to 3 days, or frozen for up to 2 weeks.

FOIE GRAS AND TÊTE DE COCHON TORCHON

500 g Marinated Foie Gras (page 298)
1 Tête de Cochon Roll

Prepare an ice bath. Line a work surface with a double layer of plastic wrap. Remove the foie gras from the sous vide bag and place between two sheets of acetate. Roll the foie gras out so that it is 1.7 cm (⅔ inch) thick, 15 cm (6 inches) long, and 23.5 cm (9¼ inches) wide. Remove the top layer of acetate and trim any excess. Remove the plastic wrap from the tête de cochon roll. Place the tête toward the bottom, longer end of the foie gras sheet. Using the acetate as an aid, roll the foie gras tightly around the tête de cochon roll. The foie gras should wrap perfectly around the tête without any gaps or overlap. Transfer the torchon to the plastic wrap–lined work surface. Cover the torchon tightly with the plastic wrap and make sure it is a perfectly round cylinder. Tie off both ends and pop any air bubbles using a small, sharp paring knife. Immediately submerge the torchon in the ice bath until firm, about 3 hours. Reserve the torchon, tightly wrapped or sealed airtight in a sous vide bag, in the refrigerator for up to 3 days.

TO FINISH

Olive oil
Fleur de sel
Horseradish Gremolata (page 298)
Horseradish, for grating
Pommery Mayonnaise (page 305)
Pickled Radishes (page 294)
Nasturtium leaves and flowers

With a hot, dry knife, cut four 2-cm (¾-inch)-thick slices from the torchon. Wrap any remaining torchon tightly with plastic wrap and reserve, refrigerated, for up to 3 days. Punch the slices with a 6.5-cm (2⅝-inch) ring cutter. Discard the trim. Brush each punched slice with olive oil and season with fleur de sel. Place a 2.5-cm (1-inch) ring cutter slightly to the right of the tête de cochon on each slice of torchon. Spoon the gremolata into the ring cutter, using it as a mold. Lightly press down the sauce so it holds its shape and is level. Place a little grated horseradish above the gremolata on each slice of torchon. Serve the torchon with pommery mayonnaise, pickled radishes, nasturtium leaves, nasturtium flowers, and additional fleur de sel.

FOIE GRAS
Torchon with Black Truffle, Mustard, and Potato

Serves 4

TRUFFLED FOIE GRAS TORCHON

460 g Marinated Foie Gras (page 298)
60 g black truffles, finely chopped

Prepare an ice bath. Place the marinated foie gras between two sheets of acetate and roll to 1.3 cm (½ inch) thick. Remove the top sheet of acetate. Cover the top surface of the foie gras evenly with the chopped truffles. Gently press the truffles into the surface of the foie gras. Refrigerate the foie gras until firm, about 2 hours. When firm, break the foie gras into large, uneven pieces. Line a work surface with a double layer of plastic wrap. Stack the foie gras pieces irregularly and slightly overlapping but evenly along the bottom edge of the plastic wrap in a line that is 15 cm (6 inches) long. Using the plastic wrap, tightly roll the foie gras into a cylinder. Twist the ends of the plastic wrap around the cylinder to make the roll as tight as possible. The diameter of the cylinder should be 7 cm (2¾ inches). Tie off the ends. Use a sharp paring knife to pop any air bubbles in the torchon. Immediately submerge the torchon in ice water until firm, about 3 hours. Reserve, tightly wrapped or sealed airtight in a sous vide bag, in the refrigerator for up to 3 days.

POTATO ONION RELISH

200 g Simple Syrup (page 300)
½ onion, diced 6 mm (¼ inch)
175 g White Balsamic Pickling Liquid (page 295)
1 Yukon Gold potato, peeled and diced 6 mm (¼ inch)
Salt
25 g Pickled Mustard Seeds (page 294)
1 g xanthan gum

Combine the syrup and onion in a saucepan over medium heat. When the syrup comes to a boil, drain the onion and discard the syrup. Transfer the onions to an airtight sealable container and cover with the pickling liquid. Seal and refrigerate overnight. Generously cover the potato dice with cold water in a saucepan and season with salt. Cook the potato dice very gently over low heat until just tender, about 25 minutes. Drain the potatoes and allow to cool to room temperature. Strain the pickling liquid

from the onions, reserve the onions, and transfer the liquid to a blender. Begin blending on low speed and slowly add the xanthan gum. Blend on medium speed for 1 minute to fully hydrate the gum. In a mixing bowl, combine the potatoes with the pickled onion and mustard seeds. Add just enough of the thickened pickling liquid to bind the mixture.

MUSTARD MARINADE

1.2 kg Chicken Stock (page 303)
30 g sherry vinegar
30 g whole-grain mustard
30 g Dijon mustard
Salt

Heat the chicken stock in a saucepan over high heat and bring to a simmer. Turn the heat to medium and continue simmering the stock until reduced to a syrup-like consistency, about 40 minutes. Remove the pan from the heat and add the sherry vinegar and both mustards. Season with salt and keep warm.

MUSTARD CREAM SAUCE

60 g cream
60 g Mustard Marinade

Heat the cream in a saucepan over medium heat to a simmer. Reduce the cream by half and remove the pan from the heat. Add the mustard marinade and stir to combine. Keep warm.

MARINATED POTATOES

24 peanut potatoes
3 sprigs thyme
1 clove garlic, crushed
Olive oil
Salt
Mustard Marinade

Preheat the oven to 150°C/300°F. Combine the potatoes with the thyme and garlic in a baking dish. Cover with olive oil and season with salt. Cover the baking dish with aluminum foil and cook the potatoes in the oven until just tender, about 1 hour. Remove the potatoes from the oven, uncover, and let cool in the oil to room temperature. Drain and discard the oil. Peel the potatoes and submerge the peeled potatoes in the remaining mustard marinade. Refrigerate the marinated potatoes in an airtight container overnight.

CONTINUED

TO FINISH

Olive oil
Fleur de sel
Black Truffle Puree (page 296)
Pickled Red Onion Rings (page 294)
Rye Crisps (page 289)
Black truffle, for shaving
Watercress sprigs
Buttermilk Vinaigrette (page 284)
4 slices Black Truffle Potato Bread (page 286), toasted

With a hot, dry knife, cut four 2-cm ($^3/_4$-inch) thick slices from the torchon. Wrap any remaining torchon tightly with plastic wrap and reserve, refrigerated, for up to 3 days. Punch the slices with a 6.7-cm ($2^5/_8$-inch) ring cutter. Discard the trim. Brush each punched slice with olive oil and season with fleur de sel.

Place each foie gras punch toward the left side of each of four plates. Shape the black truffle puree into four quenelles and place one on each plate beside the foie gras. Drain the potatoes from the marinade. Gently smash half of the potatoes with a fork. Arrange the smashed and whole potatoes in an arc along the right rim of each plate. Spoon the potato onion relish among the potatoes and arrange the pickled red onion rings on the potatoes and the relish. Spoon the mustard cream sauce on and around the potatoes. Arrange two rye crisps on each plate. Shave black truffle over the potatoes. Dress the watercress with the buttermilk vinaigrette and divide among the plates. Serve with the Black Truffle Potato Bread.

BEEF
Carpaccio with Foie Gras and Porcini

Serves 4

FOIE GRAS CURLS

1 lobe foie gras, about 800 g
770 g salt
16 g pink curing salt #1
15 g brandy

Keeping the foie gras in its original packaging, bring to room temperature. Prepare an ice bath. Remove the foie from the package. Carefully push away the foie from the veins and lift the veins out. Gently form the foie gras back into a naturally elongated shape. Using plastic wrap, wrap and further shape the foie and immediately submerge in the ice bath until very firm, about 3 hours. Combine both salts in a bowl and mix well. Unwrap the foie gras and discard the plastic wrap. Bury the foie gras in the salt mixture and let cure, refrigerated, for 12 hours. Remove the foie gras from the salt mixture and rinse under very cold running water to remove any excess salt. Prepare an ice bath. Seal the cured foie gras in a sous vide bag with the brandy and submerge in the ice bath for 6 hours. Line a baking dish with acetate and set aside.

Remove the foie gras from the bag and, using a deli slicer or mandoline, slice the foie gras lengthwise into eight (3-mm/⅛-inch) thick slices. The foie gras slices should naturally curl as they come off the slicer. Immediately transfer the curls onto the prepared baking dish. Wrap the baking dish tightly with plastic wrap and place in the freezer until ready to serve. Serve the foie gras curls within 2 hours of slicing. Any remaining unsliced foie gras may be stored, refrigerated, for up to 24 hours, or frozen for up to 3 days.

BEEF CARPACCIO

340 g beef tenderloin

Wrap the tenderloin tightly with plastic wrap. Place the beef in the freezer just until firm enough to slice, about 2 hours. Line a baking sheet with acetate and set aside. Using a deli slicer, slice the cold beef into 3-mm (⅛-inch) thick rounds. Place the rounds in a

single even layer on the prepared baking sheet. Wrap the baking sheet tightly with plastic wrap and keep refrigerated until ready to serve.

MUSHROOM VINAIGRETTE

10 g dried porcini mushrooms
15 g grapeseed oil
115 g cremini mushrooms, thinly sliced
½ onion, thinly sliced
4 cloves garlic, thinly sliced
360 g Chicken Stock (page 303)
2 g bonito flakes

In a bowl, cover the dried porcini mushrooms with hot water. Set the bowl aside to allow the mushrooms to rehydrate, about 10 minutes. When hydrated, drain the mushrooms and squeeze to remove any excess water.

Heat the oil in a saucepan over high heat. When the oil just starts to smoke, add the cremini mushrooms. Cook, stirring only occasionally, until the mushrooms are caramelized and browned, about 6 minutes. Turn the heat to low and add the onion, garlic, and drained porcini mushrooms to the pan. Cook, stirring frequently, until the vegetables are softened, about 5 minutes. Add the chicken stock and bring to a simmer. Continue to simmer until the liquid is reduced by half. Remove the pan from the heat and add the bonito flakes, stirring to incorporate. Let steep for 5 minutes at room temperature. Strain the vinaigrette through a chinois and transfer to a clean saucepan. Heat the vinaigrette over medium heat and bring to a simmer. Continue to simmer until reduced by half again. Let cool to room temperature before serving or transfer to an airtight container and reserve, refrigerated, for up to 3 days.

PICKLED PORCINI

4 porcini mushrooms
60 g White Balsamic Pickling Liquid (page 295)

Quarter the porcini and place in a heatproof container. Bring the pickling liquid to a boil in a saucepan over high heat. Pour the liquid over the mushrooms and let cool to room temperature.

CONTINUED

ROASTED PORCINI

10 porcini mushrooms
15 g grapeseed oil
Salt
15 g butter
1 clove garlic, crushed
2 sprigs thyme

Halve the mushrooms lengthwise. Heat the oil in a large sauté pan over high heat. When the oil just begins to smoke, place the halved mushrooms in the pan, cut side down. Season the mushrooms with the salt. When the cut sides of the mushrooms are golden brown, about 2 minutes, turn the heat to medium. Flip the mushrooms over and add the butter, garlic, and thyme. Continue to cook the mushrooms in the foamy butter, basting each as needed, until cooked tender, about 3 minutes. Transfer the roasted porcini to a paper towel to drain.

TO FINISH

Olive oil
Fleur de sel
15 g Parmesan
2 porcini mushrooms
Mustard greens

Brush eight foie gras curls and thirty-two beef carpaccio slices with olive oil and season with fleur de sel. Arrange two foie gras curls on each of four plates. Divide the beef carpaccio slices, roasted mushrooms, and pickled mushrooms among the plates, arranging them on and around the foie gras curls. Crumble the Parmesan on and around the beef and mushrooms. Using a mandoline, thinly slice the porcini mushrooms lengthwise. Brush the slices with olive oil and season with fleur de sel. Garnish each plate with the porcini shaves and mustard greens. Sauce each plate with the mushroom vinaigrette and break the vinaigrette with a few drops of olive oil before serving.

VEAL
Tartare with Black Truffle and Hazelnuts

Serves 4

TRUFFLE BAVAROIS

1 sheet gelatin
100 g cream
1 g salt
100 g Black Truffle Puree (page 296)

Bloom the gelatin in ice water. Combine the cream and salt in a mixing bowl and whip to soft peaks. Set aside and keep refrigerated. Heat the truffle puree in a saucepan over low heat. When the puree is warmed through, squeeze the bloomed gelatin of any excess water and stir into the warm puree. When the gelatin is completely melted, fold the whipped cream into the puree mixture in three additions with a rubber spatula. Once incorporated, place a layer of plastic wrap directly on top of the bavarois and refrigerate until set, about 3 hours. Whip the bavarois with a wire whisk until completely smooth.

TOASTED HAZELNUTS

12 hazelnuts

Preheat the oven to 165°C/325°F. Line a baking sheet with parchment paper. Using a mandoline, thinly slice the hazelnuts into rounds. Place the hazelnut slices on the prepared baking sheet and toast until golden brown, about 7 minutes. Let cool to room temperature.

PICKLED FINGERLING POTATO SLICES

2 fingerling potatoes
120 g White Balsamic Pickling Liquid (page 295)

Using a mandoline, slice the potatoes lengthwise paper thin. Place the potato slices in a heatproof container. Heat the pickling liquid to a simmer in a saucepan over high heat. Pour the liquid over the potato slices to cover. Let cool to room temperature.

POTATO CHIPS

2 fingerling potatoes
140 g water
15 g salt
Canola oil, for frying

Using a mandoline, slice the potatoes crosswise paper thin. Place the potato slices in a heatproof container. Heat the water and salt to a boil in a saucepan over high heat, stirring to dissolve the salt. Pour the hot brine over the potato slices to cover and let cool to room temperature. Heat 7.5 cm (3 inches) of canola oil in a heavy pot to 175°C/350°F. Line a baking sheet with paper towels. Drain the potato slices and rinse well under cold running water. Pat dry on a paper towel. Fry the potato slices in small batches, until golden brown and crispy, about 3 minutes. Transfer to the lined baking sheet to drain.

CHAMPAGNE HAZELNUT VINAIGRETTE

27 g champagne vinegar
10 g Dijon mustard
100 g hazelnut oil
Salt
1/2 shallot, finely chopped

Using an immersion blender, blend the vinegar, mustard, and oil together until fully emulsified. Season with salt. Reserve the vinaigrette in an airtight container, refrigerated, for up to 5 days. When ready to serve, stir in the chopped shallots.

TO FINISH

400 g veal tenderloin
Hazelnut oil
Fleur de sel
1 black truffle, for shaving

Cut the veal into four large pieces and chill in the freezer until firm, about 2 hours. Put the veal through a meat grinder, keeping it in long strands as it comes out of the grinder. Brush the veal with hazelnut oil and season with fleur de sel. Divide the ground veal in small piles among four plates. Form the truffle bavarois into quenelles and place among the veal on each plate. Divide the toasted hazelnuts, pickled potatoes, and potato chips among the plates. Sauce each plate with the champagne hazelnut vinaigrette. Shave black truffle over each plate to finish.

EGG
Slow Poached with Asparagus and Parmesan

Serves 4

GLAZED COLLARED ASPARAGUS

20 jumbo asparagus stalks
45 g Chicken Stock (page 303)
30 g butter
Salt

Trim the ends of the asparagus stalks so that they are 7.5 cm (3 inches) in length. Peel the green from the bottom 2.5 cm (1 inch) of each stalk. Bring a pot of salted water to a rolling boil and prepare an ice bath. Blanch the asparagus in the boiling water until just tender, about 4 minutes. Immediately shock in the ice bath. When the asparagus are cold, drain and pat dry.

Heat the chicken stock in a sauté pan to a simmer over medium heat. Add the butter and blanched asparagus. Season with salt. As the butter melts and emulsifies, it will glaze the asparagus evenly. Be careful not to overcook the asparagus or reduce the glaze too far, as the emulsion will break and make the asparagus greasy. Transfer the glazed asparagus to a paper towel to drain any excess glaze and keep warm.

POACHED EGGS

4 eggs

Heat a water bath to 62°C/145°F. Carefully submerge the eggs in the water bath for 27 minutes. Remove the eggs from the water bath and keep at room temperature.

TO FINISH

160 g Cooked Quinoa (page 287)
70 g Puffed Quinoa (page 289)
White Balsamic Vinaigrette (page 289)
Brown Butter Sabayon (page 302)
Parmesan Foam (page 305)
Fleur de sel
Parmesan, for shaving

Heat a saucepan of salted water to just below simmering. Remove the pan from the heat and crack the poached eggs into the pan to rewarm while preparing the rest of the dish. Combine the cooked and puffed quinoa in a mixing bowl. Dress the quinoa with the vinaigrette.

Arrange the asparagus among four bowls, placing them in a pentagon and leaving the center of each bowl empty. Divide the quinoa salad among the four bowls, filling in any holes formed by the asparagus. Expel 30 g of the brown butter sabayon in the center of each bowl. Using a slotted spoon, remove the eggs from the warm water and place one egg on top of the sabayon in each bowl. Season each egg with fleur de sel. Using an immersion blender, froth the Parmesan foam and spoon a generous amount around each egg. Shave the Parmesan with a vegetable peeler on and around the asparagus and quinoa.

TAGLIATELLE
King Crab with Meyer Lemon and Black Pepper

Serves 4

TAGLIATELLE

Semolina flour
6 sheets Pasta Dough (page 288)

Dust a baking sheet lined with parchment paper with semolina. Using the tagliatelle attachment, roll the pasta sheets one at a time through the pasta machine. Lay out the cut pasta in a single layer onto the prepared baking sheet. Dust the pasta with semolina to prevent sticking. Cover the pasta with parchment paper and keep refrigerated until ready to cook.

KING CRAB LEGS

2 king crab legs, about 450 g

Using sharp kitchen scissors, carefully cut open the crab leg shells, avoiding cutting into the meat. Remove the meat from the shells. Pick through the crabmeat to ensure there are no stray pieces of shell or cartilage while keeping the meat in pieces as large as possible. Keep refrigerated.

TO FINISH

320 g Chicken Stock (page 303)
205 g butter
40 g Meyer lemon juice
Salt
Cracked black pepper
Sliced chives

Bring a large pot of lightly salted water to a boil over high heat. Divide the chicken stock between two large sauté pans and heat over medium heat to a simmer. Divide the butter between the pans and melt the butter so that it emulsifies with the chicken stock, forming a thick glaze. Turn the heat to medium and divide the crab between the pans. Gently cook just to warm the crab through.

Cook the pasta in the water until just tender with a little bite, about 2 minutes. Drain the pasta and reserve some of the pasta cooking water. Divide the cooked pasta between the pans and stir to combine. If the glaze is too thick, add some of the reserved pasta water. Season both pans of pasta with lemon juice, salt, and black pepper. Divide the pasta and crab among four bowls and finish with sliced chives. Serve immediately.

CAVATELLI
Clams with Parsley and Chile

Serves 4

PARSLEY PASTA DOUGH

165 g flat-leaf parsley leaves
130 g ice water
300 g tipo 00 flour
4 g salt
Semolina flour

Combine the parsley and ice water in a blender and puree on high speed until smooth. Pass the puree through a fine-mesh tamis and transfer to the bowl of a stand mixer fitted with the dough hook attachment. Add the flour and salt and mix on low speed. When the dough starts to form, about 3 minutes, turn to medium speed and mix until the flour is fully hydrated and forms into a ball, about 8 minutes. Turn the dough out onto a clean work surface and knead by hand for 2 minutes. Shape the dough into a ball and cover tightly with plastic wrap. Refrigerate overnight. Line a baking sheet with parchment paper. Unwrap the dough and, using a rolling pin, roll the dough to 6-mm ($\frac{1}{4}$-inch) thickness. Cut the dough into 2.5-cm (1-inch) wide strips. Using a cavatelli maker, form the dough strips into individual cavatelli. Spread the pasta out onto the prepared baking sheet. Dust the pasta generously with semolina flour. Keep the pasta refrigerated until ready to cook.

LITTLENECK CLAMS

36 littleneck clams, about 1.4 kg, covered in cold water
*   and refrigerated overnight*
235 g dry white wine
1 shallot, thinly sliced
3 cloves garlic, crushed
3 sprigs thyme
1 bay leaf

Prepare an ice bath. Drain the clams. Heat a large saucepan over high heat. When the pan is very hot, add all of the ingredients at once and immediately cover the pan. Shake the pan occasionally to evenly steam the clams until they are all opened, about 4 minutes. Chill the clams in the cooking liquid over the ice bath. Discard any unopened clams. When cold, drain the clams and strain the liquid through cheesecloth. Separate and discard the clamshells. Trim and discard the mantle of the clams and rinse off any dirt. Reserve the cleaned clams in the strained clam stock, refrigerated.

RAZOR CLAMS

8 razor clams
3 sprigs flat-leaf parsley
$\frac{1}{2}$ shallot, thinly sliced
80 g dry white wine

Prepare an ice bath. Heat a large saucepan over high heat. When the pan is very hot, add all of the ingredients at once and immediately cover the pan. Shake the pan occasionally to evenly steam the clams until they are all opened, about 2 minutes. Chill the clams in the cooking liquid over the ice bath. Discard any unopened clams. When cold, drain the clams and strain the liquid through cheesecloth. Separate and discard the clamshells. Trim and discard all but the cleaned siphon of the clams and rinse off any dirt. Slice the clams 6 mm ($\frac{1}{4}$ inch) thick, on a bias. Reserve the cleaned clams in the strained clam stock, refrigerated.

TO FINISH

240 g Roasted Garlic Clam Stock (page 306)
180 g butter
10 g thinly sliced flat-leaf parsley leaves, plus more
*   leaves to garnish*
10 g lemon juice
4 g Chile Oil (page 284)
Salt
Dried red pepper flakes

Bring a large pot of lightly salted water to a boil over high heat. Cook the cavatelli in the boiling water until just tender, about 3 minutes. While the pasta is cooking, warm the clam stock in two large sauté pans over medium heat. When the stock is at a simmer, divide the butter between the pans. As the butter melts and emulsifies, it will form a thick glaze. When the pasta is cooked, drain it and immediately divide it between the pans. Add the littleneck and razor clams, and sliced parsley to the pans. Cook, stirring, just until the clams are warmed through. Add the lemon juice and chile oil and season with salt. Divide the pasta among four bowls. Garnish each bowl with the parsley leaves and pepper flakes.

RICOTTA
Gnocchi with Squash and Mushrooms

Serves 4

RICOTTA GNOCCHI

550 g Pressed Ricotta (page 299)
1 egg
40 g Parmesan, grated
65 g all-purpose flour
8 g salt
Semolina flour

Line a rimmed baking sheet with parchment paper. Combine the pressed ricotta in a bowl with the egg, Parmesan, flour, and salt. Mix the ingredients together with a rubber spatula until thoroughly combined. Transfer to a piping bag and set aside. Cover the bottom of a baking dish with semolina flour. Pipe 15 g portions of the gnocchi dough onto the prepared baking sheet. Roll the portions into balls and place in the semolina flour in a single layer, not touching. After shaping all the gnocchi, bury them completely in additional semolina flour. Cover the baking dish with plastic wrap and refrigerate for at least 24 hours and no longer than 2 days before cooking.

BUTTERNUT SQUASH PARISIENNES

1 butternut squash
12 g olive oil
0.5 g salt
1 sprig thyme

Bring a large pot of water to a boil and prepare an ice bath. Cut the bottom bulb from the squash and set aside for the butternut squash puree. Peel the neck of the squash. Using a #25 parisienne scoop, scoop balls from the neck of the squash. Seal the squash with the olive oil, salt, and thyme airtight in a sous vide bag. Cook the squash in the bag in the boiling water until tender, about 15 minutes. Shock the squash in the ice bath. When cold, remove the squash from the bag and set aside.

BUTTERNUT SQUASH PUREE

Reserved bottom bulb of butternut squash
25 g olive oil
Salt
2 sprigs thyme
40 g Brown Butter (page 284), melted

Preheat the oven to 165°C/325°F. Line a baking sheet with parchment paper. Halve the squash bulb and scrape out the seeds. In a bowl, coat the squash halves with the oil and season with salt. Transfer the squash to the prepared baking sheet, cut side up, with a thyme sprig on each half. Roast the squash until completely tender but with little color, about 50 minutes. When the squash is cool enough to handle, scoop out the flesh and transfer to a blender. Puree on high until completely smooth. Turn to low speed and slowly add the brown butter. Continue to blend until completely incorporated. Season with salt. Keep warm.

FRIED SAGE

8 sage leaves
Canola oil, for frying

In a large heavy pot, heat 7.5 cm (3 inches) of canola oil to 175°C/350°F. When the oil is hot, quickly fry the sage leaves until crispy, about 10 seconds. With a spider strainer, remove the leaves from the oil and place on a paper towel to drain.

GLAZED MUSHROOMS

45 g butter
16 bluefoot mushrooms
16 chanterelles
8 black trumpet mushrooms
Salt
30 g Chicken Stock (page 303)

Heat the butter in a pan over medium heat until foamy but not browned. Add the bluefoot and chanterelle mushrooms and cook just until the mushrooms soften, about 4 minutes. Add the black trumpet mushrooms and cook for 1 minute. Season the mushrooms with salt. Add the chicken stock and bring to a simmer. As the stock reduces, it will form a glaze. Be careful not to reduce the glaze too far or it will make the mushrooms greasy. Transfer the mushrooms to a paper towel to drain any excess glaze. Keep warm.

CONTINUED

ROASTED PORCINI

2 porcini mushrooms
10 g grapeseed oil
Salt
15 g butter
1 clove garlic
2 sprigs thyme

Cut the mushrooms in half lengthwise. Heat the grapeseed oil in a large sauté pan over high heat. When the oil just begins to smoke, place the halved mushrooms in the pan, cut side down. Season the mushrooms with the salt. When the cut sides of the mushrooms are golden brown, reduce the heat to medium. Turn the mushrooms over and add the butter, garlic, and thyme. Cook the mushrooms in the foamy butter, basting as necessary until cooked through. Transfer the cooked mushrooms to a paper towel to drain. Keep warm.

TO FINISH

1 porcini mushroom
Olive oil
Fleur de sel
120 g Chicken Stock (page 303)
50 g butter
Salt
Parmesan, for grating

Bring a large pot of lightly salted water to a boil. Using a mandoline, thinly slice the porcini lengthwise. Brush the slices with olive oil and season with fleur de sel. Set aside.

Drop twenty gnocchi in the boiling water and cook until they float, about 3 minutes. While the gnocchi are cooking, bring the chicken stock to a simmer in a pan. Add the butter and the butternut squash parisiennes. Season with salt. Melt the butter so that it emulsifies with the chicken stock and forms a thick glaze. When the gnocchi are cooked, using a spider strainer, carefully remove them from the water and add to the glaze in the pan. Gently coat the gnocchi with the glaze.

Divide the butternut squash puree and the butternut squash parisiennes among four bowls. Grate the Parmesan over the gnocchi in the pan. Divide the gnocchi and mushrooms among the four bowls. Garnish each bowl with the porcini slices and fried sage.

TORTELLONI
with Celery Root and Black Truffle

Serves 4

―――

CELERY ROOT FILLING

900 g peeled celery root, diced 2.5 cm (1 inch)
500 g milk
20 g Parmesan, grated
8 g finely chopped black truffle
2 g white truffle oil
30 g mascarpone
3 g salt

Preheat the oven to 95°C/200°F. Line a baking sheet with a nonstick baking mat. In a large saucepan over medium heat, cover the celery root with the milk. Bring the milk to a boil and turn the heat to low. Cover with a parchment cartouche and continue to cook the celery root at a gentle simmer until tender, about 45 minutes. Remove the pan from the heat and drain the mixture through a chinois. Press down on the celery root to drain as much liquid as possible. Transfer the strained celery root to a food processor and process until smooth, about 5 minutes. Spread the mixture 5 cm (2 inches) thick on the prepared baking sheet. Place the puree in the oven to dehydrate, stirring it every 20 minutes or so to keep a skin from forming as it dries. Continue to dehydrate the puree until it has reduced by a third, about 6 hours.

Line a baking sheet with parchment paper. Weigh out 400 g of the dried celery root puree and transfer it to a mixing bowl with the Parmesan, truffle, truffle oil, mascarpone, and salt. Using a rubber spatula, stir to mix until the filling stays bound together. Portion the filling into 15 g balls. Arrange the portions in a single layer on the lined baking sheet. Cover with plastic wrap and refrigerate until cold, about 3 hours.

―――

TORTELLONI

Semolina flour
Pasta Dough (page 288)
Celery Root Filling

Line a baking sheet with parchment paper and dust it with semolina. Cut the pasta sheets into 9-cm (3.5-inch) squares and arrange in a single layer on a clean work surface. Place a portion of filling in the center of each pasta square. Working with one tortelloni at a time, lightly dampen the edges of a square with water, using a spray bottle. Fold the square into a triangle, pressing down along the edges to seal, removing as much air as possible. Punch the pasta folds with a 5-cm (2-inch) ring cutter. Bring the two ends of each pasta fold together, pressing tightly to seal. Transfer the tortelloni to the prepared baking sheet and refrigerate until ready to serve.

―――

CELERY ROOT PUREE

225 g peeled celery root, diced 2.5 cm (1 inch)
110 g cream
110 g milk
Salt

In a saucepan, cover the celery root with the cream and milk. Heat to a boil over medium heat, then turn the heat to low and simmer until the celery root is tender, about 45 minutes. Strain the mixture through a chinois; reserve the cooking liquid. Transfer the strained mixture to a blender along with a splash of the cooking liquid and puree on high until smooth. Season with salt and keep warm.

―――

TO FINISH

100 g Chicken Stock (page 303)
80 g butter
Salt
15 g finely chopped black truffle
Black Truffle Puree (page 296)
Parmesan Foam (page 305)
Celery heart leaves
Black truffle, to shave

Bring a large pot of lightly salted water to a simmer. Cook the tortelloni in the water until tender, about 2½ minutes. While the pasta is cooking, bring the chicken stock to a simmer in a saucepan over medium heat and add the butter. As the butter melts and emulsifies, it will form a thick glaze. Season with salt. Be careful not to reduce the glaze too far, as the emulsion will break and make the pasta greasy. When cooked, use a spider strainer to remove the tortelloni from the water and add them to the glaze, along with the chopped black truffle. Stir gently to coat the tortelloni evenly. Divide the black truffle puree among four bowls. Tap the bottom of each bowl to flatten the puree slightly. Spoon the celery root puree over the black truffle puree to cover completely. Tap the bottom of each bowl to flatten the puree slightly. Divide the tortelloni among the bowls, placing them atop the purees. Using an immersion blender, froth the Parmesan foam and sauce each plate with it. Garnish with the celery leaves and shaved black truffle.

MAINS

SPRING GREENS
with Grains and Flowers

Serves 4

___

GRAIN SALAD

180 g Cooked Wheat Berries (page 287)
120 g Puffed Bulgur Wheat (page 288)
1/2 shallot, finely chopped
Lemon Vinaigrette (page 285)

Combine the wheat berries, bulgur wheat, and shallot in a bowl and dress with lemon vinaigrette. Stir to mix well.

___

SAUTÉED GREENS

45 g olive oil
100 g Bloomsdale spinach leaves
Salt
50 g pea greens
32 broccoli spigarello leaves

Heat one-third of the oil in a sauté pan over high heat. When the oil is very hot, add the spinach to the pan and immediately stir. Sauté the spinach until just slightly wilted, about 1¹/₂ minutes, and season with salt. Transfer to a paper towel to drain. Repeat this process with the pea greens and broccoli spigarello, lightly sautéing each separately. Keep warm.

___

TO FINISH

Malabar spinach leaves
Broccoli spigarello leaves
Pea greens
Lemon Vinaigrette (page 285)
Pea flowers
Broccoli rabe flowers
Ricotta salata, for shaving

Arrange the sautéed greens in several piles on each of four plates. Place the grain salad in small piles among the greens. Dress the Malabar spinach, broccoli spigarello leaves, and pea greens with the lemon vinaigrette in a mixing bowl. Toss to combine. Divide the dressed greens among each plate atop the sautéed greens. Garnish each plate with pea flowers and broccoli rabe flowers. Using a vegetable peeler, shave the ricotta salata over each plate to finish.

MORELS
with Nettles, Potatoes, and Lardo

Serves 4

NETTLE SAUCE

45 g butter
1 shallot, chopped
1/2 fennel bulb, sliced
2 celery stalks, sliced
1 carrot, peeled and sliced
2 cloves garlic, sliced
125 g dry white wine
25 g bacon, coarsely chopped
1 sprig thyme
25 g Yukon Gold potato, peeled and sliced
200 g Chicken Stock (page 303)
150 g water
100 g nettle leaves
Salt

Heat the butter in a saucepan over medium heat until foamy, but not browned. Add the shallot, fennel, celery, carrot, and garlic and sweat, stirring occasionally, until the vegetables are tender and without any color, about 12 minutes. Deglaze the pan with the white wine. Bring the wine to a simmer and reduce until almost dry. Tie the bacon and thyme in a cheesecloth sachet and add to the pan with the potato, chicken stock, and water. Bring the mixture to a gentle simmer and cook until the potato is tender, about 45 minutes. Remove and discard the sachet. Transfer the mixture to a blender and puree on high until smooth. Strain the sauce through a chinois and keep warm.

Bring a large pot of salted water to a boil over high heat and prepare an ice bath. Wearing gloves to handle the raw nettles, blanch the nettles until completely tender, about 10 minutes. When you rub the cooked leaves between your fingers, they should fall apart completely. Shock the nettles in the ice bath. When cold, drain and squeeze out any excess water. Transfer the nettles to a blender with a splash of ice water and puree on high speed until smooth. Right before serving, combine equal parts vegetable and nettle puree and whisk together to incorporate. Season with salt.

MOREL RAGOUT

70 g nettle leaves
15 g butter
1 clove garlic, finely chopped
15 g morels, finely chopped
30 g lardo, finely chopped
5 mint leaves, thinly sliced
Grated zest of 1 lemon
8 g lemon juice
Salt

Bring a large pot of salted water to a boil and prepare an ice bath. Wearing gloves to handle the raw nettles, blanch the nettles until just tender, about 6 minutes, and shock in the ice bath until cold. Drain the nettles and squeeze out any excess water. Chop coarsely and set aside. Heat the butter in a sauté pan over medium heat until foamy but not browned. Add the garlic. Cook until softened and without any color, about 4 minutes. Add the morels and lardo. Cook, stirring occasionally, until the morels are tender and the lardo starts to render, about 5 minutes. Add the nettles, stirring to incorporate. Cook the mixture until the nettles are warmed through, about 3 minutes. Remove the pan from the heat and fold in the mint, lemon zest, and juice. Season with salt and keep warm.

CONFIT POTATOES

32 peanut potatoes
2 sprigs thyme
1 clove garlic, crushed
240 g olive oil
Salt

Preheat the oven to 150°C/300°F. Combine the potatoes with the thyme and garlic in a baking dish. Cover with olive oil and season with salt. Cover the baking dish with aluminum foil and cook the potatoes in the oven until just tender, about 1 hour. Remove the potatoes from the oven, uncover, and let cool in the oil until warm enough to handle. Drain the potatoes and reserve the cooking oil. Set aside half of the potatoes and keep warm. Lightly smash the remaining potatoes with the palm of your hand. Heat 45 g of the reserved oil in a large sauté pan over high heat. When the oil just starts to smoke, add the smashed potatoes to the pan in a single layer and turn the heat to medium. Cook the potatoes, stirring occasionally, until evenly browned and crispy on all sides, about 6 minutes. Season with salt and transfer the potatoes to a paper towel to drain. Keep warm.

CONTINUED

PICKLED MORELS

60 g morels, sliced into rings 6 mm (¼ inch) thick
1 sprig thyme
175 g White Balsamic Pickling Liquid (page 295)

Combine the morel rings and thyme in a heatproof container and set aside. Heat the pickling liquid to a boil in a saucepan over high heat. Remove the pan from the heat and pour the hot liquid over the mushrooms to cover. Let cool to room temperature.

MOREL PANNA COTTA

15 g butter
½ shallot, thinly sliced
1 clove garlic, crushed
30 g morels
15 g dried morels
500 g half-and-half
10 g sherry
2 sprigs thyme
2 g porcini powder
4 g salt
1 egg, beaten
2 g agar-agar
50 g water

Heat the butter in a saucepan over medium heat until foamy but not browned. Add the shallot and garlic. Cook, stirring occasionally, until softened and without any color, about 5 minutes. Add the morels and continue to cook until the mushrooms are tender, about 5 minutes. Add the half-and-half, sherry, thyme, and porcini powder to the pan, stirring to incorporate. Bring to a simmer and remove the pan from the heat. Cover and let steep at room temperature for 1 hour. Strain the mixture through a chinois. Season the strained liquid with the salt and transfer to a clean saucepan. Heat over low heat and bring to just under a simmer. Crack the egg into a mixing bowl and slowly whisk in one-third of the hot liquid to temper. Slowly whisk the egg mixture into the remaining morel base and continue to whisk together until fully incorporated. Remove the pan from the heat and keep warm.

Line a 23 by 33-cm (9 by 13-inch) baking sheet with acetate. Lightly coat with nonstick baking spray and wipe off any excess spray with a paper towel. Combine the water and agar-agar in a saucepan and bring to a simmer over medium heat, whisking constantly. Continue to simmer the mixture, whisking, until the agar-agar is fully hydrated and appears translucent, about 5 minutes. Remove the pan from the heat and slowly whisk in the warm morel mixture. Continue to whisk together until fully incorporated and transfer to the prepared baking sheet. Refrigerate, undisturbed and level, until fully set and firm, about 3 hours. When ready to serve, tear the panna cotta into 2.5-cm (1-inch) pieces by hand.

MORELS

45 g butter
32 morels
50 g Chicken Stock (page 303)
Salt

Heat two-thirds of the butter in a large sauté pan over medium heat until foamy but not browned. Add the morels and sweat until the mushrooms soften without any color, about 4 minutes. Add the chicken stock and remaining butter. Season the mushrooms with salt. As the butter melts and emulsifies, it will glaze the mushrooms evenly. Transfer the mushrooms to a paper towel to drain any excess glaze. Keep warm.

TO FINISH

8 slices lardo, 1.5 mm (¹⁄₁₆ inch) thick
Lamb's-quarter leaves
Chickweed tops
Nepitella blossoms

Place two pieces of panna cotta on each of four plates. Spoon the nettle sauce in between the panna cotta pieces. Arrange the morels, morel ragout, confit potatoes—smashed and whole—and pickled morels over the sauce. Drape two slices of lardo over each arrangement. Garnish each plate with the herbs and flowers.

ASPARAGUS
with Smoked Potatoes and Black Truffle

Serves 4

LEEK PUREE

25 g olive oil
325 g leeks, white and pale green parts only
2 shallots, thinly sliced
Salt
75 g dry white wine
1 sprig thyme
300 g water

Heat the oil in a sauté pan over medium heat. Sweat the
leeks and shallots in the oil until slightly softened and
without any color, about 7 minutes. Season the vegetables
with salt. Add the white wine and thyme. Bring the wine
to a simmer and reduce until almost dry, about 3 minutes.
Add the water and bring to a simmer. Turn the heat to
low and continue to cook until the vegetables are tender,
about 30 minutes. Strain the vegetables through a chinois,
reserving the cooking liquid for the truffle leek vinaigrette. Remove and discard the thyme sprig. Transfer the
vegetables to a blender and puree on high until smooth.
If necessary, add a splash of the reserved cooking liquid to
help attain a smooth consistency. Pass the puree through
a chinois and season with salt. Keep warm.

TRUFFLE LEEK VINAIGRETTE

85 g white balsamic vinegar
56 g Leek Puree
20 g reserved leek puree cooking liquid
30 g olive oil
3 g black truffles, finely chopped
Salt

Combine the vinegar, leek puree, and cooking liquid
in a blender. Blend the mixture on low speed while
slowly adding the olive oil. Blend on medium speed until
emulsified. Stir in the black truffles, season with salt, and
keep at room temperature.

MELTED LEEKS

35 g butter
*100 g leeks, white and pale green parts only,
    finely chopped*
Salt

Heat the butter in a sauté pan over low heat until foamy
but not browned. Add the leeks. Cook, stirring occasionally,
until tender and without any color, about 15 minutes.
Season with salt. If necessary, add a splash of water during
the cooking process to prevent the leeks from browning.
Remove the pan from the heat and set aside.

SMOKED POTATO ÉCRASER

500 g fingerling potatoes, peeled
Salt
100 g Chicken Stock (page 303)
50 g butter
Melted Leeks
40 g Smoked Butter (page 285)
10 g black truffles, finely chopped

Cover the potatoes with cold water in a large saucepan
and heat over medium heat. Bring the water to a simmer
and season with salt. Turn the heat to low and continue
cooking the potatoes until just tender, about 45 minutes.
Drain the potatoes and set aside. In a separate pan, bring
the chicken stock to a simmer over medium heat. Add
the butter and cooked potatoes. Crush the potatoes with
a large fork until evenly crumbled. Fold in the melted
leeks, smoked butter, and black truffles until thoroughly
incorporated. Season with salt and keep warm.

TRUFFLE LEEK DASHI

1 (15-cm/6-inch) square piece of kombu
*100 g leeks, white and pale green parts only,
    thinly sliced*
275 g water
0.5 g bonito flakes
15 g cornstarch
3 g black truffles, finely chopped
Salt

Rinse the kombu under cold running water until softened
and pliable. Place the kombu, leeks, and 250 g of the
water in a saucepan over medium heat. Heat the water to
65°C/150°F and maintain the temperature for 35 minutes.
Remove the pan from the heat and add the bonito. Let
steep at room temperature for 30 minutes. Strain the

CONTINUED

dashi through a chinois and transfer to a clean saucepan. Heat the dashi over medium heat and bring to a simmer. Whisk the cornstarch and remaining 25 g water together in a bowl to form a slurry. Whisk the cornstarch slurry into the simmering dashi to thicken. Continue to simmer the thickened dashi, whisking constantly, until the cornstarch cooks out, about 5 minutes. Remove the pan from the heat and stir in the black truffle. Season with salt and keep warm.

GLAZED ASPARAGUS

12 jumbo asparagus stalks, trimmed
to 18 cm (7 inches)
80 g Chicken Stock (page 303)
50 g butter
Salt

Peel the bottom 2.5 cm (1 inch) of each asparagus stalk. Bring a large pot of salted water to a rolling boil and prepare an ice bath. Blanch the asparagus in the boiling water until just tender, about 3 minutes. Shock in the ice bath. Meanwhile, heat the chicken stock to a simmer in a sauté pan over medium heat. When the asparagus is cold, remove it from the ice bath and add to the simmering chicken stock with the butter. As the butter melts and emulsifies, it will glaze the asparagus evenly. Be careful not to overcook the asparagus or reduce the glaze too far, as the emulsion will break and make the asparagus greasy. Season the asparagus with salt. Transfer the glazed asparagus to a paper towel to drain any excess glaze. Keep warm.

ROASTED ASPARAGUS

12 jumbo asparagus stalks, trimmed
to 18 cm (7 inches)
Olive oil
Salt

Peel the bottom 2.5 cm (1 inch) of each asparagus stalk. Heat a large sauté pan over high heat. Add just enough oil to coat the bottom of the pan. Place the asparagus in the pan in a single layer. Roast the asparagus, without stirring, until deeply caramelized on one side, about 2 minutes. Season with salt. Turn the asparagus and continue cooking until tender and caramelized on all sides, about 3 minutes. Transfer the roasted asparagus to a paper towel to drain and keep warm.

TOASTED BREAD

75 g baguette, crusts removed, torn
into 2.5-cm (1-inch) pieces
20 g olive oil
Salt
Truffle Leek Vinaigrette
Sliced chives

Preheat the oven to 190°C/375°F. Line a baking sheet with parchment paper. Toss the baguette pieces in a mixing bowl with the olive oil and season with salt. Place the bread in a single layer on the prepared baking sheet and toast until golden brown, about 11 minutes. The bread pieces should be crisped on the outside but remain soft in the center. Dress the bread with truffle leek vinaigrette in a mixing bowl and toss to evenly coat. Let the bread sit for 5 minutes to lightly soak in the vinaigrette. Garnish with sliced chives.

TO FINISH

Black truffle, for shaving

Divide the smoked potato écraser among four plates. Arrange the roasted and glazed asparagus parallel to each other atop the potato écraser, alternating the two types of asparagus. Place the toasted bread in between the asparagus spears. Sauce each plate with the truffle leek dashi and finish with freshly shaved black truffle.

BROCCOLI
Variations with Parmesan, Lardo, and Lemon

Serves 4

BROCCOLI PLANKS

  2 long-stemmed heads broccoli
  35 g grapeseed oil
  Salt
  Fleur de sel

Preheat the oven to 175°C/350°F. Remove the leaves from the stems and reserve them for garnish. Slice the broccoli heads lengthwise into four 1.3-cm (1/2-inch) thick planked cross sections, including the head and the stem. Peel the lower stems of the planks to remove the woody outer layers. Reserve the trim for the broccoli lemon puree.

Divide the oil between two large sauté pans and heat over high heat. Carefully place two broccoli planks in each pan. Roast the planks until deeply caramelized and brown on one side, about 3 minutes. Season with salt and flip the planks to sear the other side. Put the pans in the oven to cook the broccoli through, about 4 minutes. When the broccoli planks are tender, transfer to a paper towel to drain and finish with fleur de sel. Keep warm.

BROCCOLI COUSCOUS

  1 head broccoli

Using a sharp knife, shave the top buds off of the surface of the broccoli head. Reserve the remaining parts of the broccoli for the broccoli lemon puree.

BROCCOLI LEMON PUREE

  250 g reserved broccoli trim, chopped
  35 g Lemon Oil (page 284)
  Salt

Bring a pot of salted water to a rolling boil over high heat and prepare an ice bath. Blanch the broccoli in the boiling water until completely tender, about 6 minutes. Shock in the ice bath. When cold, drain the broccoli and transfer to a blender. Add a splash of ice water and puree on high until smooth. Turn to low speed and slowly blend in the lemon oil. Continue to blend until emulsified; season with salt. The puree should have a velvety smooth

texture. Transfer to an airtight container and keep cold. Before serving, let the puree sit at room temperature for 30 minutes to temper.

PARMESAN CHIPS

  200 g Parmesan, coarsely grated

Preheat a convection oven to 105°C/225°F, low fan. Spread the cheese out in a thin and even layer on a baking sheet lined with a nonstick baking mat. Place in the oven and bake until golden brown and crispy, about 20 minutes. Let cool to room temperature. Break the sheet into 5-cm (2-inch) chips and store in a dry, airtight container.

TO FINISH

  16 broccoli florets
  White Balsamic Vinaigrette (page 285)
  Salt
  Broccoli leaves
  Grated zest of 1 lemon
  Fleur de sel
  8 slices lardo, 1.5 mm (1/16 inch) thick
  Broccoli flowers

Bring a pot of salted water to a rolling boil over high heat and prepare an ice bath. Blanch the broccoli florets in the boiling water until tender, about 4 minutes. Shock in the ice bath. When cold, drain the broccoli and set aside. In a mixing bowl, combine the broccoli couscous with the lemon zest, dress with white balsamic vinaigrette, and season with salt. In another mixing bowl, dress the blanched broccoli florets and broccoli leaves with white balsamic vinaigrette and season with fleur de sel.

Divide the broccoli lemon puree among four plates. Place one broccoli plank on each plate over the puree. Arrange the dressed broccoli florets, broccoli couscous, and Parmesan chips on and around each plank. Drape two slices of lardo over each plank. Garnish each plate with dressed broccoli leaves and the broccoli flowers.

SUMMER SQUASH
with Sheep's Milk Feta and Pistachios

Serves 4

PARISIAN GNOCCHI

120 g water
60 g butter, diced 1.3 cm (1/2 inch)
3 g salt
95 g flour
2 eggs
90 g French-style sheep's milk feta, drained
3 g basil leaves, finely chopped
3 g mint leaves, finely chopped
5 g sliced chives
Grated zest of 1 lemon
30 g grapeseed oil

Heat the water, butter, and salt in a saucepan over low heat. When the butter has completely melted, turn the heat to medium. Bring to a simmer and add all of the flour at once. Stir the mixture with a rubber spatula to incorporate and hydrate the flour. Turn the heat to low and continue to cook, stirring constantly, until the flour cooks out, about 3 minutes. The dough should pull away from the sides of the pan without sticking. Transfer the dough to the bowl of a stand mixer and paddle on low speed until the dough stops steaming, about 5 minutes. Turn to medium speed and add the eggs one at a time, allowing the first egg to incorporate into the dough before adding the next. Mix in the cheese, herbs, and lemon zest until just combined. Transfer the dough to a piping bag fitted with a #807 piping tip. Refrigerate the dough until firm, about 2 hours.

Bring a pot of salted water to a simmer and prepare an ice bath. Spray a paring knife with nonstick baking spray. Pipe the dough out over the water, using the prepared knife to cut 2.5-cm (1-inch) pieces into the water. Simmer the gnocchi until firm enough to hold its shape, about 4 minutes. Remove the gnocchi from the pot and shock in the ice bath. When cold, transfer the gnocchi to a paper towel to drain any excess water.

Heat the oil in a sauté pan over medium heat. Place the gnocchi in the pan in a single layer and cook, stirring occasionally, until browned and crispy on all sides, about 2 minutes. Transfer the gnocchi to a paper towel to drain and lightly season with salt. Keep warm.

OLIVE OIL SQUASH

14 baby summer squash
40 g lemon juice
35 g olive oil
1 sprig mint
4 g salt

Bring a large pot of water to a boil over high heat. Seal the squash, lemon juice, oil, mint, and salt airtight in a sous vide bag. Submerge the bag in the boiling water and cook until the squash is just tender, about 10 minutes. Remove the squash from the bag and transfer to a paper towel to drain. Depending on size, halve some of the squash lengthwise. Keep warm.

ROASTED SQUASH

30 g olive oil
8 baby summer squash
Salt

Heat the oil in a sauté pan over medium heat. Depending on size, halve some of the squash lengthwise. Add the squash and cook, stirring occasionally, until tender and deeply caramelized on all sides, about 8 minutes. Drain the squash on paper towels to drain. Keep warm.

ZUCCHINI BASIL PUREE

2 green zucchini
20 g basil leaves
15 g fermented pistachio paste
25 g Lemon Oil (page 284)
105 g grapeseed oil
Salt

Cut the skins off the zucchini. Thinly slice the skins. Reserve the inner white flesh for the feta nage. Heat a large pot of salted water to a rolling boil and prepare an ice bath. Blanch the basil leaves in the boiling water until completely tender, about 6 minutes. When you rub the basil between your fingers, it should fall apart. Immediately shock the basil in the ice bath. When cold, remove the basil from the ice water and squeeze out any excess water. Blanch the zucchini skins in the boiling water until completely tender, about 13 minutes. When you rub the skins between your fingers, they should fall apart. Immediately shock the zucchini in the ice bath. When cold, drain the zucchini and combine in a blender with the blanched basil and the pistachio paste. Puree

CONTINUED

on high until smooth. Turn to low speed and slowly add both oils. Blend until fully emulsified. Season with salt and keep at room temperature until ready to serve.

_____

FETA NAGE

> *15 g olive oil*
> *70 g reserved squash from Zucchini Basil Puree, sliced*
> *1 shallot, sliced*
> *2 cloves garlic, sliced*
> *8 g lemongrass, coarsely chopped*
> *Pinch of saffron*
> *125 g dry white wine*
> *150 g water*
> *Peeled zest of 1 lemon*
> *1 sprig mint*
> *1 sprig basil*
> *1 sprig thyme*
> *145 g French-style sheep's milk feta, drained*
> *50 g crème fraîche*
> *Salt*

Heat the oil in a large saucepan over medium heat. Add the squash, shallot, garlic, lemongrass, and saffron. Sweat the vegetables, stirring frequently, until tender and without any color, about 10 minutes. Add the white wine and bring to a simmer. Reduce the wine until almost dry. Add the water to the pan and bring to a simmer. Reduce the liquid by half. Add the lemon zest and herbs and remove from the heat. Cover and let steep at room temperature for 20 minutes. Strain through a chinois. Using an immersion blender, blend in the feta and crème fraîche until fully incorporated. Season with salt and keep warm.

_____

TO FINISH

> *10 pistachios*
> *45 g French-style sheep's milk feta, crumbled*
> *6 Bing cherries, halved and pitted*
> *Squash blossoms*
> *Mint tops*

Preheat the oven to 175°C/350°F. Spread the pistachios on a baking sheet lined with parchment paper and toast until lightly browned and aromatic, about 8 minutes. Shape the zucchini basil puree into quenelles and place two on each of four plates. Divide the toasted pistachios, olive oil squash, roasted squash, Parisian gnocchi, crumbled feta, and cherry halves among the plates. Garnish each plate with squash blossoms and mint tops. With an immersion blender, lightly froth the feta nage and sauce each plate.

FENNEL
with Bottarga and Anchovy

Serves 4

ANCHOVY PASTE

5 anchovy fillets
65 g pitted and drained green olives
1 egg yolk
Pinch of dried red pepper flakes
20 g olive oil
15 g lemon juice
Grated zest of 1/2 orange

Combine the anchovies, olives, egg yolk, and pepper flakes in a blender and puree on high until smooth. Turn to low speed and slowly add the olive oil. Blend until emulsified. Blend in the lemon juice and orange zest and keep at room temperature.

FENNEL PLANKS

2 fennel bulbs, tops attached
125 g dry white wine
Peeled zest of 1 lemon
25 g lemon juice
2 star anise pods
1 g fennel seeds
2 sprigs thyme
4 g salt
40 g olive oil
4 cloves garlic, crushed

Trim the tops of the fennel bulbs so they are 7.5 cm (3 inches) long. Cut the fennel lengthwise into 1.3-cm (1/2-inch) thick planked cross sections. Using a vegetable peeler, peel away the woody outer layer of the stems and the outside layer of the bulbs. Prepare an ice bath. Combine the wine, lemon zest and juice, star anise, fennel seeds, thyme, and salt in a saucepan. Heat to a simmer over medium heat and reduce by half. Remove the pan from the heat and chill over the ice bath.

Bring a large pot of water to a rolling boil over high heat. Line a baking sheet with parchment paper. Seal the fennel planks with the cooking liquid airtight in a sous vide bag. Submerge the bag in the boiling water and cook until the fennel is tender, about 20 minutes. Shock the

bagged fennel in the ice bath. When cold, remove the fennel from the bag, place on the prepared baking sheet, and keep at room temperature. Strain and reserve the cooking liquid for the barigoule sauce.

BARIGOULE SAUCE

100 g reserved cooking liquid from Fennel Planks
40 g crème fraîche
2 g salt

Heat the cooking liquid in a saucepan over medium heat. Bring to a simmer and remove the pan from the heat. Blend in the crème fraîche using an immersion blender and season with salt. Keep warm.

TO FINISH

Olive oil
Slow-Poached Quail Eggs (page 300)
Parmesan Sauce (page 305)
Bottarga, for grating
1 fennel bulb
Fleur de sel
4 Sour Rye Crisps (page 289)
Bronze fennel
Fennel blossoms
Fennel pollen

Preheat the oven to 175°C/350°F. Brush the fennel planks with olive oil and place in the oven to heat through, about 5 minutes. Heat a large saucepan of water to 71°C/160°F. Crack open the quail eggs into the hot water to warm through, about 2 minutes. Lightly brush each warm fennel plank with the Parmesan sauce. Grate bottarga over each fennel plank and place one at the center of each of four plates. Using a mandoline, slice the fennel bulb lengthwise into paper thin shaves. Lightly dress the shaved fennel with Parmesan sauce in a mixing bowl. Place a small pile of dressed shaved fennel next to each fennel plank. Using a slotted spoon, carefully remove the quail eggs from the water and season with fleur de sel. Divide the quail eggs among the plates. Spread the anchovy paste onto each crisp and place one over each fennel plank. Garnish each plate with the bronze fennel, fennel blossoms, and fennel pollen. Using an immersion blender, froth the barigoule sauce and sauce each plate.

BUTTERNUT SQUASH
Roasted with Apples and Quinoa

Serves 4

SPICED PICKLING LIQUID

5 g whole coriander seeds
5 g cardamom seeds
5 g star anise pods
2 cinnamon sticks
400 g White Balsamic Pickling Liquid (page 295)

Combine the spices in a wide saucepan. Toast until fragrant, stirring occasionally to prevent burning, about 3 minutes. Add the pickling liquid to the toasted spices. Heat the liquid to a simmer and remove the pan from the heat. Let the liquid cool to room temperature. Strain through a chinois. Reserve the pickling liquid in an airtight container, refrigerated, for up to 1 week.

PICKLED APPLES

300 g Simple Syrup (page 300)
1 Granny Smith apple
Spiced Pickling Liquid

Preheat the oven to 95°C/200°F. Line a baking sheet with parchment paper. Heat the syrup in a saucepan over medium heat until warmed through. Remove the pan from the heat and keep warm. Quarter the apples and cut each quarter into three wedges. Cut the peel from each apple wedge using a 6-cm (2⅜-inch) ring cutter. Punch out the cores of the apple wedges to form half-moons, using a 2.2-cm (⅞-inch) ring cutter. Place the apple moons in a mixing bowl and cover with the warm syrup. Let steep at room temperature for 5 minutes. Drain and discard the syrup. Spread the moons in a single layer on a baking sheet lined with parchment paper. Place in the oven to dehydrate until they appear shriveled on the outside, yet still retain some juice, about 3 hours. Place the apples in a heatproof container. Heat the pickling liquid to a simmer in a saucepan over medium heat. Pour the liquid over the apples to cover and let cool to room temperature.

APPLE DICE

15 g glucose syrup
1 Granny Smith apple, peeled and diced
  6 mm (¼ inch)
Salt

Heat the syrup in a saucepan over medium heat until melted. Add the diced apple and cook, stirring occasionally, until the apples start to soften, about 4 minutes. Turn the heat to low and continue to cook until the apples are soft and translucent without any color, about 15 minutes. Remove the pan from the heat and set aside.

MELTED LEEKS

30 g butter
175 g leek, white and pale green parts only,
  finely chopped
Salt

Heat the butter in a sauté pan over low heat until foamy but not browned. Add the leek to the pan. Cook, stirring occasionally, until tender and without any color, about 15 minutes. Season with salt. If necessary, add a splash of water during the cooking process to prevent the leeks from browning. Remove the pan from the heat and set aside.

MORCILLA SAUSAGE RAGOUT

220 g Chicken Jus (page 303)
75 g morcilla sausage, casings removed
Melted Leeks
Apple Dice
25 g butter
Salt

Heat the chicken jus in a saucepan over medium heat. Bring the jus to a simmer and reduce by half. Add the morcilla and melted leeks to the pan. Continue to simmer and reduce the liquid until thickened to a glaze consistency. Fold in the apple dice and butter. Continue to cook until the butter is melted and fully incorporated. Season with salt and keep warm.

CONTINUED

BUTTERNUT SQUASH ROASTED WITH APPLES AND QUINOA, CONTINUED

TO FINISH

2 butternut squash
Grapeseed oil
Salt
1 Granny Smith apple
95 g Cooked Quinoa (page 287)
25 g Puffed Quinoa (page 289)
5 g sliced chives
Lemon Vinaigrette (page 285)
Baby Russian kale leaves

Preheat the oven to 175°C/350°F. Line a baking sheet with paper towels. Carefully cut the butternut squash lengthwise into four 1.3-cm (1/2-inch) thick planked cross sections. Remove the seeds with a spoon and discard. Only use planks with a large cavity left by the seeds. Peel the squash planks and score the neck portions. Heat 1.3 cm (1/2 inch) of oil in each of two large sauté pans over high heat. Place two planks in each pan and sear until deeply caramelized on one side, about 3 minutes. Turn the planks over and season with salt. Transfer the pans to the oven and cook until the planks are tender, about 10 minutes. Turn the planks over and season with salt before transferring to the paper towel–lined baking sheet to drain.

Quarter the apple and cut each quarter into three wedges. Cut the peel from each apple wedge using a 6-cm (2³/₈-inch) ring cutter. Punch out the cores of the apple wedges to form half-moons, using a 2.2-cm (7/8-inch) ring cutter. Set aside. Combine both quinoas in a mixing bowl with the chives and dress with lemon vinaigrette. In a separate mixing bowl, lightly dress the baby kale leaves with lemon vinaigrette.

Place one cooked plank in the center of each plate and spoon the morcilla sausage ragout into each seed cavity, allowing the sauce to spill over a touch. Spoon the quinoa mixture on and around each plank. Finish each plate with the pickled and fresh apples and the dressed baby Russian kale leaves.

CARROT
Slow Roasted with Yogurt, Vadouvan, and Kale

Serves 4

GARLIC CURRY OIL

150 g grapeseed oil
7 cloves garlic, thinly sliced
10 g vadouvan curry powder

Heat the oil and garlic in a saucepan over medium heat. When the oil reaches 71°C/160°F, remove the pan from the heat and stir in the curry powder. Let steep at room temperature for 20 minutes. Strain the oil through a chinois and discard the garlic. Strain again through a coffee filter. Reserve the curry oil in an airtight container, refrigerated, for up to 1 week.

ROASTED CARROTS

24 small rainbow carrots
90 g lamb fat, melted
Salt
Garlic Curry Oil
Fleur de sel

Preheat the oven to 205°C/400°F. In a large mixing bowl, toss the carrots and melted fat together until evenly coated. Season the carrots with salt. Spread on a wire rack set over a baking sheet. Place in the oven and roast until tender and browned, about 50 minutes. Remove from the oven and lightly brush with garlic curry oil. Season with fleur de sel and keep warm.

KALE SAUCE

200 g lacinato kale leaves
45 g spinach leaves
80 g ice water
10 g Garlic Curry Oil
Salt

Cut the ribs from the kale leaves and discard. Thinly slice the cleaned leaves. Bring a large pot of salted water to a boil and prepare an ice bath. Blanch the spinach leaves in the boiling water until completely tender, about 5 minutes. When you rub the spinach between your fingers, it should fall apart completely. Shock the spinach in the ice bath. Blanch the kale leaves in the boiling water until completely tender, about 10 minutes. The kale should similarly fall apart when rubbed between your fingers. Shock the kale in the ice bath until cold. Drain the blanched greens and squeeze to remove any excess water. Transfer the greens to a blender and start to blend on low speed. Slowly add the ice water and puree on high speed until smooth. Turn to low speed and slowly add the garlic curry oil until emulsified. Season with salt. Reserve in an airtight container, refrigerated, for up to 2 days. When ready to serve, remove from the refrigerator and allow the sauce to come to room temperature.

TO FINISH

80 g Cooked Quinoa (page 287)
25 g Puffed Quinoa (page 289)
1/2 shallot, finely chopped
5 g sliced chives
Lemon Vinaigrette (page 285)
80 g Yogurt Gel (page 301)
8 Kale Chips (page 298)
Carrot tops

Combine both quinoas in a mixing bowl with the shallot and chives and dress with lemon vinaigrette. Swirl yogurt gel and kale sauce on each of four plates. Divide the roasted carrots over the sauces on each plate. Spoon the quinoa salad into small piles between the carrots. Garnish each plate with kale chips and carrot tops.

SALSIFY
with Blood Pudding and Lady Apples

Serves 4

——

POACHED SALSIFY

*20 salsify roots, peeled and trimmed
    to 16 cm (6¹/₂ inches) in length
Salsify Cooking Liquid (page 306)
100 g Chicken Stock (page 303)
65 g butter
Salt*

Combine the salsify in a large saucepan with enough
salsify cooking liquid to cover. Heat to a gentle simmer
over low heat and cook the salsify until just tender, about
1 hour. Remove the pan from the heat and let the salsify
cool to room temperature in the liquid. Heat the chicken
stock to a simmer in a large saucepan over medium heat.
Remove the salsify from the cooking liquid and place in
the pan with the chicken stock; add the butter. As the
butter melts and emulsifies, it will glaze the salsify evenly.
Season with salt. Be careful not to overcook the salsify or
reduce the glaze too far, as the emulsion will break and
make the salsify greasy. Transfer to a paper towel to drain
any excess glaze.

——

BLOOD PUDDING

*170 g cream
35 g panko
35 g pork fatback, diced 3 mm (¹/₈ inch)
¹/₂ onion, finely chopped
2 cloves garlic, finely chopped
85 g lean pork, diced 2.5 cm (1 inch)
1 g quatre épices
12 g apple brandy
1 g thyme leaves
8 g sugar
6 g salt
175 g pork blood*

Preheat the oven to 150°C/300°F. Line the bottom of
a 22 by 11-cm (8¹/₂ by 4¹/₂-inch) loaf pan with acetate.
Combine the cream and panko in a bowl and stir to fully
incorporate. Soak the panko in the cream for 1 hour at
room temperature. Fill a large mixing bowl with ice. Heat
a sauté pan over high heat. When the pan is hot, add the

diced fatback and sauté just enough to cook but not fully
render, about 30 seconds. Transfer the cooked fatback
to a plate using a slotted spoon. Leave the rendered fat in
the pan. Turn the heat to low. Add the onion and garlic.
Cook, stirring frequently, until softened without any
color, about 6 minutes. Remove the pan from the heat
and let cool to room temperature. Combine the diced
pork, vegetables, quatre épices, brandy, thyme, sugar,
and salt in a mixing bowl set over the ice. Stir to fully
incorporate. Pass the mixture through a meat grinder,
using the small die, into a clean, dry mixing bowl set over
the ice. Stir to combine and pass the mixture though the
grinder a second time into a clean, dry mixing bowl set
over the ice. Add the soaked panko, cooked fatback, and
pork blood to the ground pork mixture. Stir together
until well incorporated. The mixture should have the
consistency of applesauce.

Pour the mixture into the prepared loaf pan. Cover the
pan with foil and place it in a larger baking dish. Pour
enough hot water into the larger baking dish to come
to the level of the blood pudding in the loaf pan. Bake
the pudding in the water bath in the oven until just set,
about 30 minutes. Remove the baking dish from the
oven and remove the loaf pan from the water bath. Let
cool to room temperature. Cover with plastic wrap and
refrigerate overnight to fully set. Use a hot, dry knife to
cut around the edges of the loaf pan and unmold the
pudding onto a cutting board. Remove the acetate and
cut the pudding into 2-cm (³/₄-inch) cubes. Reserve,
refrigerated, until ready to serve.

——

APPLE BLOOD SAUCE

*15 g grapeseed oil
1 Granny Smith apple, peeled and sliced
1 shallot, sliced
120 g apple cider
120 g Chicken Stock (page 303)
120 g white verjus
180 g Chicken Jus (page 303)
2 sprigs thyme
5 g pork blood
Salt*

Heat the oil in a saucepan over medium heat. Add the
apple and shallot. Cook, stirring occasionally, until
softened and without any color, about 7 minutes. Add
the apple cider, chicken stock, and white verjus to the
pan. Bring the liquid to a simmer and reduce by half.

CONTINUED

147

Add the chicken jus and continue to simmer until the sauce is thick enough to coat the back of a spoon. Strain the sauce through a chinois and place the sauce in a clean saucepan over low heat. Add the thyme and slowly whisk in the pork blood until fully incorporated. Bring the sauce to a simmer and continue to cook until slightly thickened, about 2 minutes. Strain the sauce through cheesecloth and season with salt. Keep warm.

APPLE ÉCRASER

75 g fingerling potatoes, peeled
45 g butter
1 Granny Smith apple, peeled and cored
Salt

In a saucepan, cover the potatoes with cold water. Season with salt. Cook the potatoes gently over low heat until just tender, about 45 minutes. Drain the potatoes and smash with a fork. Keep warm. Heat the butter in a saucepan over medium heat until foamy but not browned. Add the sliced apple and turn the heat to low. Cook the apples, stirring frequently, until softened but not browned, about 8 minutes. Season with salt and remove the pan from the heat. Using a large fork, mash the cooked apples thoroughly. Combine the potatoes with the apples. Keep warm.

ROASTED SALSIFY

40 g lard
15 g grapeseed oil
16 salsify roots, peeled and trimmed to
*   16 cm (6 1/2 inches) in length*
Salt

Heat the lard and oil in a large sauté pan over medium heat. When the oil is hot, add the salsify roots to the pan and start to roast. Season with salt. Cook, stirring frequently, until evenly browned on all sides and tender, about 8 minutes. Transfer the salsify roots to a paper towel to drain. Keep warm.

SALSIFY CHIPS

Canola oil, for frying
1 salsify root
Salt

Heat 7.5 cm (3 inches) of canola oil in a large, heavy pot to 175°C/350°F. Using a vegetable peeler, peel long, lengthwise strips from the salsify. Fry the salsify strips in the oil until golden brown and crispy, about 3 minutes. Transfer the chips to a paper towel to drain. Season with salt.

TO FINISH

15 g grapeseed oil
1 1/2 Granny Smith apples, peeled
Roasted Lady Apples (page 299)

Preheat the oven to 175°C/350°F. Line a baking sheet with parchment paper. Heat the oil in a sauté pan over high heat. Sear the blood pudding cubes on two opposite sides until blackened but not burnt. Transfer the blood pudding to the prepared baking sheet and place in the oven to heat through, about 3 minutes.

Using a turning slicer, turn four ribbons from the whole apple, each about 20 cm by 2.5 cm (8 inches by 1 inch) in size. Dice the remaining half apple into 3-mm (1/8-inch) pieces and mix into the sauce. Alternate the glazed salsify and roasted salsify among four plates. Spoon the apple écraser onto each plate next to the salsify. Arrange the roasted lady apples and blood pudding cubes on and around the salsify. Garnish each plate with a salsify chip and an apple ribbon. Sauce with the apple blood sauce.

BLACK BASS
with Scallions, Rhubarb, and Green Garlic

Serves 4

PEANUT POTATO CONFIT

24 peanut potatoes
Olive oil
3 sprigs thyme
1 clove garlic, crushed
2 g salt

Preheat the oven to 150°C/300°F. Combine all of the ingredients in a baking dish. Cover with aluminum foil. Cook the potatoes in the oven until just tender, about 1 hour. Remove the potatoes from the oven and keep warm.

PICKLED GREEN GARLIC

16 cloves green garlic, peeled
120 g White Balsamic Pickling Liquid (page 295)

In a saucepan, cover the garlic cloves with cold water and place over high heat. When the water comes to a boil, drain and cover again with cold water. Heat over high heat and repeat the blanching process four more times. On the fifth blanching, do not drain the garlic; instead turn the heat to low and simmer until the garlic is tender, about 7 minutes. Drain the garlic and transfer to a heatproof container. Heat the pickling liquid in a saucepan over high heat to a boil. Pour the liquid over the blanched garlic and allow to cool to room temperature.

RHUBARB CONDIMENT

200 g rhubarb, sliced
45 g agave nectar
4 g salt
5 g raspberry vincotto
10 g olive oil
15 g green garlic, finely chopped
25 g Pickled Mustard Seeds (page 294)

Heat the rhubarb, agave nectar, and salt in a saucepan over low heat. Stir occasionally and cook until the liquid released from the rhubarb is reduced to nearly dry, about 15 minutes. Add the vincotto and stir to incorporate. Set aside. Heat the oil in a saucepan over low heat. Add the green garlic and sweat until tender without any color, about 4 minutes. Transfer the garlic to a bowl and combine with the cooked rhubarb and pickled mustard seeds. Stir to incorporate and keep at room temperature.

RHUBARB FISH SAUCE

1 black bass, about 2.3 kg
10 g grapeseed oil
80 g scallions, thinly sliced
25 g ginger, peeled and thinly sliced
1/2 jalapeño, seeded and thinly sliced
240 g rhubarb juice (from about 5 stalks)
0.5 g xanthan gum
Lime juice
Salt

Scale and fillet the fish. Reserve the fillets for the Black Bass. Remove and discard any fins or bloodline from the fish bones. Soak the cleaned bones in ice water overnight. Preheat the broiler. Drain the fish bones and cut into 5-cm (2-inch) pieces. Spread the fish bones on a wire rack set over a baking sheet. Roast the fish bones under the broiler until thoroughly browned, about 15 minutes. Turn the bones over and continue broiling until browned on the opposite side, about 10 minutes more. Set aside. Heat the oil in a saucepan over medium heat. When the oil is hot, add the scallions, ginger, and jalapeño. Cook, stirring occasionally, until the vegetables are soft, about 5 minutes. Add the rhubarb juice and roasted bones to the pan. Heat the liquid to a simmer. Remove the pan from the heat and cover the pan with a lid. Let the sauce steep at room temperature for 20 minutes. Uncover and strain the sauce through a chinois. Transfer to a blender and start to blend on medium speed. Slowly add the xanthan gum and continue to blend for 1 minute, until the xanthan gum is hydrated and the sauce is thickened. Blend in the lime juice and season with the salt. Keep warm.

SCALLIONS

8 scallions
50 g butter
45 g Chicken Stock (page 303)
Salt

Peel the scallions down to the tender hearts. In a sauté pan, melt the butter over medium heat. Add the scallion hearts and cook until they just start to wilt without any

CONTINUED

color, about 2 minutes. Season with salt. Add the chicken stock and make a glaze with the butter. Be careful to not overcook the scallions or reduce the glaze too far, as the emulsion will break and make the scallions greasy. Transfer the glazed scallions to a paper towel–lined tray to drain any excess glaze. Keep warm.

RHUBARB PLANKS

240 g rhubarb juice (from about 5 stalks)
15 g ginger juice
32 g grenadine
30 g sugar
10 g red wine vinegar
2 rhubarb stalks, halved crosswise

Preheat the oven to 150°C/300°F and prepare an ice bath. Line a baking sheet with parchment paper. Heat the rhubarb and ginger juices, grenadine, sugar, and vinegar in a saucepan over medium heat. Stir to fully dissolve the sugar. When the liquid is at a simmer, place the rhubarb stalks in the pan so that they are completely submerged in the liquid. Cover with a parchment cartouche and turn the heat to low. Gently cook the stalks until they are tender, about 15 minutes. Remove the pan from the heat and chill the stalks in the cooking liquid over the ice bath. When cold, peel and discard the outer woody layer from the rhubarb using a paring knife. Cut the stalks into 9-cm (3½-inch) long pieces and trim the ends on a bias. Place the trimmed stalks on the prepared baking sheet. Cook the rhubarb in the oven just until they are warmed through. While the stalks are in the oven, heat the cooking liquid in a saucepan over medium heat. Bring the liquid to a simmer and reduce to glazelike consistency. Remove the pan from the heat and add the warm rhubarb. Gently stir to evenly coat in the glaze. Keep warm.

BLACK BASS

2 black bass fillets
40 g grapeseed oil
Salt

Preheat the oven to 150°C/300°F. Line a baking sheet with paper towels. Cut each fillet in half, crosswise, on a bias. Season each portion of fish with salt on both sides. Thoroughly pat the skin side of each portion dry. Heat the grapeseed oil in a large ovenproof sauté pan over high heat. When the oil is very hot, carefully place each portion in the pan, skin side down. Do not crowd the pan. (It may be necessary to use two sauté pans.) The fish will seize and curl when it hits the hot oil. Reduce the heat to medium. After 1 minute, very gently press down on the flesh side of each portion. The goal is to make sure there is good contact with the skin and the oil, so that the skin crisps. However, if you press down too forcefully, the skin will tear. When the skin begins to crisp and turns a light golden brown, about 3 minutes, transfer the sauté pan to the oven to cook the fish through, about 7 minutes. When the fish is cooked through, carefully remove the fish from the pan and place on the prepared baking sheet, flesh side down. Serve immediately.

TO FINISH

Onion blossoms
Olive oil

Place one black bass portion on the center of each of four plates. Spoon the rhubarb condiment in several small piles around each piece of black bass. Drain the potatoes from the oil and divide among the four plates. Divide the scallions, rhubarb planks, and pickled green garlic among the plates. Garnish each plate with onion blossoms and sauce with the rhubarb fish sauce. Break the sauce on each plate with several drops of olive oil.

HALIBUT
*Seared with Favas
and Ramps*

Serves 4

―――

HALIBUT

1 halibut fillet, about 600 g
Salt
40 g grapeseed oil
35 g Chicken Stock (page 303)
10 g lemon juice
15 g butter

Preheat the oven to 160°C/325°F. Portion the fillet into
four portions, each about 115 g. Reserve and set aside
the trim for the smoked halibut. Season the portions with
salt on both sides. Heat the oil in a large sauté pan over
high heat. When the oil just starts to smoke, place the
portions in the pan bone side down. Reduce the heat to
medium and cook until golden brown, about 2 minutes.
Transfer the pan with the halibut to the oven to cook
through, about 6 minutes. Remove the pan from the
oven. Transfer the halibut to a paper towel, seared side
up, and set aside for a moment. Drain any fat from the
pan. Deglaze the pan with the chicken stock. Add the
lemon juice and butter. As the butter melts, it will form
a thick glaze. Season the glaze with salt. Spoon the glaze
over the halibut and keep warm.

―――

SMOKED HALIBUT

About 125 g reserved trim from the Halibut

Preheat the broiler. Soak 35 g of applewood chips in
cold water for 10 minutes. Drain. Line a roasting pan
with aluminum foil and place ten charcoal briquettes in a
single layer in it. Place the charcoal in the broiler until lit,
about 15 minutes. Remove the charcoal from the broiler
and sprinkle enough wood chips over the charcoal to
put out any live flames, but not so many that the embers
are smothered. Turn off the broiler and set the oven
to 120°C/250°F. Cut the halibut trim into small pieces,
about 5 cm (2 inches) square. Spread the halibut in a
single layer on a wire rack set over a baking sheet and
place in the oven with the charcoal to smoke. Hot-smoke
the fish until heavily smoked and cooked through, about
15 minutes. Remove the halibut from the oven and let

cool until the pan can be safely wrapped with plastic
wrap. Wrap the pan tightly and place in the refrigerator
to cool. When chilled, unwrap and reserve in an airtight
container, refrigerated, for up to 3 days.

―――

GREEN GARLIC FUMET

Smoked Halibut
20 g grapeseed oil
125 g leeks, white and pale green parts only,
*   thinly sliced*
100 g green garlic, tops and bottoms, thinly sliced
75 g spring onions, tops and bottoms, thinly sliced
240 g Fish Fumet (page 304)
75 g skim milk
Salt

Tie the smoked halibut in a cheesecloth sachet and set
aside. Heat the oil in a saucepan over medium heat. Add
the leeks, garlic, and onions to the pan and cook, stirring
occasionally, until softened without any color, about
7 minutes. Add the fumet and the sachet of smoked halibut
to the pan. Bring to a simmer and cook for 20 minutes.
Remove and discard the sachet. Strain the fumet through
a chinois, pressing to extract as much liquid as possible.
Reserve the liquid and cooked vegetables separately.
Transfer the vegetables to a blender and puree on high
until smooth. On low speed, add 45 g of the reserved
cooking liquid and the milk. Season with salt and blend
on high speed until fully incorporated. Strain the sauce
through a chinois and keep warm.

―――

PICKLED MEYER LEMONS

80 g Meyer lemon zest, diced 3 mm (1/8 inch)
240 g White Balsamic Pickling Liquid (page 295)

Combine the zest in a saucepan with enough cold water
to cover. Over high heat, bring the water to a boil. Drain
the zest and cover again with cold water. Repeat the
boiling and draining process two times. After the third
blanching, transfer the drained lemon zest to a heatproof
container. Heat the pickling liquid to a boil in a saucepan
over high heat. Pour the hot liquid over the zest to cover
and let cool to room temperature.

CONTINUED

CURED MEYER LEMON SEGMENTS

2 Meyer lemons, cut into segments with no seeds,
*   peel, or pith*
3 g salt
4 g confectioners' sugar

Place the lemon segments in a bowl and season with the salt and sugar. Transfer to a colander and let sit at room temperature for 1 hour. Chop the cured segments and transfer to a paper towel to drain.

MEYER LEMON JUICE SLURRY

120 g Meyer lemon juice
30 g water
25 g sugar
0.5 g xanthan gum

Combine the juice, water, and sugar in a blender and begin to blend at medium speed. Slowly add the xanthan gum and continue to blend for 1 minute until the gum is fully hydrated and the liquid is thickened. Reserve the slurry in an airtight container, refrigerated, for up to 2 days.

MEYER LEMON RELISH

Pickled Meyer Lemons
Cured Meyer Lemon Segments
25 g Meyer Lemon Juice Slurry

Drain the pickled Meyer lemons from the pickling liquid and combine with the remaining ingredients in a mixing bowl. Mix just to combine.

CHARRED RAMPS

8 ramps
15 g grapeseed oil
Salt

Preheat a griddle over high heat. Place the ramps in a mixing bowl and lightly dress them with the oil. Season with salt. Char the ramps on the griddle until the leaf is charred and the bulb is tender, about 2 minutes on each side. Transfer the ramps to a paper towel to drain. Keep warm.

FAVA BEANS

80 g fava beans, removed from pods
50 g Chicken Stock (page 303)
35 g butter
Salt

Bring a large pot of salted water to a boil and prepare an ice bath. Blanch the favas in the water until tender, about 3 minutes. Shock the beans in the ice bath until cold. Drain the blanched favas. Remove and discard the outer shells from the beans. Heat the stock to a simmer in a pan over low heat. Add the beans and the butter. Season with salt. As the butter melts and emulsifies, it will glaze the beans evenly. Be careful not to overcook the beans or reduce the glaze too far, as the emulsion will break and make the beans greasy. Transfer the beans to a paper towel to drain any excess glaze. Keep warm.

TO FINISH

Ramp leaves
4 slices Candied Meyer Lemon (page 296)
Olive oil

Place one halibut portion in the center of each of four bowls. Divide the favas and Meyer lemon relish among the bowls, spooning them in small piles around the fish. Lightly froth the green garlic fumet with an immersion blender and spoon around the fish in each bowl. Arrange two charred ramps over each fish. Garnish each fish with a candied Meyer lemon and a ramp leaf. Break the sauce in each bowl with several drops of olive oil.

LOBSTER
Poached with Snap Peas and Morels

Serves 4

––––

LOBSTER

4 lobsters, 575 g each

Bring a large pot of water to a rolling boil and prepare an ice bath. Place the lobsters in a large heatproof container and pour enough of the boiling water over the lobsters to submerge. Immediately cover the container with plastic wrap and cook until the lobster tails are opaque, about 2 minutes. Quickly remove the lobsters from the hot water and separate the knuckles and claws from the bodies. Return the knuckles and claws to the hot water and shock the bodies in the ice bath. Allow the knuckles and claws to continue cooking until opaque, about 3 minutes more. Remove the knuckles and claws from the hot water and shock in the ice bath.

Twist the lobster tails away from the bodies. Crack and remove the shells from the tails and remove the intestinal tracts. Separate the knuckles and claws. Pull the small pincer back from the large pincer of the claw and then pull it straight out and up. A small piece of cartilage should come away with the small pincer. Crack and remove the shells from the knuckles and claws, keeping the lobster meat as intact as possible. Keep refrigerated until ready to serve.

––––

SHERRY SABAYON

15 g dried morels
500 g cold water
25 g grapeseed oil
1 shallot, thinly sliced
250 g cremini mushrooms, thinly sliced
30 g sherry
4 sprigs thyme
1 egg
3 egg yolks
230 g butter, melted
5 g vin jaune
8 g sherry vinegar
Salt

Combine the morels and water in a large mixing bowl and let soak at room temperature for 2 hours. Heat the oil in a large saucepan over medium heat. Add the shallot to the pan. Cook, stirring occasionally, until tender and without any color, about 4 minutes. Add the sliced mushrooms and cook, stirring occasionally, until the mushrooms are caramelized and the liquid released from the mushrooms is fully evaporated, about 8 minutes. Add the sherry to deglaze and scrape the caramelized bits from the bottom of the pan. Bring the wine to a simmer and reduce until almost dry. Add the rehydrated morels with the soaking water. Bring the liquid to a simmer and add the thyme. Simmer the mixture for 20 minutes. Remove the pan from the heat and strain through a chinois. Heat a water bath to 62°C/145°F. Return the mixture to a clean saucepan and heat to a simmer over medium heat. Continue to simmer until reduced by half, to about 100 g. Crack the egg and egg yolks into a mixing bowl and whisk to combine. Whisk the warm mushroom base into the eggs, being careful not to scramble the eggs. Once combined, slowly whisk in the melted butter, vin jaune, and vinegar. Season the mixture with salt. Transfer the sabayon to an iSi canister and charge with two charges of N_2O. Cook the sabayon in the water bath for 45 minutes. Keep warm.

––––

SUGAR SNAP PEAS

12 whole sugar snap peas
120 g shelled sugar snap peas
50 g Chicken Stock (page 303)
35 g butter
Salt

Heat a large pot of salted water to a boil over high heat and prepare an ice bath. Carefully remove one side of the outer shell from the whole snap peas, while leaving the inner peas still attached to the other side of the shell. Blanch the whole snap peas in the boiling water for 20 seconds and immediately shock in the ice bath. Blanch the shelled snap peas in the boiling water for 10 seconds and immediately shock in ice water. Drain both peas and pat dry with a paper towel. Heat the chicken stock to a simmer in a sauté pan over medium heat. Add the butter and season with salt. As the butter melts and emulsifies, it will form a thick glaze. Carefully add the blanched whole snap peas and shelled snap peas to the glaze, stirring gently just to warm through. Transfer the peas to a paper towel to drain any excess glaze. Keep warm.

CONTINUED

BRAISED MORELS

30 g butter
36 morels
1/2 shallot, finely chopped
45 g vin jaune
80 g cream
50 g Sherry Sabayon
25 g lemon juice
Salt

Heat the butter in a sauté pan over medium heat. When the butter is foamy but not browned, add the morels and stir occasionally to evenly cook. When the morels begin to soften, about 2 minutes, add the shallots. Continue to stir occasionally until the morels and shallots are tender, about 3 minutes. Add the vin jaune and reduce until almost dry. Add the cream and reduce until it is a thick glaze. Remove the pan from the heat. Expel the sherry sabayon into the pan and gently fold it into the mushrooms. Season the mushrooms with the lemon juice and salt. Transfer the morels to a paper towel to drain any excess glaze. Keep warm.

TO FINISH

Citrus Beurre Blanc (page 303)
Fleur de sel
Chive blossoms
Pea tendrils
Miner's lettuce

Heat the beurre blanc in a pot to 62°C/144°F. Submerge the lobster tails, knuckles, and claws in the beurre blanc until heated through, about 7 minutes. Transfer the lobsters to a paper towel to drain any excess butter, and season with fleur de sel.

Place one tail, one knuckle, and one claw in each of four bowls. Divide the sugar snap peas and braised morels among the four bowls, arranging them on and around the lobster. Garnish the lobsters with chive blossoms, pea tendrils, and miner's lettuce. Expel 20 g of the sherry sabayon on each plate to finish.

RED SNAPPER
Poached with Corn and Tomato

Serves 4

SUMMER SWEET CORN NAGE

400 g Tomato Water (page 301)
50 g butter
15 g lemongrass, bruised and sliced
½ shallot, sliced
5 g ginger, peeled and sliced
125 g Fish Fumet (page 304)
100 g corn kernels
3 sprigs basil
15 g water
10 g cornstarch
5 g salt
Pinch of cayenne

Heat the tomato water in a saucepan over medium heat. Bring to a simmer and cook until reduced by half. Remove the pan from the heat and set aside. In a separate saucepan, heat half of the butter over medium heat until foamy but not browned. Add the lemongrass, shallot, and ginger. Cook, stirring frequently, until soft and without any color, about 7 minutes. Add the fumet and reduced tomato water to the mixture and bring to a simmer. Continue to cook until the liquid is reduced by half. Add the corn and simmer for 15 minutes. Add the basil and stir to incorporate. Remove the pan from the heat and cover with a lid. Let steep at room temperature for 15 minutes. Uncover and strain the sauce through a chinois. Transfer to a clean saucepan and place over low heat. Whisk the water and cornstarch together in a small bowl until smooth. Turn the heat to medium and bring the sauce to a simmer. Whisk in the cornstarch slurry. Continue to simmer the sauce, while whisking continuously, until the cornstarch cooks out and thickens the sauce, about 3 minutes. Turn the heat to low and whisk the remaining butter into the sauce, being careful to maintain the emulsion. Season the sauce with the salt and cayenne. Keep warm.

PEANUT POTATO RISSOLET

175 g peanut potatoes
2 sprigs thyme
1 clove garlic, smashed
Olive oil
3 g salt
50 g Chicken Stock (page 303)
30 g butter

Preheat the oven to 150°C/300°F. In a baking dish, combine the potatoes, thyme, and garlic with enough olive oil to completely cover. Add the salt and cover with aluminum foil. Cook the potatoes in the oven until just tender, about 1 hour. Remove the potatoes from the oven and uncover. Let cool to room temperature in the oil. Drain the potatoes and reserve 40 g of the cooking oil.

Heat the reserved oil in a large sauté pan over high heat. When the oil just starts to smoke, add the potatoes to the pan and turn the heat to medium. Sauté the potatoes, stirring occasionally, until evenly heated through, golden brown, and crispy on all sides, about 6 minutes. Drain and discard the oil from the pan. Add the stock and butter to the pan. As the butter melts and emulsifies, it will glaze the potatoes evenly. Be careful not to overcook the potatoes or reduce the glaze too far, as the emulsion will break and make the potatoes greasy. Place the potatoes on a paper towel to drain any excess glaze. Keep warm.

RED SNAPPER

2 red snapper fillets, each about 230 g
150 g Chicken Stock Slurry (page 303)
Fleur de sel

Preheat a water bath to 62°C/144°F. Divide each snapper fillet into two portions, each about 115 g. Place each portion individually in a zip-top bag. Divide the chicken stock slurry among the bags. Slowly lower each bag into the water bath to just below the zip top, allowing the water pressure to push the air out of the bags, and close each seal. Submerge the fish in the bath and cook until tender, about 12 minutes. Carefully remove the fish from the bags and place on a paper towel, skin side facing up, to drain any excess slurry. Season each portion with fleur de sel to finish and keep warm.

CONTINUED

RED SNAPPER POACHED WITH CORN AND TOMATO, CONTINUED

———

MARINATED TOMATOES

20 heirloom cherry tomatoes, halved
8 basil leaves, torn in half
White Balsamic Vinaigrette (page 285)

Combine the tomatoes with the basil in a mixing bowl and dress with the vinaigrette. Toss to evenly coat. Let the tomatoes marinate for at least 30 minutes, but no more than 4 hours. Remove and discard the basil before serving.

———

TO FINISH

50 g Chicken Stock (page 303)
125 g corn kernels
35 g butter
Salt
10 g lime juice
12 Roasted Tomatoes (page 299)
Borage cress
Borage flowers
Olive oil

Heat the chicken stock in a sauté pan over medium heat and bring to a simmer. Add the corn and butter to the pan. As the butter melts and emulsifies, it will glaze the corn evenly. Be careful not to overcook the corn or reduce the glaze too far, as the emulsion will break and make the corn greasy. Add the lime juice and season with salt, stirring to combine. Transfer the glazed corn to a paper towel to drain any excess glaze. Keep warm.

Place one cooked red snapper portion in the center of each of four plates. Divide the glazed corn, marinated tomatoes, roasted tomatoes, and peanut potato rissolet among the four plates, arranging them around the fish. Garnish each plate with borage cress and borage flowers. Lightly froth the corn nage using an immersion blender. Sauce each plate with the frothed sauce. Break the sauce with several drops of olive oil.

SCALLOP
Seared with Peas and Carrots

Serves 4

————

PEA PUREE

> 200 g frozen peas, thawed
> Ice water
> 25 g Lemon Oil (page 284)
> 25 g Chive Oil (page 284)
> Salt

Heat a pot of salted water to a boil over high heat and prepare an ice bath. Blanch the peas in the boiling water until tender, about 4 minutes. Immediately shock in the ice bath. When cold, drain the peas well and transfer to a blender with a splash of ice water. Puree on high speed until smooth. Turn to medium speed and slowly add both oils. Continue blending until the puree is completely emulsified. Season with salt and pass the puree through a chinois. Immediately chill the puree over the ice bath. Reserve the puree in an airtight container, refrigerated, for up to 2 days. Before serving, let the puree sit at room temperature for 30 minutes to temper.

————

CARROT SAUCE

> 30 g butter
> 35 g leeks, white and pale green parts only, sliced
> 20 g lemongrass, bruised and sliced
> 1/2 shallot, sliced
> 15 g ginger, peeled and sliced
> 1 Thai bird chile, seeded and finely chopped
> 50 g vermouth
> 50 g dry white wine
> 250 g carrot juice (from about 4 peeled carrots)
> 250 g Fish Fumet (page 304)
> 125 g Lobster Stock (page 304)
> 150 g coconut milk
> 110 g cream
> 4 sprigs mint
> 1 kaffir lime leaf
> 5 g lime juice
> Salt
> 3 g xanthan gum

Heat the butter in a large saucepan over medium heat until foamy but not browned. Add the leeks, lemongrass, shallot, ginger, and chile to the pan. Cook, stirring occasionally, until the vegetables are soft, about 7 minutes. Add the vermouth and wine. Bring to a simmer and reduce until almost dry. Add the carrot juice, fumet, and lobster stock, stirring to incorporate. Bring to a simmer and reduce by half. Stir in the coconut milk, cream, mint sprigs, and kaffir lime leaf. Bring to a simmer, stirring occasionally, and continue to simmer for 15 minutes. Add the lime juice and season the sauce with salt. Strain through a chinois, discarding the vegetables. Transfer the sauce to a blender and begin blending on low speed. Slowly add the xanthan gum and blend on medium speed for 1 minute to fully hydrate the gum. Keep the sauce warm.

————

CARROT SHAVES

> 1/2 purple carrot
> 1/2 orange carrot
> 1/2 yellow carrot
> 150 g White Balsamic Pickling Liquid (page 295)
> 25 g Lemon Oil (page 284)

Using a mandoline, slice each carrot paper thin on a bias to form oval-shaped shaves. Combine the shaves in a mixing bowl with the pickling liquid and lemon oil to cover. Keep cold until ready to plate.

————

RAINBOW CARROTS

> 1 purple carrot
> 1 orange carrot
> 1 yellow carrot
> 50 g olive oil
> Salt

Preheat the oven to 190°C/375°F. Set a wire rack on a baking sheet. Combine the carrots, oil, and salt in a mixing bowl. Toss to evenly coat. Place the carrots on the wire rack in a single layer and roast until tender, about 30 minutes. Remove from the oven and let cool to room temperature. Cut each carrot into 2.5-cm (1-inch) segments. Using a 2.2-cm (7/8-inch) ring mold, punch each piece, discarding the outer skin. Cut half of the carrot punches in half and leave the rest whole. Return the trimmed carrots to the oven to warm through and keep warm.

CONTINUED

SCALLOP SEARED WITH PEAS AND CARROTS, CONTINUED

ENGLISH PEAS

125 g English peas, removed from pods
50 g Chicken Stock (page 303)
35 g butter
Salt

Bring a large pot of salted water to a rolling boil over high heat and prepare an ice bath. Blanch the peas in the boiling water until tender, about 5 minutes. Immediately shock the peas in the ice bath until cold. Drain and shuck the peas, discarding the outer shells. Heat the stock to a simmer in a saucepan over medium heat. Add the shucked peas and butter, stirring to incorporate. Season with salt. As the butter melts and emulsifies, it will glaze the peas evenly. Be careful not to overcook the peas or reduce the glaze too far, as the emulsion will break and make the peas greasy. Transfer the peas to a paper towel to drain any excess glaze. Keep warm.

TO FINISH

12 U10 scallops
60 g grapeseed oil
Salt
30 g butter
Pea shoots

Using a ridge knife, cut the top quarter round off of each scallop. Gently pat the scallops dry with a paper towel. Divide the oil between two large sauté pans and heat over high heat. Season the scallops with salt on all sides. When the oil just starts to smoke, divide the scallops between the two pans, carefully placing them cut side down. Do not overcrowd the pan, leaving ample space between the scallops to cook. Turn heat to medium and cook the scallops until golden brown and well caramelized, about 2 minutes. Divide the butter between the two pans and heat until foamy but not browned. Turn the scallops over and gently cook, basting, just long enough to warm through, about 30 seconds. Remove the pans from the heat and transfer the scallops to a paper towel to drain. Keep warm.

Spoon the pea puree in two quenelles on each of four plates. Arrange the scallops and the rainbow carrots in a vertical line on each plate in and around the pea puree. Spoon the English peas in among the scallops and carrots. Garnish each plate with the carrot shaves and pea shoots. With an immersion blender, lightly froth the carrot sauce and sauce each plate.

HALIBUT
Poached with Fennel and Tomato

Serves 4

————

FENNEL MINESTRONE

40 g olive oil
180 g fennel, sliced
70 g leeks, white and pale green parts only, sliced
50 g green zucchini, peeled and sliced
30 g carrots, peeled and sliced
30 g celery root, peeled and sliced
1 clove garlic, sliced
120 g dry white wine
800 g Fish Fumet (page 304)
1 roma tomato, coarsely chopped
90 g Yukon Gold potato, peeled and sliced
8 sprigs basil
2 sprigs mint
Pinch of saffron
70 g butter
15 g Meyer lemon juice
5 g Pernod
Salt
Piment d'Espelette

Heat the oil in a large saucepan over medium heat. When the oil is hot, add the fennel, leeks, zucchini, carrots, celery root, and garlic and sweat until tender without any color, about 8 minutes. Add the white wine and bring to a simmer. Cook and reduce the wine by half. Add the fumet, tomato, and potato. Stir to incorporate and bring the liquid to a simmer. Continue to cook the sauce at a low simmer for 30 minutes. Add the basil, mint, and saffron and cover with a lid. Remove the pan from the heat and let steep at room temperature for 20 minutes. Strain the sauce through a chinois and transfer to a clean saucepan. Heat the sauce over medium heat and bring to a simmer. Cook the sauce until reduced by three-quarters. Using an immersion blender, add the butter in increments of about 15 g, blending until fully emulsified. Add the lemon juice and Pernod. Season with salt and piment d'Espelette. Keep warm.

————

FENNEL WINGS

1 fennel bulb
Salt

Bring a large pot of salted water to a rolling boil and prepare an ice bath. Cut the fennel bulb into twelve wedges. Blanch the fennel wedges in the boiling water until just tender, about 6 minutes. Shock the fennel in the ice bath. When cold, remove the fennel from the ice water. Set aside.

————

BABY FENNEL

12 baby fennel bulbs

Bring a large pot of salted water to a rolling boil and prepare an ice bath. Trim the baby fennel tops on a bias. Blanch the fennel in the water until just tender, about 7 minutes. Shock the fennel in the ice bath. When cold, remove the fennel from the ice water. Set aside.

————

ROASTED TOMATOES

6 cherry tomatoes, halved

Heat a sauté pan over high heat. When the pan is very hot, place the tomatoes in the pan, cut side down. Roast until charred, about 4 minutes. Remove the tomatoes from the pan and keep warm.

————

TOMATO PULP

1 beefsteak tomato
Salt

Cut both ends off the tomato. Cut the outer flesh from around the tomato revealing the seed clusters. Scoop the seed sacs from the tomato using a spoon, keeping the sacs as intact as possible. Season the seed sacs lightly with salt.

————

MARINATED CHERRY TOMATOES

8 cherry tomatoes
4 basil leaves, torn in half
White Balsamic Vinaigrette (page 285)

Cut the tomatoes in half or quarters, depending on the size of each. Combine the tomatoes with the basil in a mixing bowl and dress with the vinaigrette. Toss to evenly coat. Allow the tomatoes to marinate at room

CONTINUED

temperature for at least 30 minutes, but no longer than 4 hours. Remove and discard the basil leaves before serving.

HALIBUT

1 halibut fillet, 460 g
Salt
150 g Chicken Stock Slurry (page 303)
Fleur de sel

Heat a water bath to 62°C/144°F. Portion the halibut into four equal portions, about 115 g each. Season each portion with salt on both sides. Place each halibut portion in a separate zip-top bag. Divide the chicken stock slurry evenly among the bags. Lower each bag into the water bath to just below the zip-top line, allowing the water pressure to push the air out of the bags. Seal the bags. Let the halibut cook through in the water bath, about 6 minutes. Remove the bags from the water bath and carefully remove the halibut portions from the bags. Transfer the halibut to a paper towel to drain any excess slurry. Season the portions with fleur de sel and keep warm.

TO FINISH

60 g Chicken Stock (page 303)
45 g butter
Salt
Fennel blossoms
Saffron threads

Heat the chicken stock to a simmer in a sauté pan over medium heat. Add the butter, fennel wings, and baby fennel. Season with salt. Cook the fennel, stirring occasionally, until just until warmed through, about 2 minutes. As the butter melts and emulsifies, it will glaze the fennel evenly. Be careful not to overcook the fennel or reduce the glaze too far, as the emulsion will break and make the fennel greasy. Transfer the fennel to a paper towel to drain any excess glaze. Keep warm.

Place one portion of halibut in the center of each of four plates. Divide the marinated tomatoes, roasted tomatoes, tomato pulp, and glazed fennel among the four plates arranging them around the halibut. Garnish each plate with fennel blossoms and saffron threads. Froth the fennel minestrone with an immersion blender and sauce each plate to finish.

SEA BASS
Poached with Summer Squash and Peppers

Serves 4

———

SUMMER NAGE

100 g white fish bones, fins and bloodlines removed,
    cut into 5.1-cm (2-inch) pieces
1 red bell pepper, quartered and seeded
1 small onion, quartered
1/2 head garlic, split lengthwise
40 g olive oil
12 g tomato paste
50 g dry white wine
5 g vermouth
400 g Fish Fumet (page 304)
3 sprigs thyme
5 g lemon juice
0.5 g xanthan gum
Salt
1 g smoked paprika
Cayenne

Rinse the bones under cold running water and place in an airtight sealable container. Cover with ice water and refrigerate overnight. Preheat the broiler. Drain the fish bones and pat dry with a paper towel. Place the bones in a single layer on a baking sheet with a wire rack. Roast the bones in the broiler until deeply browned on one side. Flip the bones over and brown the other side. Remove from the broiler and set aside.

Lightly dress the pepper, onion, and garlic in a mixing bowl with 20 g of the olive oil. Transfer the vegetables onto a baking sheet with a wire rack. Roast in the broiler until well charred. Flip the vegetables over and char the other side. Heat a large saucepan over medium heat. When the pan is hot, add the charred vegetables and heat through, about 3 minutes. Add the tomato paste and stir with a rubber spatula to incorporate. Cook the mixture, stirring occasionally, until the tomato paste is well toasted, about 5 minutes. Add the roasted fish bones to the pan and stir to incorporate. Add the wine and vermouth, stirring to deglaze the pan, and simmer until reduced by half. Add the fish fumet and thyme. Heat to a simmer and reduce by half. Remove the pan from the heat and strain the sauce through a chinois.

Transfer to a blender and blend on low speed. Slowly add the remaining 20 g of olive oil, the lemon juice, and the xanthan gum. Turn to medium speed and blend for 1 minute to fully hydrate the gum. Season the sauce with salt, paprika, and cayenne. Keep warm until ready to serve.

———

RATATOUILLE

480 g tomato juice
48 g olive oil
100 g eggplant, diced 6 mm (1/4 inch)
100 g green zucchini, diced 6 mm (1/4 inch)
100 g yellow summer squash, diced 6 mm (1/4 inch)
100 g red bell pepper, seeded and diced
    6 mm (1/4 inch)
1 clove garlic, finely chopped
5 g lemon juice
Grated zest of 1/2 lemon
Salt

Heat the tomato juice in a saucepan over medium heat. Bring the juice to a simmer and turn the heat to low. Continue to simmer the juice, stirring occasionally, until reduced by half. Remove the pan from the heat and set aside.

Heat a large sauté pan over high heat with 16 g of the oil. When the oil just starts to smoke, add the diced eggplant. Cook, stirring occasionally, until softened, about 6 minutes. Season with salt and place the eggplant on a paper towel to drain any excess oil. Set aside. Heat a separate sauté pan over medium heat with 16 g of the oil. When the oil is very hot, add the zucchini, yellow squash, and garlic. Cook until softened but not browned, stirring occasionally, about 5 minutes. Season the vegetables with salt and transfer to a paper towel to drain any excess oil. Set aside. Heat the remaining 16 g of oil in a sauté pan over high heat. When the oil is very hot, add the diced pepper and sweat, stirring occasionally, until softened and slightly caramelized, about 5 minutes. Season with salt and transfer to a paper towel to drain any excess oil.

Heat a large saucepan over low heat. Combine all of the cooked vegetables in the pan with the reduced tomato juice. Stir to incorporate. Heat the liquid to a simmer and reduce until thick enough to bind the vegetables together, about 8 minutes. Remove the pan from the heat and stir in the lemon juice and zest. Season with salt and keep warm.

CONTINUED

PICKLED SQUASH

1 baby green zucchini
150 g White Balsamic Pickling Liquid (page 295)

Using a mandoline, slice the squash crosswise into 2-mm ($^1/_{16}$-inch) thick slices. Place the squash in a heat-proof container. In a saucepan over high heat, bring the pickling liquid to a boil. Pour the hot liquid over the squash and let cool to room temperature.

SEA BASS

500 g striped sea bass fillet, skinned
Salt
60 g Lemon Oil (page 284)
Fleur de sel

Heat a water bath to 62°C/144°F. Cut the fillet into four equal size portions. Season both sides of each portion with salt. Place each seasoned portion in a separate zip-top bag. Divide the lemon oil among the bags. Add the bags to the water bath to just below the zip-top line, allowing the water pressure to push the air out. Seal the bags. Cook the bass in the water bath until the fish is opaque and cooked through, about 9 minutes. Remove the bags from the water bath and carefully remove the fish, keeping each portion intact. Place the bass on paper towels to drain any excess oil. Season the fish with fleur de sel and keep warm.

TO FINISH

$^1/_2$ green zucchini
$^1/_2$ yellow zucchini
Olive oil
Fleur de sel

Using a mandoline, slice the squash crosswise into 2-mm ($^1/_{16}$-inch) thick slices. Submerge the slices in ice water for 30 minutes to crisp and curl. Drain the squash slices from the ice water, dress with olive oil in a mixing bowl, and season with fleur de sel.

Place one sea bass portion in the center of each of four bowls. Divide the ratatouille among the four bass portions, covering each piece of fish completely. Divide the summer nage among the four bowls, spooning the sauce all around the fish. Cover each fish completely with the pickled squash and the dressed squash slices, alternating colors. Break the sauce with several drops of olive oil.

LOBSTER
Poached with Beets and Smoked Potato

Serves 4

———

LOBSTER

4 lobsters, 575 g each

Bring a large pot of water to a rolling boil and prepare an ice bath. Using 15-cm (6-inch) wooden skewers, skewer each lobster tail so it remains straight when cooked. Place the skewered lobsters in a large heatproof container and pour enough of the boiling water over the lobsters to submerge. Immediately cover the container with plastic wrap and let stand until the tails are opaque, about 2 minutes. Quickly remove the lobsters from the hot water and separate the knuckles and claws from the bodies. Return the knuckles and claws to the hot water and shock the bodies in the ice bath. Allow the knuckles and claws to continue cooking until opaque, about 3 minutes more. Remove the knuckles and claws from the hot water and shock in the ice bath.

Twist the lobster tails away from the bodies. Clean the bodies by removing and discarding the top shell from the body. Scrape the gills from the body and discard. Reserve the bodies with the legs still attached and set aside for the lobster beet sauce. Remove and discard the wooden skewers from the tails. Crack and remove the shells from the tails and remove the intestinal tracts. Separate the knuckles and claws. Pull the small pincer back from the large pincer of the claw and then pull it straight out and up. A small piece of cartilage should come away with the small pincer. Crack and remove the shells from the knuckles and claws, keeping the lobster meat as intact as possible. Keep refrigerated until ready to serve.

———

LOBSTER BEET SAUCE

235 g beet juice (from about 3 large beets)
15 g bone marrow
15 g grapeseed oil
2 reserved lobster bodies, cleaned and quartered
1 shallot, thinly sliced
10 g ginger, peeled and thinly sliced
5 g lemongrass, bruised and thinly sliced
2 cloves garlic, thinly sliced
60 g dry white wine
400 g Lobster Stock (page 304)
1 sprig tarragon
1 sprig dill
3 sprigs chervil
10 g red wine vinegar
5 g lime juice
0.5 g xanthan gum
Salt

Heat the beet juice in a saucepan over medium heat. Bring to a simmer and cook, stirring occasionally to prevent burning, until reduced by two-thirds. Remove the reduced juice from heat and set aside.

Combine the bone marrow with enough cold water to cover in a saucepan. Bring to a simmer over medium heat. Remove the pan from the heat and drain the marrow. Set aside.

Heat the oil in a large saucepan over high heat. Add the lobster bodies to the pan and cook, stirring occasionally, until deeply caramelized, about 8 minutes. Add the shallot, ginger, lemongrass, and garlic and turn the heat to low. Stir occasionally and cook until the vegetables are soft and without any color, about 7 minutes. Add the wine to the pan and turn the heat to medium. Bring to a simmer and reduce until almost dry. Add the lobster stock to the pan and bring to a simmer. Cook until reduced by half. Add the reduced beet juice and bring to a simmer. Continue to cook until the sauce is reduced by half. Remove the pan from the heat and add the tarragon, dill, and chervil. Cover and let steep at room temperature for 10 minutes.

Strain the sauce through a chinois and transfer to a blender. While blending on low speed, add the blanched bone marrow, vinegar, and lime juice. Slowly add the xanthan gum. Turn the blender to medium speed and blend for 1 minute to fully hydrate the gum. Season with salt and keep warm.

CONTINUED

BEET SHEETS

90 g beet juice (from about 1 large beet)
30 g red wine vinegar
5 g salt
1 large red beet

Prepare an ice bath. Bring the beet juice in a saucepan to a simmer over medium heat. Cook, stirring occasionally, to prevent burning and reduce by half. Remove the pan from the heat. Add the vinegar and season the reduced juice with salt. Chill the juice over the ice bath. Turn the beet into a long thin sheet, using a chef's knife or a turning slicer. Cut the sheet into ribbons 18 cm (7 inches) long and 3 cm (1¼ inches) wide. Combine the ribbons with the beet vinegar mixture in a sous vide bag. Seal airtight. Bring a large pot of water to a boil. Cook the bagged beet sheets in boiling water until tender, about 5 minutes. Remove the sheets from the bag and keep warm.

SMOKED POTATO PUREE

250 g fingerling potatoes, peeled
Salt
70 g Smoked Butter (page 285)
70 g Brown Butter (page 284)
120 g cream

Cover the potatoes generously with water in a large saucepan and season with salt. Bring the potatoes to a simmer over low heat and cook gently until tender, about 45 minutes. Drain the potatoes and immediately pass through a ricer while still hot. Heat both butters in a saucepan over medium heat until melted. Add the cream, stirring to incorporate, and bring to just under a boil. Remove the pan from the heat and keep warm. Transfer the riced potatoes to a mixing bowl and add half of the scalded cream mixture. Fold together until just incorporated and pass through a fine-mesh tamis. If necessary, fold in additional cream mixture to achieve a smooth puree consistency. The puree should be thick enough to hold its shape when spooned onto a plate. Season with salt and keep warm.

TO FINISH

Citrus Beurre Blanc (page 303)
Fleur de sel
20 Demi-Dehydrated Beets (page 297)
Nasturtium leaves
Petite beet leaves
Bone Marrow Fat (page 284), melted

Preheat the oven to 150°C/300°F. Heat the beurre blanc in a pot to 62°C/144°F. Submerge the lobster tails, knuckles, and claws in the beurre blanc until heated through, about 7 minutes. Transfer the lobsters to a paper towel to drain any excess butter, season with fleur de sel, and keep warm.

Spread the dehydrated beets on a baking sheet lined with parchment paper and brush with olive oil. Rewarm the dehydrated beets in the oven until warmed through.

Place one tail, one knuckle, and one claw on each of four plates. Divide the dehydrated beets among the plates. Spoon smoked potato puree onto each plate. Drape two beet sheets over each lobster tail. Garnish each plate with the nasturtium and beet leaves. Sauce with the lobster beet sauce. Break the sauce with several drops of bone marrow fat.

BLACK BASS
Poached with Parsnips and Razor Clams

Serves 4

—

PARSLEY PUREE

> 50 g flat-leaf parsley leaves
> Ice water

Bring a large pot of salted water to a boil and prepare an ice bath. Blanch the parsley leaves in the boiling water until completely tender, about 6 minutes. When you rub the parsley between your fingers, it should fall apart completely. Immediately shock the parsley in the ice bath. When cold, drain the parsley and squeeze out any excess water. Transfer the blanched parsley and a splash of ice water to a blender and puree on high speed until completely smooth. Pass the puree through a fine-mesh tamis. Reserve the puree, refrigerated, in an airtight container.

—

PARSLEY PEAR SAUCE

> 15 g olive oil
> 1 green Anjou pear, cored and sliced
> 80 g ginger, peeled and sliced
> 1 shallot, sliced
> 18 littleneck clams, about 680 g
> 5 sprigs flat-leaf parsley
> 1 bay leaf
> 300 g dry white wine
> 180 g pear juice (from about 2 pears)
> 1 g xanthan gum
> Parsley Puree
> Lemon juice
> Salt

Heat the oil in a saucepan over medium heat. Add the pear, ginger, and shallot to the pan. Cook, stirring occasionally, until softened without any color, about 7 minutes. Turn the heat to high and add the clams, parsley, bay leaf, wine, and pear juice all at once. Quickly stir to incorporate and immediately cover the pan with a lid. Once the liquid comes to a simmer, reduce the heat to medium and cook the clams for 30 minutes. Uncover and simmer for an additional 10 minutes. Strain the sauce through a chinois and discard the clams. Transfer to a

blender and start to blend on medium speed. Slowly add the xanthan gum and blend for 1 minute until the sauce is thickened and the gum is fully hydrated. Keep the sauce warm. Just before serving, whisk the parsley puree into the warm sauce and season with lemon juice and salt.

—

RAZOR CLAMS

> 12 razor clams
> 4 sprigs flat-leaf parsley
> 1/2 shallot, thinly sliced
> 115 g dry white wine

Prepare an ice bath. Heat a large saucepan over high heat. When the pan is very hot, add all the ingredients at once and immediately cover the pan. Shake the pan occasionally to evenly steam the clams until they are all opened, about 2 minutes. Chill the clams in the cooking liquid over the ice bath. Discard any unopened clams. When cold, drain the clams and strain the liquid through cheesecloth. Separate and discard the clamshells. Trim and discard all but the cleaned siphons of the clams and rinse off any dirt. Reserve the cleaned clams in the strained clam stock, refrigerated.

—

ROASTED PARSNIPS

> 2 parsnips, peeled and quartered lengthwise, cores removed
> 30 g Brown Butter (page 284)
> 2 sprigs thyme
> 2 cloves garlic, crushed
> 3 g salt
> 40 g grapeseed oil

Bring a large pot of water to a boil and prepare an ice bath. Seal the parsnips, brown butter, thyme, garlic, and salt in an airtight sous vide bag. Cook the sealed parsnips in the boiling water until tender, about 25 minutes. Shock in the ice bath. When cold, remove the parsnips from the bag. Heat the oil in a sauté pan over high heat. Roast the cooked parsnips until evenly caramelized on all sides, about 5 minutes. Transfer to a paper towel to drain. Keep warm.

CONTINUED

BLACK BASS

2 black bass fillets, each about 240 g
Salt
150 g Chicken Stock Slurry (page 303)
Fleur de sel

Slice each fillet in half, crosswise, on a bias. Season each portion of fish with salt, on both sides. Place each bass portion in a separate zip-top bag. Divide the chicken stock slurry evenly among the bags. Lower each bag into the water bath to just below the zip-top line, allowing the water pressure to push the air out of the bags. Seal the bags. Let the bass cook in the water bath until cooked through, about 9 minutes. Remove the bags from the water bath. Carefully remove the bass from the zip-top bags and transfer to a paper towel to drain any excess slurry. Season the portions with fleur de sel and keep warm.

TO FINISH

1 green Anjou pear
45 g Chicken Stock (page 303)
30 g butter
Salt
Parsley Oil (page 285)

Cut the cheeks off the pear and thinly slice twelve whole shaves using a mandoline. Heat the chicken stock to a simmer in a saucepan over medium heat. Add the butter and season with salt. As the butter melts, it will emulsify with the stock and form a thick glaze. Add the pear slices and razor clams to the pan and cook just until warmed through, about 1 minute. Transfer the pear slices and clams to a paper towel to drain any excess glaze.

Place one bass portion on the center of each of four plates. Arrange the roasted parsnips, clams, and pear shaves over each fish. Sauce each plate with the parsley pear sauce and break the sauce with the parsley oil.

JOHN DORY
Seared with Fennel, Preserved Lemon, and Yogurt

Serves 4

———

JOHN DORY

4 John Dory fillets, no skin, each about 115 g
Salt
35 g grapeseed oil
30 g Chicken Stock (page 303)
15 g lemon juice
25 g butter

Season the fillets with salt on both sides. Heat the oil in a large sauté pan over high heat. When the oil is hot, turn the heat to medium. Place the fillets in the pan, bone side down. Sear the fillets until golden brown, about 2 minutes. Gently flip the fillets over and cook for 1 minute. Transfer the fish to a paper towel to drain. Drain the pan of any oil and deglaze with the chicken stock. Add the lemon juice and butter. As the butter melts, it will form a thick glaze. Season the glaze with salt. Over low heat, gently place the fillets back in the pan, seared side facing up. Spoon the glaze over the fillets to finish cooking the fish, about 3 minutes. Be careful not to overcook the fish or reduce the glaze too far, as the emulsion will break and make the fish greasy. Transfer the fillets to a paper towel to drain any excess glaze. Keep warm.

———

PRESERVED LEMON RELISH

3 Preserved Meyer Lemons (page 299)
15 g glucose syrup
25 g sugar
1 g powdered apple pectin
Salt

Drain the Meyer lemons and place on a paper towel to drain. Thinly slice the lemons crosswise. Remove and discard any seeds. Heat the lemon slices with the glucose, sugar, and pectin in a saucepan over low heat. Season with salt. Cook, stirring occasionally, until thickened to a jamlike consistency, about 5 minutes. Keep warm.

———

FENNEL BARIGOULE

75 g dry white wine
Peeled zest of 1 lemon
1 star anise pod
1 g fennel seeds
1 g salt
20 g olive oil
1 fennel bulb, cut into 16 wedges

Prepare an ice bath. Heat the wine, lemon zest, star anise, and fennel seeds in a saucepan over medium heat. Bring the liquid to a simmer and cook until reduced by half. Season with the salt and remove the pan from the heat. Chill the liquid over the ice bath. When cold, seal the cooking liquid, oil, and fennel wedges airtight in a sous vide bag. Bring a pot of water to a rolling boil. Submerge the bag in the boiling water and cook until the fennel is tender, about 40 minutes. Shock the bagged fennel in the ice bath.

———

TO FINISH

2 baby fennel bulbs
Lemon Vinaigrette (page 285)
Bronze fennel fronds
Yogurt Sauce (page 306)
Olive oil
Fennel pollen

Using a mandoline, thinly slice the fennel lengthwise. Immediately submerge the fennel shaves in ice water to curl. Remove the cooked fennel barigoule from the bag and place in a saucepan with the cooking liquid. Heat over low heat until warmed through. Transfer the fennel to a paper towel to drain and keep warm.

Place one John Dory fillet to the left of center of each of four plates. Spoon the preserved lemon relish over each fillet. Arrange the fennel barigoule over the relish on each fillet. Drain the fennel shaves on a paper towel and transfer them to a mixing bowl. Dress the fennel shaves with lemon vinaigrette. Garnish each John Dory fillet with the dressed fennel shaves and bronze fennel fronds. Sauce each plate with the yogurt sauce. Break the yogurt sauce on the plate with several drops of olive oil. Sprinkle fennel pollen over the yogurt sauce to finish.

SCALLOP
Seared with Grapes and Parsnips

Serves 4

PARSNIP-GRAPE PUREE

40 g butter
175 g peeled parsnips, thinly sliced
5 green grapes, seedless
140 g milk
5 g white verjus
Salt

Heat half of the butter in a saucepan over medium heat until foamy but not browned. Add the parsnips to the pan and cook, stirring occasionally, until just softened, about 4 minutes. Add the milk to the pan and bring to a simmer. Turn the heat to low and cover with a parchment cartouche. Cook the parsnips until tender, about 15 minutes. Remove the pan from the heat and strain the mixture through a chinois. Reserve the cooking liquid and set aside. Transfer the mixture, with the grapes, to a blender and puree on high speed until smooth. If necessary, add a splash of the cooking liquid to attain a smooth consistency. Turn to low speed and blend in the remaining butter and the verjus. Season with salt. Pass the puree through a fine-mesh tamis. Keep warm.

PRESSED PARSNIPS

4 parsnips
45 g olive oil
7 g salt

Preheat the oven to 175°C/350°F. Line a baking sheet with parchment paper. Combine the parsnips, 30 g of the oil, and the salt in a mixing bowl and toss to evenly coat. Place the parsnips in a single layer on the baking sheet, then cover the parsnips with another piece of parchment paper and place another baking sheet on top. Place a heavy, heatproof object on the top baking sheet to act as a weight. Place the parsnips in the oven to roast until tender, about 1½ hours. Remove the parsnips from the oven and let cool, still being pressed, to room temperature. Trim off both ends of the parsnips, halve the parsnips lengthwise, and trim the edges to form

straight planks. Heat the remaining 15 g of oil in a large saute pan over medium heat. Place the trimmed planks in the pan skin side down. Cook until the skins are crispy and browned, about 2 minutes, then turn them over and brown and crisp the opposite sides, about 2 minutes more. Remove the parsnips from the heat and keep warm.

PARSNIP BARK

2 parsnips
Salt
Canola oil, for frying

Preheat the oven to 175°C/350°F. Line a baking sheet with parchment paper. Place the parsnips on top of the prepared baking sheet in a single layer and roast in the oven until tender, about 1 hour. Remove the tray from the oven and let rest at room temperature until cool enough to handle. Using a sharp paring knife, cut a straight incision lengthwise to pierce through the outer skin. Gently scrape away and discard all the roasted flesh, while leaving the skin completely intact. Cut the skin into 5-cm (2-inch) square pieces. Heat 7.5 cm (3 inches) of canola oil to 175°C/350°F in a large, heavy pot. Fry the parsnip skins in the oil until golden brown and crispy, about 45 seconds. Spread the bark in a single layer on a paper towel to drain and season with salt.

LOBSTER VERJUS NAGE

690 g Lobster Stock (page 304)
50 g butter
6 seedless green grapes
20 g white verjus
6 g lobster roe
5 g lemon juice
Salt
1 g xanthan gum

Heat the lobster stock in a saucepan over medium heat. Bring to a simmer and turn the heat to low. Simmer the stock until reduced by two-thirds. Add the butter and whisk until emulsified. Transfer the nage to a blender and start to blend on low speed. Blend in the grapes, verjus, and lobster roe. Add the lemon juice and season with salt. Slowly add the xanthan gum and turn to high speed for 1 minute to thicken and fully hydrate the gum. Strain through a chinois and keep warm.

CONTINUED

DEMI-DEHYDRATED GRAPES

280 g Simple Syrup (page 300)
16 seedless red grapes
8 green seedless grapes

Preheat the oven to 79°C/175°F. Line a baking sheet with parchment paper. Heat the syrup in a saucepan over medium heat until warmed through. Remove the pan from the heat and add the grapes so they are covered. Let steep at room temperature for 5 minutes. Drain the grapes and discard the syrup. Transfer the grapes to the baking sheet and dehydrate the grapes in the oven until wrinkled on the outside, but still juicy, about 2 hours. Let cool to room temperature.

TO FINISH

4 seedless green grapes
4 seedless red grapes
White Balsamic Vinaigrette (page 285)
1/2 parsnip
8 U10 scallops
60 g grapeseed oil
Salt
Parsnip tops

Slice the grapes into rounds. In a mixing bowl, dress with enough white balsamic vinaigrette to heavily coat. Let sit at room temperature for 5 minutes to marinate.

Using a mandoline, slice the parsnip crosswise into paper thin rounds and immediately submerge in ice water to curl slightly.

Using a ridge knife, cut four scallops in half crosswise and halve the rest lengthwise. Gently pat the scallops dry with a paper towel. Divide the oil between two large sauté pans and heat over high heat. Season the scallops with salt on all sides. When the oil just starts to smoke, turn the heat to medium and carefully place the scallops in the pan, cut sides down. Do not overcrowd the pan, leaving ample space in between the scallops to cook. Cook the scallops until well caramelized and warmed through, about 2 minutes for the scallops halved lengthwise, and 3 minutes for the scallops halved crosswise. Remove the scallops from the pan and transfer to a paper towel to drain. Keep warm.

Drain the parsnip shaves from the ice water and transfer to a mixing bowl with the parsnip tops. Dress the shaves and tops with white balsamic vinaigrette.

Spoon the puree onto the center of four plates. Arrange the pressed parsnips, marinated grapes, demi-dehydrated grapes, and seared scallops over the puree on each plate. Garnish each plate with the dressed parsnip shaves, parsnip tops, and parsnip bark. Sauce each plate with the lobster nage.

SWEETBREADS
Pan Roasted with Spring Vegetables

Serves 4

COURT BOUILLON

1/2 onion, chopped
1 carrot, peeled and chopped
1 celery stalk, chopped
400 g dry white wine
400 g water
1 lemon, halved
3 sprigs thyme
6 g salt

Prepare an ice bath. Heat the ingredients in a saucepan over high heat. When the liquid comes to a simmer, remove the pan from the heat and let steep at room temperature for 30 minutes. Strain the liquid through a chinois and chill over the ice bath. Reserve the court bouillon in an airtight container, refrigerated, for up to 1 week.

SWEETBREADS

4 veal sweetbreads, each about 100 g
Court Bouillon
50 g grapeseed oil
Cornstarch
2 sprigs thyme
2 cloves garlic, crushed
Fleur de sel

Trim away and discard any excess fat or blood from the sweetbreads. Place the sweetbreads in a heatproof container. Heat the court bouillon to a boil in a saucepan over high heat. Pour the hot court bouillon over the sweetbreads to cover. Let the sweetbreads sit at room temperature to poach until slightly firm to the touch, about 20 minutes. Drain the sweetbreads, discarding the cooking liquid, and pat dry with a paper towel. Peel the membrane from the sweetbreads. Dredge each sweetbread in cornstarch to evenly coat. Dust off any excess cornstarch and set aside. Heat the oil in a large sauté pan over high heat. When the oil is hot, carefully place the sweetbreads in the pan. Turn the heat to medium and cook until golden brown on one side, about 3 minutes. Turn the sweetbreads over and add the

thyme and garlic to the pan. Baste the sweetbreads with the oil until evenly golden brown on all sides and cooked through, about 3 minutes. Remove the sweetbreads from the pan and place on a paper towel to drain. Season with fleur de sel and keep warm.

MORELS AND BABY GEM LETTUCE

2 baby gem lettuce heads
45 g butter
48 morels
90 g Morel Cream (page 305)
Salt

Bring a large pot of salted water to a rolling boil and prepare an ice bath. Trim and discard the loose outer leaves of the lettuce heads. Blanch the lettuce in the boiling water until just tender, about 7 minutes. Shock the lettuce in the ice bath. When cold, drain the lettuce and pat dry with a paper towel. Halve each lettuce head lengthwise and set aside.

Heat the butter in a large sauté pan over medium heat until foamy but not browned. Add the morels to the pan and cook until softened, about 2 minutes. Add the blanched lettuce and morel cream to the pan. Season with salt. Bring the cream to a simmer. Continue to cook until the mushrooms are tender and the cream glazes the vegetables, about 3 minutes. Remove the pan from the heat and place the vegetables on a paper towel to drain any excess cream. Keep warm.

SPRING VEGETABLES

12 Thumbelina carrots, peeled
Salt
8 jumbo asparagus
28 romanesco florets
20 snap peas
90 g Chicken Stock (page 303)
65 g butter

Prepare an ice bath. Place the carrots in a saucepan and cover with cold water. Season with salt. Heat the water to a simmer and continue to cook the carrots in simmering water until just tender, about 7 minutes. Shock the carrots in the ice bath. Trim the asparagus so that they are 7.5 cm (3 inches) in length. Peel the bottom 1.3 cm (1/2 inch) of each stalk. Bring a pot of salted water to a rolling boil. Blanch the green vegetables separately in the salted water until just tender, about 4 minutes for the

CONTINUED

asparagus, 3 minutes for the romanesco, and 20 seconds for the snap peas, and immediately shock in the ice bath. When cold, remove the vegetables from the ice bath. Cut the peas on a bias into 1.3-cm (¹/₂-inch) pieces.

Heat the chicken stock in a sauté pan over medium heat and bring to a simmer. Add the butter, carrots, asparagus, romanesco, and snap peas and stir to incorporate. As the butter melts and emulsifies, it will glaze the vegetables evenly. Transfer the vegetables to a paper towel to drain any excess glaze. Keep warm.

_____

SPRING ONIONS

90 g Chicken Stock (page 303)
75 g butter
4 spring onions, dark green top removed,
*   halved lengthwise*
Salt

Heat the chicken stock in a saucepan over medium heat. When the stock begins to simmer, add the butter and spring onions. Season with salt. As the butter melts and emulsifies, it will glaze the onions evenly. Cover the onions with a parchment cartouche. Continue cooking the onions in the glaze over low heat until tender, about 15 minutes. If the glaze starts to break, add a few tea-spoons of water to bring the glaze back together. When the onions are tender, transfer them to a paper towel to drain any excess glaze. Keep warm.

_____

TO FINISH

Morel Cream (page 305)
Chive blossoms

Heat the morel cream in a saucepan over low heat and gently rewarm through. Remove the pan from the heat and keep warm.

Place the sweetbreads, morels, carrots, asparagus, lettuce, romanesco, spring onions, and snap peas in separate piles on each of four plates. Garnish the snap peas and spring onions with the chive blossoms. Using an immersion blender, froth the warm morel cream. Spoon the froth over the morels to finish.

SUCKLING PIG
Confit with Apricots, Bacon, and Arugula

Serves 4

SUCKLING PIG CONFIT

2 bone-in suckling pig shoulders, skin on,
   about 2 kg each
Salt
6 sprigs thyme
6 cloves garlic, crushed
5 kg duck fat, melted

Debone the shoulders; reserve the bones for the apricot pork jus. Season the meat generously with salt inside and out, then place it, skin side down, on a baking sheet lined with parchment paper. Evenly cover with the thyme and garlic. Refrigerate overnight, uncovered, to cure.

Preheat the oven to 105°C/225°F. Rinse the shoulders well under cold running water and pat dry with paper towels. Place in a large roasting pan, skin side down, flat, with enough duck fat to cover, then cover with aluminum foil. Cook until tender, about 4 hours. Carefully remove the shoulders from the fat, without tearing the skin. Place the shoulders on a baking sheet lined with parchment paper, skin side down. Pour the fat from the roasting pan through a chinois and allow it to separate. Remove the fat and reserve it for another use. Reserve the remaining cooking liquid. Carefully pick the meat from the skin, discarding any veins and large pieces of fat. Be careful not to tear the skin while picking the meat. Place the cleaned confit meat in a large mixing bowl and mix with just enough of the reserved cooking liquid to moisten; season with salt. The seasoned confit meat should be very moist, but there should be no liquid pooling at the bottom of the mixing bowl. Scrape any excess meat or fat still attached to the skin. Line one 23 by 33-cm (9 by 13-inch) baking sheet with parchment paper. Line the prepared baking sheet with the scraped skin in a single, even layer. Fill the skin-lined tray with the seasoned confit meat, filling the tray and forming an evenly packed layer. Wrap the tray with plastic wrap and place another tray on top with a weight. Press the tray overnight, refrigerated. Unwrap the tray of pressed confit and carefully turn it out onto a cutting board. Cut the confit into 7.5-cm (3-inch) squares. Reserve tightly covered with plastic wrap, refrigerated, for up to 1 week.

APRICOT PORK JUS

15 g grapeseed oil
150 g reserved pork bones from the Suckling
   Pig Confit
240 g Chicken Jus (page 303)
20 g Apricot Gastrique (page 302)
Salt

Heat the oil in a saucepan over high heat. When the oil just starts to smoke, add the pork bones to pan. Sear the pork bones, while turning occasionally, until caramelized and browned on all sides, about 6 minutes. Turn the heat to low and add the chicken jus to the pan. Bring to a simmer and reduce until thick enough to coat the back of a spoon. Add the apricot gastrique and season the sauce with salt. Strain the sauce through a chinois. Keep warm.

PICKLED APRICOTS

3 firm apricots, halved and pitted
400 g Apricot Pickling Liquid (page 294)

Place the apricots in a heatproof container. Heat the liquid to a simmer in a saucepan over low heat. Pour the simmering liquid over the apricots and let cool to room temperature. Cut two of the apricot halves into quarters. Keep the pickled apricots in the pickling liquid until ready to serve.

SLOW-ROASTED ONION

1 onion, unpeeled
25 g olive oil
Salt
35 g Chicken Stock (page 303)
25 g butter

Preheat the oven to 150°C/300°F. In a mixing bowl, dress the whole onion with the olive oil and season with salt. Toss to evenly coat. Wrap the dressed onion tightly in an aluminum foil packet and place in a baking dish. Roast the onion in the oven until tender, about 3¹/₂ hours. Remove from the oven and unwrap, discarding the foil. Cut the onion in half from the stem end and discard the outer skins. Separate the individual layers and cut the onion into petals. Heat the stock to a simmer in a sauté pan over medium heat. Add the onion petals and butter, stirring to incorporate. Season with salt. As the butter melts and emulsifies, it will coat the onions evenly. Be careful not to overcook the onions or reduce the glaze

CONTINUED

SUCKLING PIG CONFIT WITH APRICOTS, BACON, AND ARUGULA, CONTINUED

too far as it will break and make the onions greasy. Transfer onions to a paper towel to drain any excess glaze. Keep warm.

_____

TO FINISH

100 g grapeseed oil
160 g arugula
Salt
4 apricots, halved and pitted
Brown Butter, melted (page 284)
Fleur de sel
130 g Bacon Marmalade (page 296), warm
40 g Pickled Mustard Seeds (page 294)
Mustard greens

Preheat the oven to 160°C/325°F. Heat 25 g of the oil in a large sauté pan over medium heat. When the oil is warm, place four suckling pig confit portions in the pan, skin sides down. Turn the heat to low and cook the confit until the skin is crispy and browned, about 15 minutes. Place the pan in the oven and cook until the confit is warmed through, about 5 minutes. Remove the pan from the oven and, using an offset spatula, carefully release the confit portions from the pan and transfer to a paper towel, skin side facing up, to drain.

Heat 50 g of the oil in a large sauté pan over high heat. When the oil is very hot, add the arugula to the pan, stirring to lightly wilt. Season with salt and transfer to a paper towel to drain.

Heat the remaining oil in a large sauté pan over high heat. When the oil is very hot, place the apricots in the pan, cut sides down. Cook the apricots until caramelized and warmed through. Remove the pan from the heat and transfer the apricots to a paper towel to drain. Brush the apricots and confit portions with brown butter and season with fleur de sel.

Arrange the suckling pig, pan-roasted apricots, pickled apricots, sautéed arugula, and slow-roasted onions among each of four plates. Spoon the bacon marmalade and pickled mustard seeds around the pig and apricots. Garnish the plates with the mustard greens. Sauce each plate with the apricot pork jus.

LAMB
Variations with Olives and Summer Vegetables

Serves 4

LAMB RACK

1 lamb rack with 4 bones, about 1 kg
Salt
20 g grapeseed oil
35 g butter
1 clove garlic, crushed
2 sprigs thyme

Preheat the oven to 160°C/325°F. Truss the rack with butcher's twine to help keep the eye of the lamb round. Season the lamb rack generously with salt. Heat the oil in a large sauté pan over high heat. When the oil is hot, turn the heat to low and place the rack in the pan, fat side facing down. Cook until the fat side is rendered and golden brown, about 5 minutes. Add the butter, garlic, and thyme. Baste the rack as the butter turns foamy, focusing on where each bone is connected to the meat. Continue basting until the rack is evenly browned, about 5 minutes. Transfer to a wire rack set over a baking sheet and place in the oven. Roast the lamb to medium, about 35 minutes. Remove the lamb from the oven and let rest at room temperature for 20 minutes before slicing to serve.

LAMB SADDLE MEDALLIONS

1 lamb saddle, about 250 g
Salt
25 g butter
1 clove garlic, crushed
1 sprig thyme
Olive Brioche Crusts (page 288)

Cut and remove any silver skin from the saddle, reserving the trim for the lamb jus. Heat a water bath to 62°C/144°F. Season the lamb saddle with salt. Roll the saddle in plastic wrap to form an evenly cylindrical shape about 3 cm (1¼ inches) in diameter. Seal the rolled saddle airtight in a sous vide bag. Cook the saddle in the water bath until medium, about 35 minutes. Remove the saddle from the water bath and let rest at room temperature for 10 minutes. Remove the saddle from the bag and unwrap. Heat a pan over medium heat and melt the butter until foamy but not browned. Place

the lamb saddle in the pan with the garlic and thyme. Roll the saddle in the foamy butter until lightly browned on all sides, about 3 minutes. Remove the saddle from the pan and transfer onto a wire rack set over a baking sheet. Rest the lamb at room temperature for 15 minutes. Preheat the broiler. Slice the saddle into 3 cm (1¼ inch) thick rounds. Place the slices, cut side up, on an unlined baking sheet. Top each slice with a piece of olive brioche crust. Heat the crust in the broiler until golden brown, about 1 minute. Keep warm.

TOMATO CONFIT

2 large beefsteak tomatoes
15 g olive oil
4 sprigs thyme
2 cloves garlic, sliced
Salt

Preheat the oven to 105°C/225°F. Line a baking sheet with parchment paper. Bring a pot of salted water to a rolling boil and prepare an ice bath. Blanch the tomatoes, just until the skin loosens, about 15 seconds. Shock the tomatoes in the ice bath. Peel and discard the skins, leaving the tomatoes intact. Halve the tomatoes crosswise. Scrape out and discard the inner flesh and seeds. Pat dry with a paper towel and combine with the olive oil, thyme, and garlic in a mixing bowl. Salt to taste. Gently toss to evenly coat and transfer to the lined baking sheet, cut sides down. Cook the tomatoes in the oven until nearly dehydrated, about 4 hours. The tomatoes should still retain a bit of moisture. Using a 6.4-cm (2½-inch) ring cutter, punch each tomato half into a round. Keep warm.

SUMMER VEGETABLES

12 yellow and orange baby carrots, peeled
*   and tops trimmed*
Salt
120 g English peas, removed from pods
100 g Chicken Stock (page 303)
90 g butter
6 Swiss chard leaves

Bring a large pot of salted water to a rolling boil and prepare an ice bath. Combine the carrots with enough cold water to cover in a large saucepan. Heat over high heat and bring to a simmer. Season with salt. Reduce the heat to medium and continue to cook in the simmering water until just tender, about 10 minutes. Shock the carrots in the ice bath. Blanch the peas in the boiling

CONTINUED

water until just tender, about 5 minutes, and shock in the ice bath. When cold, drain the blanched vegetables. Heat half of the chicken stock and half of the butter in a large sauté pan over medium heat. Add the blanched vegetables to the pan. Season with salt and stir occasionally while the butter and stock form a thick glaze to evenly coat the vegetables. Be careful not to overcook the vegetables or reduce the glaze too far, as the emulsion will break and make them greasy. Transfer to a paper towel to drain any excess glaze. Keep warm. Cut and discard the stems from the Swiss chard leaves. Cut into 5-cm (2-inch) pieces. Heat the remaining butter in a large sauté pan over medium heat until foamy but not browned. Add the chard leaves to the pan and stir occasionally until evenly wilted, about 3 minutes. Season with salt. Add the remaining chicken stock to the pan and bring to a simmer. As the stock simmers and reduces, it will form a thick glaze. Be careful not to overcook the chard or reduce the glaze too far, as the emulsion will break and make them greasy. Transfer the glazed Swiss chard to a paper towel to drain any excess glaze. Keep warm.

CHANTERELLE MUSHROOMS

45 g butter
24 chanterelle mushrooms
Salt
30 g Chicken Stock (page 303)

Over medium heat, heat half the butter in a large sauté pan until foamy but not browned. Add the mushrooms. Cook until the mushrooms are soft and without any color, about 4 minutes. Season with salt and add the chicken stock and remaining butter to the pan. Bring the stock to a simmer and reduce until thickened to a glaze, evenly coating the mushrooms. Transfer the mushrooms to a paper towel to drain any excess glaze. Keep warm.

LAMB JUS

20 g grapeseed oil
100 g reserved trim from the Lamb Rack and Lamb
    Saddle Medallions
1 sliced shallot
2 garlic cloves, thinly sliced
100 g dry white wine
240 g Chicken Jus (page 303)
1 sprig thyme
2 g Banyuls vinegar
Salt

Heat the oil in a pan over medium heat. When the oil just starts to smoke, add the lamb trim. Caramelize the lamb trim on all sides, turning occasionally, about 6 minutes. Remove the lamb from the pan and set aside. Add the shallot and garlic to the pan. Cook, stirring frequently, until soft, about 4 minutes. Add the wine and bring to a simmer. Reduce the wine until almost dry. Add the caramelized lamb trim, chicken jus, and thyme. Bring the sauce to a simmer and reduce until thick enough to coat the back of a spoon. Add the vinegar and season with salt. Strain the sauce through a chinois and keep warm.

TO FINISH

Brown Butter, melted (page 284)
Fleur de sel
Roasted Garlic (page 299)
Pickled Radishes (page 294)
8 Taggiasca olives
Chive blossoms
Lemon thyme tips

Remove and discard the string from the lamb rack. Slice the rack into individual chops. Brush each chop with brown butter and season with fleur de sel. Place a lamb chop and medallion on each of the four plates. Divide the tomato confit, roasted garlic cloves, pickled radishes, Swiss chard, chanterelle mushrooms, English peas, baby carrots, and olives among the plates. Garnish the peas with the chive blossoms. Garnish the tomato confit with the lemon thyme. Sauce each plate with lamb jus to finish.

BEEF
Roasted with Tomato and Artichokes

Serves 4

BEEF TENDERLOIN

1 beef tenderloin, about 600 g
Salt
30 g butter
2 cloves garlic, crushed
2 sprigs thyme
4 Bone Marrow Crusts (page 286)

Heat a water bath to 62°C/144°F and preheat the broiler. Trim the beef of any fat or connective tissue and reserve for the artichoke beef jus. Season the tenderloin with salt. Roll the tenderloin in several layers of plastic wrap to form into a smooth cylinder. Cut the tenderloin crosswise into four portions, each about 120 g. Seal the portions airtight in a single layer in a sous vide bag. Cook the beef in the water bath to medium, about 30 minutes. Remove the bag from the water bath and take the beef portions out of the bag. Remove and discard the plastic wrap from the portions and drain on a paper towel.

Heat the butter in a sauté pan over medium heat until foamy but not browned. Place the beef portions in the pan with the garlic and thyme. Baste the beef with the foamy butter until the thyme and garlic become aromatic, about 2 minutes. Remove the portions from the pan and place on a paper towel to drain. Transfer the beef to an unlined baking sheet, cut side facing up. Top each portion with a bone marrow crust punch. Cook the beef in the broiler until the crust is evenly golden brown, about 1 minute. Keep warm.

SMOKED CRÈME FRAÎCHE

60 g crème fraîche

Preheat the broiler and soak 35 g of applewood chips in cold water for 10 minutes. Drain the chips and line a roasting pan with aluminum foil. Arrange ten briquettes of charcoal in a single layer in the pan and place under the broiler until lit, about 15 minutes. Remove the pan from the broiler and sprinkle enough wood chips on top to put out any live flames, but not so much that the embers are smothered. Turn off the broiler. Place the crème

fraîche and the charcoal together with two roasting pans full of ice in the oven that is shut off. Tightly close the oven door and, after 10 minutes, check to make sure the ice has not completely melted. After 10 more minutes, remove the crème fraîche from the oven and immediately cover with plastic wrap. Refrigerate to cool. When chilled, reserve the smoked crème fraîche in an airtight container, refrigerated, for up to 3 days.

SMOKED ARTICHOKE PUREE

5 globe artichokes, turned and thinly sliced
265 g water
115 g dry white wine
75 g olive oil
1 lemon, halved
1 shallot, thinly sliced
Smoked Crème Fraîche
Salt

Heat the artichokes, water, wine, oil, lemon, and shallot in a saucepan over medium heat. The artichokes should be completely submerged in the cooking liquid. Bring the liquid to a simmer and turn the heat to low. Cover with a parchment cartouche and cook until the artichokes are completely tender, about 45 minutes. Strain through a chinois, reserving the cooking liquid. Combine the cooked artichokes with a splash of the cooking liquid in a blender and puree on high until smooth. Turn to low speed and add the smoked crème fraîche. Blend until completely emulsified and pass through a chinois. Season with salt and keep warm.

BLOOMED ARTICHOKE

Canola oil, for frying
4 baby artichokes, turned
Salt

Heat 1.3 cm (1/2 inch) of canola oil in a wide and heavy saucepan over medium heat. When the oil is just warm, not hot, place the artichokes in the pan, top sides down. Cover the pan with a lid. Cook the artichokes until the tops are flattened, golden brown, and crispy and the stem is tender, about 7 minutes. Remove the artichokes from the pan and season with salt. Place on a paper towel to drain and keep warm.

CONTINUED

ARTICHOKE PLANKS

2 globe artichokes, turned
150 g dry white wine
250 g olive oil
115 g Chicken Stock (page 303)
115 g lemon juice
Peeled zest of 3 lemons
4 sprigs thyme

Slice the artichokes 1.3 cm (1/2 inch) thick to form planked cross sections. Combine with the remaining ingredients in a saucepan to cover and heat over medium heat. Bring the liquid to a gentle simmer and cover with a parchment cartouche. Turn the heat to low and cook until the artichoke planks are tender, about 30 minutes. Reserve 50 g of the cooking liquid for the artichoke beef jus. Remove the pan from the heat and keep the planks warm in the remaining cooking liquid.

ARTICHOKE BEEF JUS

15 g grapeseed oil
About 100 g beef trim from the Beef Tenderloin
1 shallot
1/2 head garlic, split
240 g Chicken Jus (page 303)
2 sprigs thyme
50 g reserved Artichoke Planks cooking liquid
Salt

Heat the oil in a pan over high heat. When the oil just starts to smoke, add the beef trim. Caramelize the beef trim on all sides, turning occasionally, about 3 minutes. Remove the beef from the pan and set aside. Turn the heat to medium and add the shallot and garlic to the pan. Cook the vegetables until soft, stirring occasionally, about 5 minutes. Add the chicken jus, caramelized beef trim, and thyme sprigs. Bring the sauce to a simmer and reduce until thick enough to coat the back of a spoon. Remove the pan from the heat and add the artichoke cooking liquid. Strain the sauce through a chinois and season with salt. Keep warm.

TO FINISH

Brown Butter, melted (page 284)
Fleur de sel
Cracked black pepper
Tomato Relish (page 300)
Arugula leaves
Arugula flowers

Cut each beef portion in half horizontally. Brush the cut sides of the beef with brown butter and season with fleur de sel and black pepper. Place one beef portion in the center of each of four plates. Spoon the smoked artichoke puree onto each plate beside the beef. Arrange the artichoke planks and bloomed artichokes around the beef on each plate. Generously spoon tomato relish around the beef and artichokes. Sauce each plate with the artichoke beef jus. Garnish each plate with arugula leaves and flowers.

LAMB
Roasted with Summer Beans and Savory

Serves 4

ROASTED LAMB SADDLE

50 g grapeseed oil
2 lamb saddles, each about 300 g
Salt
40 g butter
2 cloves garlic, crushed
4 sprigs thyme

Preheat the oven to 150°C/300°F. Divide the oil between two large sauté pans and heat over high heat. Trim any excess fat or connective tissue from the saddles, then season generously with salt on all sides. When the oil is hot, place the saddles in the pan, fat sides down. Turn the heat to low and start to render the fat cap, periodically draining the fat from the pans. When each fat side is rendered crispy and golden brown, about 6 minutes, divide the butter, garlic, and thyme between the pans. Baste the lamb as the butter turns foamy, to evenly brown on all sides. Remove the pans from heat and transfer the lamb to a wire rack set on a baking sheet, fat sides down. Place in the oven and roast to medium, about 30 minutes. Remove the lamb from the oven and let rest at room temperature for at least 20 minutes before slicing to serve.

COCO BEAN ÉCRASER

150 g drained Coco Beans (page 297),
*   cooking liquid reserved*
20 g butter
Salt

Heat the beans with enough cooking liquid just to cover over medium heat. Bring the liquid to a simmer and turn the heat to low. Using a large fork, start to crush the beans to form a mash. Continue to crush the beans while cooking until thoroughly and evenly mashed. Add the butter and stir until melted and emulsified into a lumpy puree. Season with salt and keep warm.

CRANBERRY BEANS

1/4 onion, cut into 1.3-cm (1/2-inch) pieces
1/2 carrot, peeled and cut into 1.3-cm (1/2-inch) pieces
1/2 celery stalk, cut into 1.3-cm (1/2-inch) pieces
2 sprigs thyme
1 bay leaf
1 kg water
150 g shelled fresh cranberry beans
Salt

Tie the onion, carrot, celery, thyme, and bay leaf in a cheesecloth sachet and combine with the cranberry beans in a pot. Cover with the water and place over medium heat. Bring the water to a simmer and turn the heat to low. Continue to cook the beans at a low simmer until tender, about 2 hours. Remove the beans from the heat and season with salt. Let the beans cool to room temperature in the cooking liquid and reserve in an airtight container, refrigerated for up to 3 days.

SUMMER BEANS

8 haricots verts
4 yellow wax beans
4 yellow romano beans
4 green romano beans
40 g Chicken Stock (page 303)
50 g drained Cranberry Beans
35 g butter
Salt

Bring a large pot of salted water to a rolling boil and prepare an ice bath. Blanch the beans separately by type in the boiling water until just tender, about 3 minutes for the haricots verts and wax beans, and 4 minutes for the romano beans. Shock the beans in ice water. When cold, drain the beans. Cut the yellow romano beans on a bias into 1.3-cm (1/2-inch) pieces. Cut the yellow wax beans on a bias into 2.5-cm (1-inch) pieces. Split the haricots verts lengthwise. Thinly slice the green romano beans lengthwise. Heat the chicken stock in a large sauté pan over medium heat and bring to a simmer. Add the blanched cut beans, cranberry beans, and butter to the pan, stirring to incorporate. Season with salt. As the butter melts and emulsifies, it will glaze the beans evenly. Be careful not to overcook the beans or reduce the glaze too far, as the emulsion will break and make the beans greasy. Transfer the beans to a paper towel to drain any excess glaze. Keep warm.

CONTINUED

SAVORY LAMB JUS

15 g grapeseed oil
About 100 g reserved trim from the
  Roasted Lamb Saddle
1 shallot, sliced
240 g Chicken Jus (page 303)
115 g dry white wine
2 sprigs savory
Banyuls vinegar
Salt

Heat the oil in a pan over medium heat. When the oil just starts to smoke, add the lamb trim. Sear the lamb, while turning occasionally, until caramelized on all sides, about 6 minutes. Remove the trim from the pan and set aside. Add the sliced shallots to the pan. Cook, stirring frequently, until softened and caramelized, about 3 minutes. Add the wine to the pan and bring to a simmer. Reduce until almost dry. Add the caramelized lamb trim back to the pan, along with the chicken jus and savory. Bring the sauce to a simmer. Turn the heat to low. Reduce until thick enough to coat the back of a spoon. Remove the pan from the heat and strain the sauce through a chinois. Add the vinegar and season with salt. Keep warm.

TO FINISH

Dragon tongue beans
Lemon Vinaigrette (page 285)
Yogurt Gel (page 301)
Brown Butter, melted (page 284)
Fleur de sel
Savory Oil (page 285)
Savory tops
Savory flowers

Using a mandoline, thinly slice the dragon tongue beans lengthwise and place in a mixing bowl. Lightly dress with lemon vinaigrette and toss to combine. Spoon the yogurt gel onto each of four plates down the center. Divide the coco bean écraser among the plates, placing the écraser in one pile toward the left of the yogurt gel. Arrange the summer beans over the coco bean écraser on each plate. Garnish the summer beans with the sliced dragon tongue beans. Trim the long edges from both lamb saddles. Slice each trimmed saddle in half lengthwise. Brush the cut sides of the lamb with brown butter and season with fleur de sel. Place one slice of lamb saddle on each plate to the right of the yogurt gel. Sauce with the lamb jus between the yogurt and the lamb. Break the sauce with several drops of savory oil. Garnish with the savory tops and flowers.

DUCK
Roasted with Apricots, Chamomile, and Swiss Chard

Serves 4

APRICOT PUREE

30 g butter
1/2 shallot, sliced
2 cloves garlic, sliced
8 apricots, pitted and quartered
60 g Chamomile Simple Syrup (page 296)
Salt

Heat the butter in a saucepan over medium heat until foamy but not browned. Add the shallots and garlic to the pan. Cook, stirring occasionally, until softened without any color, about 5 minutes. Add the apricots to the pan and cook until tender, about 25 minutes. Transfer the cooked mixture to a blender and puree on high until smooth. Turn to low speed and blend in the chamomile syrup. Season with salt. Keep warm.

ROASTED DUCK BREASTS

4 duck breasts, each about 550 g
Salt
60 g butter

Preheat the oven to 150°C/300°F. Trim and remove any silver skin or meat that overlaps the fat side. Set aside and reserve for the Chamomile Jus. Pat the duck breasts dry with a paper towel. Season both sides of each portion with salt.

Divide the duck breasts between two large sauté pans and place skin-side facing down. Heat the pans over low heat to begin rendering. Periodically drain the fat from each pan as the ducks render, reserving the rendered fat to finish the chamomile jus. When the skin has fully rendered crispy and turned a deep golden brown, about 12 minutes, transfer the breasts to a baking sheet lined with a wire rack, skin side facing down and place in the oven to cook to medium, about 4 minutes. Remove the duck from the oven and let rest in a warm place for at least 15 minutes before slicing to serve.

CHAMOMILE JUS

15 g grapeseed oil
About 150 g reserved trim from Roasted Duck Breasts
1/2 shallot, sliced
60 g dry white wine
240 g Chicken Jus (page 303)
10 g dried chamomile
Salt
Reserved rendered fat from Roasted Duck Breasts

Heat the oil in a saucepan over high heat. Add the duck trim to the pan and sear until deeply caramelized, about 4 minutes. Remove the trim from the pan and set aside. Drain and discard the rendered fat from the pan. Turn the heat to medium and add the shallots to the pan. Cook, stirring occasionally, until softened, about 3 minutes. Add the wine to the pan and deglaze. Bring to a simmer and reduce until almost dry. Add the caramelized duck trim and chicken jus to the pan. Heat to a simmer and turn the heat to low. Gently simmer and reduce the sauce until thick enough to coat the back of a spoon. Remove the pan from the heat and stir in the dried chamomile. Cover the pan and let steep at room temperature for 7 minutes. Strain the sauce through cheesecloth and season with salt. Break the sauce with the rendered duck fat and keep warm.

ROASTED APRICOTS

3 apricots, halved and pitted
25 g olive oil
Salt
Confectioners' sugar
Brown Butter (page 284), melted
Fleur de sel
Cracked black pepper

Preheat the oven to 135°C/275°F. Line a baking sheet with parchment paper. Combine the apricot halves, oil, and salt in a mixing bowl, tossing to evenly coat. Transfer the apricots to the baking sheet, cut sides down, and dust lightly with the confectioners' sugar. Roast the apricots until tender, about 1 hour. Remove from the oven and cut two of the halves into quarters. Brush the cut side of each apricot with brown butter and season with fleur de sel and cracked black pepper. Keep warm.

CONTINUED

SWISS CHARD

10 Swiss chard leaves
40 g butter
Salt
45 g Chicken Stock (page 303)

Remove the stems from the chard leaves and set the leaves aside. Trim the stems down to 10 cm (4 inches) in length. Using a mandoline, thinly slice the stems lengthwise and immediately submerge in cold water. Set aside and reserve to garnish the plates. Cut the cleaned leaves into 5-cm (2-inch) pieces. Heat the butter in a large sauté pan over medium heat until foamy but not browned. Add the chard leaves to the pan and stir occasionally until evenly wilted, about 3 minutes. Season with salt. Add the chicken stock to the pan and bring to a simmer. As the stock simmers and reduces, it will form a thick glaze. Be careful not to overcook the chard or reduce the glaze too far, as the emulsion will break and make them greasy. Transfer the glazed Swiss chard to a paper towel to drain any excess glaze. Keep warm.

TO FINISH

Brown Butter (page 284), melted
Fleur de sel
Pickled Apricot (page 294)
White Balsamic Vinaigrette (page 285)
Chamomile greens and flowers

Slice the duck breasts in half lengthwise. Brush the cut side of each portion with brown butter and season with fleur de sel. Place both halves of each portion in the center of each of four plates. Spoon the apricot puree onto each plate next to the ducks. Divide the glazed Swiss chard into one pile on each plate. Divide the roasted and pickled apricots among the plates, arranging them next to the duck. Drain the Swiss chard stem shaves from the ice water and pat dry. In a bowl, dress the Swiss chard stem shaves with white balsamic vinaigrette. Garnish each plate with the dressed Swiss chard stem shaves and chamomile flowers and greens. Sauce each plate with the chamomile jus.

SQUAB
Variations with Kale and Bluefoot Mushrooms

Serves 4

ROASTED SQUAB

4 New York–dressed squab, each about 550 g
40 g grapeseed oil
Salt
60 g butter
4 cloves garlic, crushed
4 sprigs thyme

Remove the gizzards and livers from the squab. Reserve the livers for Liver Mousse (page 298). Cut and separate the head, neck, wings, and lower half of the spine from each squab and set aside for the squab jus. Make sure to leave as much of the skin intact and still attached to the body as possible. Cut and separate the legs as well and set aside for the squab leg confit. Stuff the cavity of each squab with a paper towel and place on a wire rack set over a baking sheet, spine sides facing down. Refrigerate uncovered for 24 hours to air dry.

Preheat the oven to 175°C/350°F. Heat two large sauté pans over high heat. Divide the oil between the two pans. Season the squab on all sides with salt. When the oil just starts to smoke, carefully place two squab in each pan, skin side facing down. Turn the heat to medium and gently roll the birds in the oil to evenly brown the breast sides. When the skins have browned and crisped, about 4 minutes, turn the birds over. Divide the butter, garlic, and thyme between the two pans and baste the birds with the foamy butter to evenly cook. When the birds are browned and crispy on all sides, about 3 minutes, transfer them to a wire rack set over a baking sheet and place in the oven to cook until medium rare, about 15 minutes. Remove the birds from the oven and let rest at room temperature for 15 minutes before slicing to serve.

SQUAB LEG CONFIT

8 reserved squab legs from the Roasted Squab
100 g salt
25 g sugar
5 sprigs thyme
600 g duck fat, melted
30 g grapeseed oil

Preheat the oven to 150°C/300°F. Remove the thigh-bones from the legs. Separate the feet from half of the squab legs. Trim the nails from the remaining feet still intact. Combine the salt and sugar in a mixing bowl. Place the legs in a baking dish and generously season on all sides with the mixture. Let cure, refrigerated, for 20 minutes. Rinse the squab legs under cold running water and pat dry with a paper towel. Place in a clean baking dish with the thyme. Pour the duck fat over the legs to cover and cover the dish with aluminum foil. Place the legs in the oven to cook until tender, about 1 hour. Remove the baking dish from the oven, uncover, and let cool to room temperature in the fat.

When ready to finish, remove the legs from the fat and pat dry with a paper towel. Heat a large sauté pan with the oil over high heat. When the oil just starts to smoke, place the legs in the pan, skin side down. Turn the heat to low and cook until the skin is evenly golden brown and crispy, about 4 minutes. Remove the legs from the pan and place on a paper towel to drain. Keep warm.

PICKLED PLUMS

2 Italian plums, halved and pitted
Plum Pickling Liquid (page 295)
20 g grapeseed oil

Cover the plums with the pickling liquid in an airtight container. Refrigerate for at least 1 week to pickle, and reserve for up to 2 months. When ready to cook, drain the plums and reserve the pickling liquid. Pat the plums dry with a paper towel. Heat the oil in a sauté pan over high heat. When the oil just starts to smoke, turn the heat to medium and place the plums in the pan, cut sides down. Cook until the plums are evenly seared, about 2 minutes. Transfer the plums to a paper towel, cut side up. Drain and discard the oil and add 200 g of the pickling liquid to the pan. Bring to a simmer and reduce to a glaze consistency. Spoon the glaze over the plums and keep warm.

CONTINUED

SQUAB JUS

15 g grapeseed oil
About 450 g reserved parts from the Roasted Squab
1 shallot, sliced
40 g dry white wine
240 g Chicken Jus (page 303)
2 sprigs thyme
5 g balsamic vinegar
Salt
15 g foie gras fat, melted

Heat the oil in a saucepan over high heat. When the oil just starts to smoke, add the reserved squab parts to the pan. Sear and caramelize the squab trim on all sides, turning occasionally, about 3 minutes. Remove the squab from the pan and set aside. Turn the heat to medium and add the shallot to the pan. Cook, stirring occasionally, until softened, about 4 minutes. Add the wine and bring to a simmer. Reduce until almost dry. Add the seared squab trim, jus, and thyme. Bring the sauce to a simmer and reduce until thick enough to coat the back of a spoon. Strain the sauce through a chinois and add the balsamic vinegar. Season with salt and break the sauce with the foie gras fat. Keep warm.

GLAZED KALE

12 lacinato kale leaves
45 g butter
50 g Chicken Stock (page 303)
Salt

Bring a large pot of salted water to a rolling boil over high heat and prepare an ice bath. Line a baking sheet with paper towels. Cut the ribs from the kale leaves and discard. Trim the kale leaves into squares about 5 cm (2 inches) in size. Blanch the kale squares in the water until just tender, about 4 minutes. Shock the kale squares in the ice bath. When cold, drain the kale and gently squeeze out any excess water. Heat the stock in a sauté pan over medium heat to a simmer. Add the blanched kale and butter. As the butter melts and emulsifies, it will glaze the kale evenly. Be careful not to overcook the kale or reduce the glaze too far, as the emulsion will break and make the kale greasy. Season with salt and transfer the glazed kale to the prepared baking sheet to drain any excess glaze. Keep warm.

SAUTEED MUSHROOMS

45 g butter
28 chanterelle mushrooms
4 bluefoot mushrooms
Salt
8 mousseron mushrooms
30 g Chicken Stock (page 303)

Heat two-thirds of the butter in a sauté pan over medium heat until foamy but not browned. Add the bluefoot and chanterelle mushrooms and sweat until the mushrooms soften without any color, about 4 minutes. Season with salt. Add the mousseron mushrooms, chicken stock, and remaining butter. As the butter melts and emulsifies, it will glaze the mushrooms evenly. Be careful not to overcook the mushrooms or reduce the glaze too far, as the emulsion will break and make the mushrooms greasy. Transfer the mushrooms to a paper towel to drain any excess glaze. Keep warm.

TO FINISH

Brown Butter (page 284), melted
Fleur de sel
1 slice miche, toasted
80 g Liver Mousse (page 298)
80 g Squash Écraser (page 300)
Kale Chips (page 298)

Carve the breasts from the ribcage. Brush the flesh with brown butter and season with fleur de sel. Cut the miche toast into four long pieces. Spread the liver mousse on half of each piece of toast and squash écraser on the other halves. Divide the squab breast, squab legs, liver mousse toasts, pickled plums, glazed kale, and sauteed mushrooms among four plates. Garnish each plate with the kale chips. Sauce with the squab jus to finish.

BEEF
Roasted with Parsnips and Royal Trumpet Mushrooms

Serves 4

———

BEEF TENDERLOIN

1 beef tenderloin, about 600 g
Salt
40 g butter
2 cloves garlic, crushed
2 sprigs thyme
4 Bone Marrow Crusts (page 286)

Heat a water bath to 62°C/144°F and preheat the broiler. Trim the beef of any fat or connective tissue and reserve for the bone marrow bordelaise. Season the tenderloin with salt. Roll the tenderloin in several layers of plastic wrap to form into a smooth cylinder. Cut the tenderloin crosswise into four portions, each about 120 g. Seal the portions airtight in a single layer in a sous vide bag. Cook the beef in the water bath to medium, about 30 minutes. Remove the bag from the water bath and take the beef portions out of the bag. Remove and discard the plastic wrap from the portions and drain on a paper towel. Heat the butter in a sauté pan over medium heat until foamy but not browned. Place the beef portions in the pan with the garlic and thyme. Baste the beef with the foamy butter until the thyme and garlic become aromatic, about 2 minutes. Remove the portions from the pan and place on a paper towel to drain. Transfer the beef to an unlined baking sheet, cut side up. Top each portion with a bone marrow crust punch. Cook the beef in the broiler until the crust is evenly golden brown, about 1 minute. Keep warm.

———

ROASTED PARSNIPS

4 parsnips, peeled, quartered, and cored
30 g Brown Butter (page 284)
2 cloves garlic, crushed
2 sprigs thyme
3 g salt
45 g Bone Marrow Fat (page 284)

Heat a large pot of water to a rolling boil and prepare an ice bath. Seal the parsnips, brown butter, garlic, thyme, and salt in a sous vide bag. Submerge the bag in the boiling water and cook until tender, about 25 minutes.

Immediately shock the parsnips in their bag in the ice bath. When cold, remove the parsnips from the bag, discarding the garlic and thyme.

Heat the bone marrow fat in a sauté pan over high heat. When the marrow fat is hot, place the cooked parsnips in the pan in a single layer. Roast, turning occasionally, until caramelized and browned on all sides, about 4 minutes. Transfer the parsnips to a paper towel to drain and keep warm.

———

BONE MARROW BORDELAISE

15 g grapeseed oil
About 100 g beef trim from the Beef Tenderloin
1 shallot, sliced
120 g dry red wine
480 g Chicken Jus (page 303)
5 g red wine vinegar
Salt
10 g bone marrow, diced
1/2 shallot, finely chopped
2 sprigs thyme, picked

Heat the oil in a saucepan over high heat. When the oil just starts to smoke, add the beef trim in a single layer. Caramelize the beef trim on all sides, turning occasionally, about 3 minutes. Remove the beef from the pan and set aside. Turn the heat to medium and add the shallot to the pan. Cook, stirring frequently, until softened, about 4 minutes. Add the red wine and bring to a simmer. Reduce the wine until almost dry. Add the caramelized beef trim back to the pan, along with the chicken jus. Heat the sauce to a simmer and reduce the sauce until thick enough to coat the back of a spoon. Remove the pan from the heat and strain the sauce through a chinois. Add the vinegar and season with salt. Keep warm.

Preheat the broiler. In a mixing bowl, combine the bone marrow dice, chopped shallots, and picked thyme. Spread the bone marrow mixture on an unlined baking sheet. Cook the bone marrow in the broiler until the bone marrow just starts to soften but still holds its shape, about 1 minute. Immediately transfer the bone marrow to the refrigerator to cool. Just before serving, add the bone marrow to the warm sauce.

CONTINUED

TO FINISH

8 royal trumpet mushrooms, halved
25 g olive oil
Salt
25 g butter
Brown Butter (page 284), melted
Fleur de sel
Cracked black pepper
Watercress sprigs

Score the cut side of each mushroom. Heat the oil in a sauté pan over high heat. When the oil just starts to smoke, place the mushrooms in the pan, cut side down. Turn the heat to medium and continue roasting the mushrooms until caramelized on one side, about 2 minutes. Turn the mushrooms over and season with salt. Add the butter to the pan and cook the mushrooms in the foamy butter until cooked through, about 3 minutes. Transfer the mushrooms to a paper towel to drain.

Cut each beef portion in half horizontally. Brush the cut sides of the beef with brown butter and season with fleur de sel and black pepper. Place a portion in the center of each plate. Divide the roasted parsnips and trumpet mushrooms among the plates, arranging them around the beef. Garnish each plate with the watercress. Sauce each plate with the bone marrow bordelaise to finish.

VEAL
Braised with Chestnuts, Cauliflower, and Black Truffle

Serves 4

———

BRAISED VEAL CHEEKS

50 g grapeseed oil
1 onion, diced 2.5 cm (1 inch)
1 carrot, peeled and diced 2.5 cm (1 inch)
1 celery stalk, peeled and diced 2.5 cm (1 inch)
15 g tomato paste
1 (750-ml) bottle dry red wine
4 sprigs thyme
12 veal cheeks, trimmed of any fat or connective tissue, about 600 g
480 g Chicken Jus (page 303)
Salt

Prepare an ice bath. Heat half of the oil in a large saucepan over medium heat. Add the onion, carrot, and celery to the pan and cook, stirring occasionally, until caramelized and tender, about 10 minutes. Add the tomato paste and continue to cook, stirring frequently, until well toasted, about 5 minutes. Add the wine and thyme to the pan. Bring the wine to a simmer and reduce by half. Remove the pan from the heat and chill the marinade over the ice bath until cold. Cover the veal cheeks with the marinade in an airtight container and refrigerate for 48 hours to marinate.

Preheat the oven to 150°C/300°F. Remove the cheeks from the marinade and pat dry with a paper towel. Strain the marinade through a chinois into a saucepan over medium heat and bring to a simmer, stirring occasionally. Add the chicken jus to the pan and bring to a simmer. Keep warm.

Heat the remaining oil in a large saucepan over high heat. Season the cheeks with salt on all sides. When the oil just starts to smoke, transfer the cheeks to the pan in a single layer. Sear on all sides, while turning occasionally, until deeply caramelized, about 6 minutes. Transfer the cheeks to a baking dish and pour the marinade over to cover. Cover the baking dish with aluminum foil and place in the oven to cook until tender, about 2½ hours. Remove

the dish from the oven and let cool to room temperature. Remove the cheeks from the liquid and set aside. Strain the cooking liquid through a chinois into a saucepan and bring to a simmer over medium heat. Reduce the liquid until thick enough to coat the back of a spoon. Turn the heat to low and place the veal cheeks in the pan to gently warm through. Keep warm.

———

CHESTNUT PUREE

15 g butter
175 g peeled chestnuts, chopped
15 g brandy
120 g Chicken Stock (page 303)
30 g mascarpone
10 g sugar
4 g salt

Heat the butter in a saucepan over medium heat until foamy but not browned. Add the chestnuts to the pan and cook, stirring occasionally, until deeply caramelized, about 15 minutes. Add the brandy to the pan and bring to a simmer. Reduce the brandy until almost dry and add the chicken stock to the pan. Bring to a simmer and turn the heat to low. Cook the chestnuts until very tender, stirring occasionally to prevent burning, about 40 minutes. Transfer the mixture to a blender and puree on high until completely smooth. Turn to low speed and add the mascarpone, sugar, and salt. Continue to blend until fully incorporated. Keep warm.

———

CAULIFLOWER PUREE

½ head cauliflower, coarsely chopped
350 g half-and-half
Salt

Cover the cauliflower with the half-and-half in a saucepan and heat over medium heat. Bring the liquid to a simmer. Turn the heat to low and cover the pan with a parchment cartouche. Continue to cook the cauliflower until very tender, about 40 minutes. Thoroughly drain the cauliflower through a chinois and reserve the cooking liquid. Combine the drained cauliflower with a splash of the cooking liquid in a blender and puree on high speed until very smooth. Season with salt. Keep warm.

CONTINUED

CHESTNUT CHIPS

2 chestnuts, peeled
Canola oil, for frying
Salt

Heat 7.5 cm (3 inches) of the oil in a heavy pot to 150°C/300°F. Using a mandoline, slice the chestnuts 1.5 mm (¹/₁₆ inch) thick. Fry the shaved chestnuts in the oil until golden brown and crispy, about 1 minute. Transfer the chestnut chips to a paper towel to drain. Season with salt.

CAULIFLOWER FLORETS

12 florets cauliflower
60 g Chicken Stock (page 303)
45 g butter
Salt

Bring a large pot of salted water to a boil and prepare an ice bath. Cook the cauliflower in the boiling water until just tender, about 5 minutes. Shock the cauliflower in the ice bath. When cold, drain and pat the cauliflower dry.

Heat the stock in a sauté pan over medium heat and bring to a simmer. Add the butter and cauliflower. Season with salt. As the butter melts and emulsifies, it will glaze the cauliflower evenly. Be careful not to overcook the cauliflower or reduce the glaze too far, as the emulsion will break and make the cauliflower greasy. Transfer the glazed cauliflower to a paper towel to drain. Keep warm.

TO FINISH

2 large cauliflower florets
Fleur de sel
1 black truffle, broken into 6-mm (¹/₄-inch) pieces
Olive oil

Using a mandoline, thinly slice the cauliflower florets into shaves and set aside. Transfer the veal cheeks to a paper towel to drain any excess glaze and season with fleur de sel. Spoon and spread the cauliflower puree onto each of four plates. Scoop two quenelles of the chestnut puree onto each plate. Divide the veal cheeks, glazed cauliflower florets, and truffle pieces among the plates and arrange them around the purees. Dress the cauliflower shaves in a bowl with olive oil and season with fleur de sel. Garnish each plate with the dressed shaves and chestnut chips. Sauce with the remaining veal cheek glaze.

VENISON
Medallions with Black Truffle, Squash, Parsnips, and Savoy Cabbage

Serves 4

VENISON LOIN

1 venison loin, about 600 g
Salt
45 g butter
4 cloves garlic, crushed
6 sprigs thyme
25 g grapeseed oil

Heat a water bath to 62°C/144°F. Trim any connective tissue and fat from the loin. Trim the loin so it is no wider than 7.5 cm (3 inches). Set aside and reserve the trim for the sauce poivrade. Divide the loin into three equal sections. Set aside two of the sections and season the third with salt on all sides. Roll the seasoned loin in plastic wrap to form a cylindrical shape. Seal the rolled venison airtight in a sous vide bag. Submerge the sealed venison in the water bath and cook to medium, about 45 minutes. Take the venison out of the bath and remove from the bag. Heat one-third of the butter in a sauté pan over medium heat until foamy but not browned. Place the cooked loin in the pan. Add a garlic clove and two thyme sprigs to the pan. Baste the venison with the foamy butter on all sides until evenly browned, about 3 minutes. Transfer the venison to a paper towel to drain any excess butter and let rest at room temperature for 10 minutes before slicing to serve.

Cut the remaining two sections of the loin into eight equal rounds. Heat the oil in a large sauté pan over medium heat. Season the medallions with salt on all sides. When the oil is very hot, place them in the pan, cut sides down. Sear and caramelize the rounds on one side, about 2 minutes, and turn over to sear the opposite sides, about 2 minutes. Add the remaining butter, garlic, and thyme to the pan. Baste the medallions in the foamy butter until evenly browned on all sides, about 2 minutes. Transfer the venison to a paper towel to drain and let rest at room temperature for 5 minutes before serving.

SAVOY CABBAGE

10 savoy cabbage leaves
45 g Chicken Stock (page 303)
35 g butter
Salt
5 g black truffle, finely chopped

Bring a large pot of salted water to a rolling boil over high heat and prepare an ice bath. Trim and discard the ribs from the cabbage leaves. Cut the leaves into squares about 5 cm (2 inches) in size. Blanch the cabbage in the water until tender, about 3 minutes. Shock the cabbage in the ice bath until cold. Drain the cabbage and gently squeeze dry.

Heat the chicken stock to a simmer in a sauté pan over medium heat. Add the butter and the blanched cabbage. Season with salt. As the butter melts and emulsifies, it will glaze the cabbage evenly. Be careful not to overcook the cabbage or reduce the glaze too far, as the emulsion will break and make the cabbage greasy. Add the truffle to the pan and stir to combine. Transfer the cabbage to a paper towel to drain any excess glaze. Keep warm.

TRUFFLE PARSLEY CONDIMENT

20 g flat-leaf parsley leaves, finely chopped
20 g black truffle, finely chopped
50 g olive oil
5 drops black truffle oil
Salt

Combine the parsley leaves, truffle, olive oil, and truffle oil in a mixing bowl. Stir to combine and season with salt.

PARSNIP PUREE

2 parsnips, peeled, quartered, and cored
30 g butter
Salt
150 g half-and-half

Thinly slice the trimmed parsnips. Heat the butter in a saucepan over medium heat until foamy but not browned. Add the parsnips to the pan, season with salt, and sweat, stirring occasionally until softened without any color, about 5 minutes. Add the half-and-half to the pan and bring the liquid to a simmer. Cover the pan with a parchment cartouche and turn heat to low. Continue to cook the parsnips until tender, about 10 minutes. Drain the mixture through a chinois, reserving the cooking liquid. Place the

CONTINUED

parsnips in a blender and start to blend on low speed. Slowly add 50 g of the strained liquid and puree on high speed until smooth. Season the puree with salt and keep warm.

———

CHANTERELLE MUSHROOMS

35 g butter
20 chanterelle mushrooms
Salt
25 g Chicken Stock (page 303)

Heat the butter in a sauté pan over medium heat until foamy but not browned. Add the chanterelle mushrooms and sweat until the mushrooms soften without any color, about 4 minutes. Season the mushrooms with salt. Add the chicken stock and bring to a simmer. As the stock reduces and forms an emulsion, it will glaze the mushrooms evenly. Transfer the mushrooms to a paper towel to drain any excess glaze. Keep warm.

———

SAUCE POIVRADE

2 allspice berries
5 juniper berries
1 whole clove
1 g black peppercorns
15 g grapeseed oil
About 150 g reserved trim from Venison Loin
115 g dry red wine
70 g blueberries
30 g red currants
240 g Chicken Jus (page 303)
1 bay leaf
2 sprigs thyme
10 g Dijon mustard
15 g pork blood
2 g 70 percent cacao chocolate, chopped
Salt

Toast the allspice, juniper, clove, and peppercorns in a sauté pan over low heat until the spices are fragrant, about 3 minutes. Remove the pan from the heat and set aside. Heat the oil in a saucepan over high heat. When the oil just starts to smoke, add the venison trim. Sear and caramelize the venison on all sides, turning occasionally, about 4 minutes. Remove the venison from the pan and drain the pan. Add the wine to the pan along with the toasted spices and bring to a simmer. Reduce until almost dry. Add the berries and crush with the back of a spoon. Continue to cook, stirring occasionally, until the liquid released from the berries is reduced to almost dry. Add the jus and the caramelized venison trim to the pan and bring to a simmer. Reduce the sauce until thick enough to coat the back of a spoon. Combine the mustard and pork blood in a small bowl. Whisk together until smooth. Slowly add the pork blood mixture to the sauce, whisking constantly. Remove the pan from the heat and whisk in the chocolate until melted. Strain the sauce through cheesecloth and season with salt. Keep warm.

———

TO FINISH

Brown Butter (page 284), melted
Fleur de sel
80 g Squash Écraser (page 300)

Slice the sous vide venison loin into four even rounds. Brush the cut side of each round with brown butter and season with fleur de sel. Place one round on each of four plates. Divide the truffle parsley condiment among the seared venison medallions, covering the top of each medallion. Place two medallions on each plate on either side of the venison round. Place one spoonful of the kabocha squash écraser and parsnip puree on each plate. Place a small pile of savoy cabbage on each plate in between the écraser and the puree. Divide the chanterelles among the plates, arranging them around the venison. Sauce each plate with the sauce poivrade to finish.

PORK
Variations with Cabbage and Beans

Serves 4

PORK RACK

1 pork rack with 4 bones, about 1 kg, frenched
Salt
25 g grapeseed oil
40 g butter
2 cloves garlic, crushed
4 sprigs thyme

Preheat the oven to 160°C/325°F. Trim the rack of any excess fat or silver skin and reserve the trim for the pork cabbage jus. Truss the rack with butcher's twine to help keep the eye of the pork round. Season the pork rack generously with salt on all sides. Heat the oil in a large sauté pan over high heat. When the oil just starts to smoke, place the rack in the pan, fat side facing down. Turn the heat to medium and sear the fat side until golden brown, about 6 minutes. Add the butter, garlic, and thyme to the pan. Baste the rack with the foamy butter to evenly brown, focusing on where the bone runs into the meat. When the rack is browned on all sides, transfer to a wire rack set over a baking sheet, fat side down, and place in the oven. Cook until medium, about 35 minutes. Remove the pork from the oven and let rest at room temperature for 20 minutes before slicing to serve.

PORK BELLY

500 g pork belly
Pork Brine (page 306)

Cover the belly with the brine in an airtight container and refrigerate for 24 hours. Heat a water bath to 58°C/136°F. Drain and discard the brine. Pat the pork belly dry with a paper towel and seal airtight in a sous vide bag. Submerge the belly in the water bath to cook until tender, 48 hours. Take the belly out of the bath and sandwich between two baking sheets, skin side facing down. Place a heavy object on the top baking sheet to press down on the belly. Refrigerate overnight to flatten. Uncover the belly and remove from the bag. Portion into irregularly shaped pieces about 5 cm (2 inches) in size. Reserve the pork belly tightly covered in plastic wrap refrigerated for up to 3 days.

RED CABBAGE PUREE

45 g butter
1/2 shallot, sliced
250 g red cabbage leaves, thinly sliced
Salt
About 250 g water
80 g dry red wine
80 g port
80 g red wine vinegar, plus more for seasoning
35 g Chicken Jus (page 303)

Heat two-thirds of the butter in a large saucepan over medium heat until foamy but not browned. Add the shallot and sweat until soft without any color, about 4 minutes. Add the cabbage and cook, stirring occasionally, until wilted down, about 5 minutes. Season with salt. Add just enough water to cover the cabbage and cover with a parchment cartouche. Turn the heat to low and cook the cabbage until very soft, about 40 minutes. Uncover and continue to cook, stirring occasionally, until the water is nearly evaporated, about 10 minutes. Add the wine and port to the pan and bring to a simmer. Reduce the liquid until the pan is nearly dry. Add the vinegar and also reduce until almost dry. Remove the pan from the heat and transfer the mixture to a blender. Puree on high until smooth. Add the remaining butter and chicken jus. Blend until emulsified. Season with salt and red wine vinegar. Keep warm.

COCO BEAN PUREE AND RAGOUT

400 g Coco Beans with cooking liquid (page 297)
Salt
Sherry vinegar
15 g olive oil
40 g brussels sprout leaves, thinly sliced
30 g butter
5 g lemon juice

Heat the cooked coco beans in their cooking liquid in a saucepan over medium heat to a boil. Drain and reserve the cooking liquid. Place half the beans in a blender with a splash of the liquid and puree on high speed until smooth. Season the puree with salt and sherry vinegar. Keep the puree warm.

Heat the olive oil in a sauté pan over high heat. When the oil is very hot, add the brussels sprout leaves and cook, stirring occasionally, until wilted. Turn the heat to medium and add the remaining coco beans to the pan. Add the butter, 50 g of the cooking liquid, and lemon

CONTINUED

213

juice. Stir to incorporate and season with salt. As the butter melts and emulsifies, it will glaze the beans evenly. Transfer to a paper towel to drain any excess glaze. Keep warm.

——

SAVOY CABBAGE

1 head savoy cabbage, halved
25 g sliced pancetta
1 sprig thyme
1 clove garlic, crushed
1 bay leaf
2 g salt
300 g White Balsamic Pickling Liquid (page 295)

Bring a large pot of water to a boil and prepare an ice bath. Separate the outer leaves from the cabbage halves and set aside for the pickled cabbage. Cut each cabbage half into four wedges, leaving the core intact. Seal the cabbage, pancetta, thyme, garlic, bay leaf, and salt airtight in a sous vide bag. Submerge the bag in the boiling water and cook until the cabbage is tender, about 30 minutes. Shock in the ice bath. When the cabbage is cold, remove from the bag and place in a heatproof container in a single layer.

Heat the pickling liquid to a boil in a saucepan over medium heat. Pour the liquid over the cabbage to cover and keep warm. When ready to serve, transfer to a paper towel to drain any excess liquid.

——

PICKLED CABBAGE

8 reserved leaves from the Savoy Cabbage
200 g White Balsamic Pickling Liquid (page 295)

Using a 5-cm (2-inch) ring cutter, punch out the center ribs of the cabbage leaves. Punch again slightly off center to form an oval shape. Place the trimmed pieces in a heatproof container. Heat the pickling liquid to a boil in a saucepan over medium heat. Pour the liquid over the cabbage ribs and let cool to room temperature.

PORK CABBAGE JUS

15 g grapeseed oil
About 150 g reserved pork trim from Pork Rack
1/2 shallot, sliced
60 g red cabbage juice (from about 1/2 head cabbage)
60 g red verjus
120 g Chicken Jus (page 303)
5 g red wine vinegar
Salt

Heat the oil in a pot over medium heat. When the oil just starts to smoke, add the pork trim. Caramelize the pork trim on all sides, turning occasionally, about 4 minutes. Remove the pork from the pan and set aside. Add the shallot to the pan and sweat, stirring frequently, until softened, about 4 minutes. Add the cabbage juice and verjus to the pan. Bring to a simmer and reduce the liquid by half. Add the seared pork trim and chicken jus to the pan. Bring the sauce to a simmer and reduce until thick enough to coat the back of a spoon. Strain the sauce through a chinois. Add the red wine vinegar and season with salt. Keep warm.

——

TO FINISH

20 g grapeseed oil
Brown Butter (page 284), melted
Fleur de sel

Preheat the oven to 160°C/325°F. Heat the oil in a sauté pan over medium heat. When the oil just starts to smoke, place the pork belly pieces in the pan, skin side facing down. Turn heat to low and gently cook until the skin is crispy and browned, about 10 minutes. Transfer the pan to the oven and cook until heated through, about 2 minutes. Remove the pork belly from the pan and using an offset spatula, carefully release the pork belly pieces from the pan and transfer to a paper towel, skin side up, to drain. Remove and discard the string from the pork rack. Slice the pork rack into individual chops and brush the cut sides with brown butter. Season the chops with fleur de sel. Arrange one chop and one piece of pork belly on each of four plates. Spoon the coco bean puree onto each plate, making a well in the center. Divide the coco bean ragout into each well. Spoon the red cabbage puree onto each plate. Place one piece of savoy cabbage on each plate and garnish with the pickled cabbage. Sauce each plate with the pork cabbage jus.

CHICKEN
Whole Roasted with Black Truffle Brioche Stuffing

Serves 4

At The NoMad, the whole roasted chicken has become a very important dish, one that has been on the menu since our opening. The basic whole roasted chicken recipe never changes, but the vegetables and plating do, with different recipes used for the spring, summer, fall, and winter. In the following pages you will find the basic chicken recipe, followed by four recipes to keep the chicken seasonal year-round.

⸻

ROASTED CHICKEN

> *185 g butter, softened, plus more for brushing*
>   *on the chickens*
> *135 g Brioche Bread Crumbs (page 287)*
> *125 g Marinated Foie Gras (page 298),*
>   *at room temperature*
> *35 g black truffle, finely chopped*
> *Salt*
> *2 chickens, head and feet on, about 1.6 kg each*
> *2 lemons, halved*
> *10 sprigs thyme*

Combine the butter, bread crumbs, foie gras, truffle, and 16 g of salt in the bowl of a stand mixer. Paddle on medium speed until thoroughly incorporated, about 5 minutes. Transfer the stuffing to a piping bag and use immediately, or reserve in an airtight container, refrigerated, for up to 2 days. Let the stuffing come to room temperature before using.

Remove the heads from both chickens (see page 220). Using your hands, loosen the skin from the breast meat and from the legs and thighs. Pipe 70 g of the stuffing under the skin of each breast in both chickens. Pipe 40 g of the stuffing under the skin of each leg and thigh of both chickens. Smooth the stuffing so that it is in an even layer. Fill the cavity of each chicken with one lemon, cut in half, and 5 thyme sprigs. Using butcher's twine, tie the chicken so that the wings are tight against the body and the feet are propped up above the legs. Wrap the chickens with plastic wrap and refrigerate overnight.

Preheat a convection oven to 220°C/425°F, high fan. Using a pastry brush, brush a layer of soft butter over the entire exterior of both chickens. Season the chickens with salt. Space the chickens on a wire rack set over a baking sheet. Roast the chickens in the oven, rotating the baking sheet once, until the skin is dark brown, about 15 minutes. Lower the oven temperature to 175°C/350°F, low fan. Continue cooking the chickens until cooked through and the internal temperature reaches 70°C/155°F at the leg joint, about 30 minutes more. Let the chickens rest at room temperature for 25 minutes.

⸻

6-MINUTE EGGS

> *2 eggs*

Bring a pot of water to a rolling boil and prepare an ice bath. Carefully submerge the eggs in the water and cook the eggs at a simmer for 6 minutes. Shock the eggs in the ice bath. When cold, drain and peel the eggs. Refrigerate until ready to serve.

⸻

PICKLED SHALLOT RINGS

> *1 shallot, sliced into rings 1.5 mm (1/16 inch) thick*
> *250 g White Balsamic Pickling Liquid (page 295)*

Place the shallot rings in a heatproof container. Heat the pickling liquid to a boil in a saucepan over medium heat. Pour the liquid over the shallot rings to cover and let cool to room temperature.

⸻

CRISPY CHICKEN SKIN

> *Canola oil, for frying*
> *40 g chicken skin*
> *Salt*

Heat the oil in a large, heavy pot to 160°C/325°F. Fry the chicken skin until golden brown and crispy, about 10 minutes. Remove the chicken skin from the oil and place on a paper towel to drain. Season with salt. Coarsely chop the chicken skin.

TO FINISH

60 g butter
1 shallot, finely chopped
80 g Chicken Stock (page 303)
40 g Chicken Jus (page 303)
Salt
20 g whole-grain mustard
Sliced chives
Brown Butter Sabayon (page 302)
Chervil tops
Brown Butter (page 284), melted
Fleur de sel

Cut the legs and thighs from both birds. Remove and discard the feet and the skin. Pick the dark meat from the legs and thighs, removing and discarding the tendons, and set aside.

Heat a saucepan of water to just under a simmer over medium heat. Remove the pan from the heat and submerge the 6-minute eggs in the water until warmed through, about 3 minutes. Meanwhile, to make a fricassee with the reserved dark meat, heat half of the butter in a saucepan over medium heat until foamy, but not browned. Add the shallot and sweat until softened, about 4 minutes. Add the reserved dark meat and stir to combine. Add the stock and jus to the pan and bring to a simmer. Add the remaining butter and season with salt. As the butter melts and emulsifies, it will glaze the chicken evenly. Be careful not to overcook the chicken or reduce the glaze too far, as the emulsion will break and make the chicken greasy. When the chicken is thickly glazed, remove the pan from the heat. Fold in the pickled shallot rings, whole-grain mustard, and sliced chives. Expel 30 g of the brown butter sabayon into the pan and fold into the chicken.

With a slotted spoon, remove the eggs from the warm water and place on a paper towel to drain. Expel about 15 g more of the sabayon in the center of each of two bowls to share. Place the eggs in the center of the sabayon. Spoon the fricassee around the eggs and top with the crispy chicken skin. Garnish with chervil.

Carve the breasts off the ribcage and brush the bone sides of the breasts with brown butter and season with fleur de sel. Serve the breasts with the desired vegetables and plating (see pages 224–7 and 230–2) with the chicken fricassee on the side to share.

ROAST CHICKEN
STEP-BY-STEP

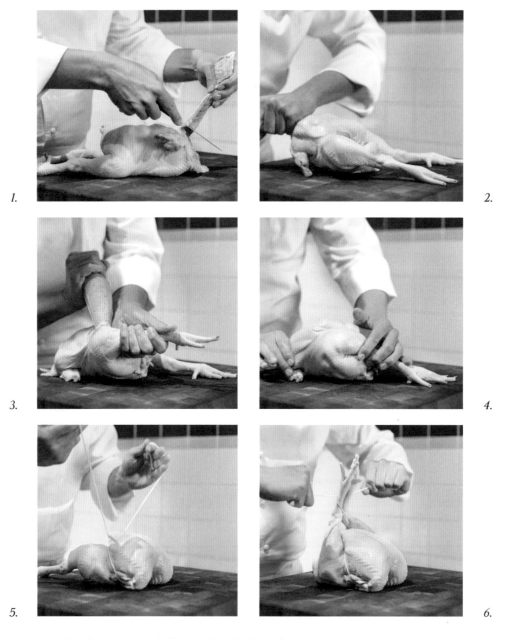

1.

2.

3.

4.

5.

6.

1. Cut and separate the head and neck from the chicken, making sure to keep the skin flap attached to the body.

2. Loosen the skin from the breast and pipe the stuffing underneath the skin. Be careful to prevent tearing.

3. Loosen the skin from the legs and thighs and pipe the stuffing underneath the skin.

4. Smooth the stuffing to evenly disperse.

5. Tuck the butcher's twine under the rib cage and tie the wings against the breast. Loop the string behind the rib cage and pull tight.

6. Loop the string around the legs and tie the legs together up behind the rib cage.

7. Liberally brush softened butter over the entire surface of the chicken.

7.

CHICKEN
Whole Roasted with White Asparagus, Nettles, Potatoes, and Morels

Serves 4

Chicken Whole Roasted with Black Truffle Brioche
Stuffing (page 218)

_____

WHITE ASPARAGUS

4 jumbo white asparagus stalks
20 g olive oil
1 shallot, sliced
1 clove garlic, crushed
1 sprig thyme
120 g dry white wine
25 g water
35 g lemon juice
35 g Chicken Stock (page 303)
25 g butter
Salt

Trim the woody end from each stalk, leaving the top 15 cm (6 inches). Using a vegetable peeler, peel the outer layer of each stalk from just below the tip to the bottom of the stalk. Set aside. Bring a large pot of water to a rolling boil over high heat and prepare an ice bath. Heat the oil in a saucepan over medium heat. Add the shallot and garlic. Cook, stirring occasionally, until tender, about 5 minutes. Add the thyme and wine. Bring the liquid to a simmer and turn the heat to low. Simmer until the wine reduces by half. Add the water and lemon juice, stirring to combine. Remove the pan from the heat and chill the liquid over the ice bath until cold.

Seal the asparagus and cooking liquid airtight in a sous vide bag. Submerge in the boiling water and cook until very tender, about 35 minutes. Shock in the ice bath until cold. Remove the asparagus from the bag and place on a paper towel to drain. Cut each spear in half on a bias. Heat the stock in a sauté pan over medium heat to a simmer. Add the asparagus and butter to the pan. Season with salt. As the butter melts and emulsifies, it will glaze the asparagus evenly. Be careful not to overcook the asparagus or reduce the glaze too far, as the emulsion

will break and make the asparagus greasy. Transfer the glazed asparagus to a paper towel–lined tray to drain any excess glaze. Keep warm.

_____

CREAMED NETTLES

60 g butter
100 g spinach leaves
100 g nettle leaves
Salt
200 g skim milk
5 g Ultratex 3
1 g xanthan gum
15 g grapeseed oil
1/2 shallot, finely chopped
30 g Garlic Confit (page 298)
55 g mascarpone
Grated zest of 1/2 lemon

Prepare an ice bath. Heat the butter in a saucepan over medium heat until foamy but not browned. Add the spinach and nettle leaves (always wear gloves when handling uncooked nettles). Cook, stirring frequently, until wilted, about 3 minutes. Season with salt. Immediately chill the cooked greens over the ice bath. When cold, squeeze out any excess liquid from the greens. Coarsely chop and set aside. Pour the milk into a blender and, on low speed, slowly blend in the Ultratex 3 and xanthan gum. Blend for 1 minute to fully hydrate the gum. Set aside.

Heat the oil in a sauté pan over medium heat. Add the shallots and sweat until soft, about 4 minutes. Add the garlic and mash with a large fork. Add the chopped spinach and nettles. Cook, stirring frequently, until warmed through. Season with salt. Turn heat to low and fold in the mascarpone until incorporated. Remove the pan from the heat and fold in the thickened milk. Keep warm.

_____

PICKLED POTATO SLICES

1 fingerling potato
100 g White Balsamic Pickling Liquid (page 295)

Using a mandoline, slice the potato lengthwise paper thin and place in a heatproof container. Heat the pickling liquid to a boil in a saucepan over medium heat. Pour over the potato to cover and let cool to room temperature.

PEANUT POTATO CONFIT

12 peanut potatoes
2 sprigs thyme
1 clove garlic, crushed
Olive oil
35 g Chicken Stock (page 303)
25 g butter
Salt

Preheat the oven to 150°C/300°F. Combine the potatoes, thyme, garlic, and enough olive oil to generously cover in a baking dish. Cover with aluminum foil and place in the oven. Cook the potatoes until just tender, about 1 hour. Remove from the oven and let cool to room temperature in the oil, then drain and discard the oil. Transfer the cooked potatoes to a sauté pan with the chicken stock and heat over medium heat. Add butter and season the potatoes with salt. As the butter melts and emulsifies, it will glaze the potatoes evenly. Be careful not to overcook the potatoes or reduce the glaze too far, as the emulsion will break and make the potatoes greasy. Place the glazed potatoes on a paper towel to drain any excess glaze. Keep warm.

MORELS

25 g butter
12 morels
Salt
40 g Morel Cream (page 305)

Heat the butter in a large sauté pan over medium heat until foamy but not browned. Add the morels and cook until the morels start to soften, about 3 minutes. Season the morels with salt. Add the morel cream to the pan and bring to a simmer. Continue to cook, stirring occasionally, until the mushrooms are tender and the cream forms a thick glaze, about 2 minutes. Transfer the mushrooms to a paper towel to drain any excess cream. Keep warm.

TO FINISH

Morel Cream (page 305)
Chive blossoms
Black Truffle Jus (page 302)

Heat the morel cream in a saucepan over low heat to gently rewarm. Remove the pan from the heat and keep warm. Place one chicken breast in the center of each of four plates. Sandwich the creamed nettles between the pickled fingerling potato slices and place two of these sandwiches on each plate. Divide the peanut potato confit, white asparagus, and morels among the four plates, arranging them around the chicken breasts. Froth the morel cream with an immersion blender and spoon the froth over the morels. Garnish each plate with chive blossoms and sauce with truffle jus. Serve the chicken fricassee on the side to share.

CHICKEN
Whole Roasted with Corn, Wheat Berries, and Chanterelles

Serves 4

Chicken Whole Roasted with Black Truffle Brioche Stuffing (page 218)

———

MADEIRA JUS

15 g grapeseed oil
150 g chicken wings
1 shallot, sliced
50 g Madeira
240 g Chicken Jus (page 303)
1 clove garlic, crushed
15 g sherry vinegar
Salt

Heat the oil in a saucepan over high heat. Add the chicken wings to the pan and sear, turning occasionally, until deeply caramelized, about 8 minutes. Remove the wings from the pan and set aside. Drain the pan of any excess fat and turn the heat to medium. Add the shallot to the pan and cook, stirring occasionally, until soft, about 5 minutes. Add the Madeira to deglaze and bring to a simmer. Reduce the wine until almost dry. Add the jus, chicken wings, and garlic and bring to a simmer. Reduce the sauce until thick enough to coat the back of a spoon. Strain the sauce through a chinois, and again through cheesecloth. Add the sherry vinegar and season with salt. Keep warm.

CHANTERELLE PUREE

30 g butter
1/2 shallot, sliced
50 g cremini mushrooms, sliced
200 g chanterelle mushrooms, sliced
30 g dry white wine
25 g mascarpone
10 g crème fraîche
Salt

Heat the butter in a saucepan over medium heat until foamy but not browned. Add the shallot and cook, stirring occasionally, until soft and without any color, about 4 minutes. Add the mushrooms and cook, stirring occasionally, until the liquid released from the mushrooms is nearly evaporated, about 10 minutes. Add the wine and bring to a simmer. Reduce the wine until almost dry. Add enough water to just cover the mushrooms. Bring the water to a simmer, stir and scrape any bits from the bottom of the pan, and cook the mushrooms until tender, about 10 minutes. Drain the mushrooms through a chinois and reserve the cooking liquid. Transfer the mushrooms to a blender with a splash of the cooking liquid. Puree on high speed until smooth. Turn to low speed and add the mascarpone and crème fraîche. Continue to blend until fully emulsified and season the puree with salt. Pass the puree through a chinois and keep warm.

———

PICKLED CORN

45 g corn kernels
250 g White Balsamic Pickling Liquid (page 295)

Place the corn in a heatproof container and prepare an ice bath. Heat the pickling liquid in a saucepan over medium heat and bring to a boil. Pour the liquid over the corn to cover and immediately chill over the ice bath.

WHEAT BERRY AND CORN RAGOUT

60 g butter
32 chanterelle mushrooms
Salt
180 g Cooked Wheat Berries (page 287)
50 g corn kernels
65 g Chicken Stock (page 303)
Pickled Corn, drained

Heat half of the butter in a saucepan over medium
heat until foamy but not browned. Add the mushrooms
and sweat, stirring occasionally, until tender, about
3 minutes. Season with salt. Add the wheat berries, corn
kernels, and stock to the pan. Bring the stock to a simmer
and add the remaining butter. As the butter melts and
emulsifies, it will glaze the ragout evenly. Be careful not
to break the emulsion as it will make the ragout greasy.
Fold in the pickled corn and keep warm.

TO FINISH

Purslane tops
15 g foie gras fat, melted

Divide the chanterelle puree among four plates. Place
one chicken breast at the center of each plate. Spoon
the wheat berry and corn ragout among the four plates
around the chicken and on the chanterelle puree. Garnish
the plate with the purslane tips. Sauce each plate with the
foie Madeira jus and break the jus with the foie gras fat.
Serve the chicken fricassee on the side to share.

CHICKEN
Whole Roasted with Lentils and Brussels Sprouts

Serves 4

Chicken Whole Roasted with Black Truffle Brioche Stuffing (page 218)

ONION JUS

2 white onions, halved crosswise
1/2 shallot, sliced
1 head unpeeled garlic, split lengthwise
36 g olive oil
Salt
5 sprigs thyme
2 sprigs rosemary
3 sprigs savory
3 sprigs marjoram
115 g dry white wine
120 g Chicken Jus (page 303)
900 g Chicken Stock (page 303)
30 g apple cider vinegar
Pinch of cayenne

Preheat the oven to 205°C/400°F. Heat a griddle pan over high heat. When the pan is very hot, sear the onions, cut sides down until deeply charred on one side, about 10 minutes. Remove the onions from the pan and set aside. Combine the shallot, garlic, and one-third of the oil in a mixing bowl. Season with salt and toss together to combine. Spread the shallot and garlic out in a single layer on a wire rack set over a baking sheet. Roast in the oven until caramelized, about 10 minutes. Heat the remaining oil in a large saucepan over high heat. When the oil just starts to smoke, add the roasted shallot and garlic to the pan and cook until the vegetables start to stick to the bottom of the pan, about 4 minutes. Add the wine and stir to deglaze the pan. Reduce the wine until almost dry. Add the jus, stock, herbs, and charred onions to the pan. Bring the liquid to a simmer and turn the heat to low. Reduce the jus until thick enough to coat the back of a spoon. Add the vinegar. Strain the sauce through a chinois and again through cheesecloth. Season with salt and cayenne. Keep warm.

PICKLED PEARL ONIONS

3 white pearl onions, peeled
100 g yuzu juice
15 g honey
5 g salt

Using a mandoline, slice the onions from the stem end 1.5 mm (1/16 inch) thick. Place the sliced onions in a heatproof container and set aside. Heat the yuzu juice, honey, and salt in a saucepan over medium heat. Bring the liquid to a simmer, stirring to incorporate. Remove the pan from the heat and pour over the onions to cover. Let cool to room temperature.

ROASTED BRUSSELS SPROUTS

30 g grapeseed oil
6 brussels sprouts, trimmed and halved
Salt

Heat the oil in a large sauté pan over high heat. When the oil just begins to smoke, add the halved sprouts, cut sides down, and turn the heat to medium. Season with salt and cook until deeply caramelized on one side, about 2 minutes. Continue to cook the sprouts, stirring occasionally, until tender, about 6 minutes. Transfer the sprouts to a paper towel to drain and keep warm.

GLAZED BRUSSELS SPROUTS

6 brussels sprouts, trimmed and halved
25 g chicken stock
15 g butter
Salt

Bring a pot of salted water to a rolling boil over high heat and prepare an ice bath. Blanch the sprouts in the water until tender, about 6 minutes. Shock the sprouts the ice bath. When cold, drain the sprouts and set aside. Heat the stock to a simmer in a sauté pan over medium heat. Add the butter and sprouts to the pan. Season with salt. As the butter melts and emulsifies, it will glaze the sprouts evenly. Be careful not to reduce the glaze too far, as the emulsion will break and make the brussels sprouts greasy. Keep warm.

GREEN AND BLACK LENTILS

1 shallot, sliced
2 heads unpeeled garlic, split lengthwise
6 sprigs thyme
3 sprigs savory
2 sprigs rosemary
75 g black lentils
75 g green lentils
Salt

Tie the shallot, garlic, and herbs in a cheesecloth sachet. Combine the sachet and lentils in a large saucepan with enough water to generously cover. Heat to a simmer over medium heat. Season with salt and turn the heat to low. Continue to cook the lentils at a gentle simmer until tender, about 40 minutes. Remove the pan from the heat and let cool to room temperature in the cooking liquid. Remove and discard the sachet. Reserve the lentils in the cooking liquid in an airtight container, refrigerated, for up to 3 days.

LENTIL HERB RAGOUT

40 g butter
20 g brussels sprout leaves, thinly sliced
Salt
Green and Black Lentils, drained
Picked leaves from 3 sprigs savory
Picked leaves from 3 sprigs thyme
10 g apple cider vinegar
35 g Chicken Stock (page 303)

Heat half of the butter in a saucepan over medium heat until foamy but not browned. Add the brussels sprout leaves and sweat until tender, about 2 minutes. Season with salt. Add the lentils, savory, thyme, vinegar, and chicken stock. Bring to a simmer and add the remaining butter. As the butter melts and emulsifies, it will glaze the ragout evenly. Be careful not to overcook the lentils or break the emulsion as it will make the ragout greasy. Season with salt and keep warm.

TO FINISH

4 broccoli spigarello leaves
White Balsamic Vinaigrette (page 285)
Brown Butter, melted (page 284)

Place one chicken breast in the center of each plate. Arrange the lentil ragout in small piles around each breast. Place the pickled pearl onions and roasted and glazed brussels sprouts on and around the lentils. In a mixing bowl, dress the broccoli spigarello leaves with white balsamic vinaigrette. Garnish each plate with a dressed leaf. Sauce each plate with the onion jus. Break the onion jus with several drops of brown butter. Serve the chicken fricassee on the side to share.

CHICKEN
Whole Roasted with Potatoes and Black Radish

Serves 4

Chicken Whole Roasted with Black Truffle Brioche Stuffing (page 218)

TRUFFLE POTATO ÉCRASER

1 head unpeeled garlic, halved
3 sprigs rosemary
300 g fingerling potatoes, peeled
Salt
250 g butter
25 g Chicken Stock (page 303)
30 g black truffle, finely chopped

Tie the garlic and rosemary in a cheesecloth sachet. Cover the potatoes and sachet generously with water in a large saucepan and season with salt. Bring the potatoes to a simmer over low heat and cook gently until tender, about 45 minutes. Remove and discard the sachet. Drain the potatoes well. Return the potatoes to a saucepan over low heat. Using a large fork, crush the potatoes. Add the butter and stock to the pan and continue to thoroughly mash the potatoes until the butter is completely melted in and emulsified. Fold in the truffles, season with salt, and keep warm.

PICKLED BLACK RADISH

2 black radishes
30 g Lemon Vinaigrette (page 285)

Bring a large pot of water to a rolling boil over high heat and prepare an ice bath. Cut the cheeks from the radishes. Using a 2.5-cm (1-inch) ring cutter, punch sixteen rounds from the outer cheeks. Seal the radish rounds and lemon vinaigrette airtight in a sous vide bag. Submerge the bag in the boiling water and cook until the radishes are tender, about 20 minutes. Shock in the ice bath. When cold, remove the radishes from the bag and set aside at room temperature.

TO FINISH

30 g Chicken Stock (page 303)
25 g butter
Salt
5 g black truffle, finely chopped, plus 1 black truffle, to shave
New Zealand spinach
Black Truffle Jus (page 302)

Combine the pickled black radishes and stock in a saucepan and place over medium heat. Bring the stock to a simmer and turn the heat to low. Add the butter to the pan and season with salt. As the butter melts and emulsifies, it will glaze the radishes evenly. Be careful not to overcook the radishes or reduce the glaze too far, as the emulsion will break and make them greasy. Add the chopped black truffle and stir to incorporate. Transfer the radishes to a paper towel to drain any excess glaze. Keep warm.

Place one chicken breast in the center of each of four plates. Spoon the truffle potato écraser in three small piles around each chicken breast. Divide the pickled black radishes among the four plates. Garnish each plate with New Zealand spinach. Sauce each plate with truffle jus. Shave black truffle over each chicken breast to finish. Serve with chicken fricassee on the side to share.

DESSERTS

CARROT
Cake with Walnuts and Raisins

Serves 4

CARROT PUREE

  260 g carrots, peeled and thinly sliced
  240 g carrot juice (from about 4 peeled carrots)
  20 g orange blossom honey
  15 g orange juice
  8 g lemon juice

Combine the carrots and carrot juice in a saucepan over medium heat. Bring to a simmer and cover the pan with a parchment cartouche. Cook until the carrots are tender, about 25 minutes. Remove the carrots from the heat and strain through a chinois, reserving the cooking liquid. Combine the cooked carrots and a splash of the cooking liquid in a blender and puree on high until completely smooth. Let the puree cool to room temperature. Reserve 110 g of the puree for the carrot cake. Combine the rest of the puree with the honey and orange and lemon juices in a mixing bowl and whisk together until fully incorporated. Reserve in an airtight container, refrigerated, for up to 3 days.

CINNAMON GLAZE

  140 g confectioners' sugar
  1 egg white
  10 g water
  1 g ground cinnamon

Combine the ingredients in a bowl and whisk together until completely smooth.

CARROT CAKE

  110 g granulated sugar
  110 g light brown sugar
  110 g Carrot Puree
  1 egg
  1 egg yolk
  7 g vanilla extract
  95 g walnut oil
  50 g olive oil
  170 g flour
  5 g baking soda
  5 g salt
  1 g ground cinnamon
  1 g ground ginger
  250 g carrots, peeled and coarsely grated
  Cinnamon Glaze

Preheat the oven to 175°C/350°F. Spray a 20-cm (8-inch) square cake pan and four 8 by 3-cm (3 by 1-inch) rectangular silicone cake molds with nonstick cooking spray and set aside. Using a stand mixer, paddle the sugars, carrot puree, egg, yolk, and vanilla together on medium speed until smooth, about 3 minutes. Turn to low speed and slowly mix in both oils until emulsified. Combine the flour, baking soda, salt, cinnamon, and ginger in a bowl. Remove the bowl from the mixer and gently fold the dry ingredients into the batter using a rubber spatula. Do not overmix the batter. Gently fold in the grated carrots. Divide the batter among the prepared pans and bake until a cake tester inserted in the centers comes out clean, about 40 minutes. Let the cakes cool to room temperature on wire racks. Break the large cake by hand into a coarse crumble. Glaze the bars with the cinnamon glaze. Slice each of the glazed cakes into three pieces.

CREAM CHEESE

  120 g cream cheese, softened
  12 g sugar

Using a stand mixer, paddle the cream cheese and sugar together on medium speed until smooth, about 3 minutes. Transfer to a piping bag and refrigerate until ready to serve.

CONTINUED

WALNUT BRITTLE

170 g walnuts, coarsely chopped
195 g sugar
60 g butter
45 g glucose syrup
30 g water
3 g baking soda
8 g salt

Preheat the oven to 175°C/350°F. Line one baking sheet with parchment paper and another with a nonstick baking mat. Place the walnuts in a single layer on the parchment-lined baking sheet and toast until aromatic, about 6 minutes. Heat the sugar, butter, glucose, and water in a heavy saucepan over medium heat. Cook, stirring frequently with a rubber spatula, until the sugar is fully dissolved and turns amber colored, about 6 minutes. Stir in the baking soda and salt. Once these are fully incorporated, fold in the walnuts and remove the pan from the heat. Quickly turn the caramel out onto the mat-lined baking sheet and spread thinly and evenly. Let cool to room temperature. Transfer to a food processor and pulse several times for a coarse crumble. Reserve the brittle in a dry, airtight container.

PICKLED RAISINS

20 g golden raisins
60 g lime juice
40 g orange blossom honey
20 g water
1/2 vanilla bean, split and scraped

Heat the ingredients in a saucepan over low heat, stirring to incorporate. When the liquid comes to a simmer, remove the pan from the heat and let cool to room temperature. When ready to serve, discard the vanilla bean and drain the pickling liquid from the raisins.

TO FINISH

Pineapple Sorbet (page 292)
Small carrot tops

Spoon the seasoned carrot puree onto each of four plates. Dot the cream cheese onto several places on each plate. Divide the glazed carrot cakes, cake pieces, walnut brittle, and pickled raisins among the plates, arranging them in and around the puree and cream cheese. Scoop a quenelle of pineapple sorbet onto each plate. Garnish each plate with carrot tops.

STRAWBERRY
Cheesecake with Graham Crumble and Meyer Lemon

Serves 4

STRAWBERRY POACHING LIQUID

750 g strawberries
250 g sugar
45 g lemon juice

Heat a large pot of water to a boil over high heat. Seal the strawberries airtight in a sous vide bag. Submerge the bag in the boiling water until the strawberries release all of their juices, about 1 hour. Strain the strawberries through cheesecloth, reserving the liquid. Discard the berries. Combine 125 g of the strained liquid, sugar, and lemon juice in a saucepan. Heat to a boil over medium heat, whisking to dissolve the sugar. Skim and discard any impurities that may float to the surface. Let cool to room temperature and reserve the liquid in an airtight container, refrigerated, for up to 1 week.

POACHED STRAWBERRIES

20 Tristar strawberries, hulled
Strawberry Poaching Liquid

Place the strawberries in a heatproof container. Heat the poaching liquid to a boil in a saucepan over medium heat. Pour the liquid over the strawberries to cover. Place a paper towel directly on top of the berries to keep covered and let cool to room temperature. Reserve the berries in the liquid in an airtight container, refrigerated.

STRAWBERRY CREAM CHEESE

125 g cream cheese, softened
25 g strawberry puree, 10 percent added sugar
15 g sugar

Combine the ingredients in a food processor and mix until fully incorporated and smooth. Reserve in an airtight container, refrigerated, for up to 3 days. When ready to serve, transfer to a piping bag and let sit at room temperature for 30 minutes to temper.

GRAHAM CRUMBLE

140 g butter, cold, cubed
65 g light brown sugar
125 g all-purpose flour
50 g finely ground whole wheat flour
40 g coarsely ground whole wheat flour
3 g salt
25 g buckwheat honey

Preheat the oven to 175°C/350°F. Line a baking sheet with parchment paper. Using a stand mixer, paddle all of the ingredients on medium speed until the mixture is crumbly in texture. Do not overmix. Transfer to the baking sheet and spread in an even layer. Bake until golden brown, about 15 minutes. Allow to cool to room temperature. Break into small pieces and transfer to a dry, airtight container.

COTTON CAKE

70 g milk
45 g butter
160 g cream cheese, softened
5 eggs, separated
Grated zest of 1 lemon
15 g lemon juice
15 g vanilla extract
3 g salt
20 g cornstarch
20 g flour
2 egg whites
75 g sugar
2 g cream of tartar

Preheat the oven to 165°C/325°F. Heat the milk and butter in a saucepan over low heat. Melt the butter completely and bring to a simmer. Remove the pan from the heat. Combine the mixture with the cream cheese in a blender and blend on high speed until fully emulsified, about 2 minutes. Turn to low speed and slowly blend in the egg yolks, lemon zest and juice, vanilla, and salt. Once fully incorporated, blend in the cornstarch and flour. Transfer the batter to a large mixing bowl and set aside. Using a stand mixer, whip all of the egg whites on low speed until foamy, about 3 minutes. Turn to medium speed and slowly add the sugar and cream of tartar. Whip the egg whites to soft peaks, about 4 minutes. Remove from the mixer and gently fold the whipped whites into the cream cheese mixture in three additions. Transfer the batter to a 20-cm (8-inch) square cake pan

CONTINUED

and smooth the surface with a spatula. Place the pan inside a large baking dish. Carefully pour warm water into the larger baking dish so that the level of water is equal to that of the cake batter. Place the baking dish in the oven and bake the cake until just set, about 50 minutes. Remove the dish from the oven and let the cake cool to room temperature in the water bath. Using a large spoon, scoop the cake out in pieces and reserve in a dry, **airtight container.**

——

MEYER LEMON GEL

115 g Meyer lemon juice
60 g sugar
60 g water
3 g agar-agar

Heat the lemon juice and sugar in a saucepan over medium heat to a simmer. Stir to dissolve the sugar. Remove the pan from the heat and keep warm.

Combine the water and agar-agar in a saucepan and bring to a simmer over medium heat, whisking constantly. Continue to simmer and whisk until the agar-agar is fully hydrated and appears translucent, about 1 minute. Slowly whisk the warm lemon juice into the agar mixture until thoroughly combined, then remove the pan from the heat.

Transfer the mixture to a shallow baking dish and refrigerate until fully set, about 3 hours. Break the gel into small pieces and transfer to a blender. Puree on high speed until smooth. Pass the gel through a fine-mesh tamis. Reserve in an airtight container, refrigerated, for up to 3 days. When ready to serve, transfer the gel to a piping bag.

——

TO FINISH

8 strawberries, hulled and sliced 6 mm (¼ inch) thick
Strawberry Sorbet (page 293)

Pipe the cream cheese into three places on each of four plates. Using a spoon, spread one spot on each plate. Break the cake into 5-cm (2-inch) pieces and divide the pieces among the plates. Divide the fresh strawberries, poached strawberries, and graham crumble among the plates, arranging them around the cake. Dot the Meyer lemon gel around the strawberries. Scoop a quenelle of strawberry sorbet over the center of each arrangement.

CHERRY
Sundae with Mascarpone and Pistachios

Serves 4

TOASTED PISTACHIOS

430 g pistachios, shelled

Preheat the oven to 175°C/350°F. Place the pistachios in a single layer on a baking sheet lined with parchment paper and toast until golden brown and aromatic, about 8 minutes. Let cool to room temperature and reserve in a dry, airtight container.

PISTACHIO PASTE

150 g Toasted Pistachios
100 g confectioners' sugar
4 g salt
50 g pistachio oil

Blend the pistachios, confectioners' sugar, and salt in a food processor until coarsely ground, about 6 minutes. Slowly add the oil and blend until the mixture resembles crunchy peanut butter. Transfer the paste to a blender and puree on high speed until smooth. Reserve 65 g for the pistachio sponge cake. Pass the remaining half through a fine-mesh tamis and reserve in a dry, airtight container for up to 1 week, refrigerated. When ready to serve, let sit at room temperature for 30 minutes to temper.

PISTACHIO BRITTLE

150 g sugar
45 g butter
32 g glucose syrup
45 g water
2 g baking soda
6 g salt
130 g Toasted Pistachios

Line a baking sheet with a nonstick baking mat. Heat the sugar, butter, glucose, and water in a heavy saucepan over medium heat. Cook, stirring frequently with a rubber spatula, until the sugar is fully dissolved and turns amber colored, about 6 minutes. Stir in the baking soda and salt. Once fully incorporated, fold in the nuts and remove the pan from the heat. Quickly turn the caramel out onto the prepared baking sheet and spread thinly and evenly. Let the brittle cool to room temperature. Break twenty of the whole pistachios from the sheet of brittle and set aside. Transfer the remaining brittle to a food processor and pulse several times to make a coarse crumble. Reserve the crumble and whole pistachios separately in dry, airtight containers.

GLAZED CHERRIES

265 g pitted Bing cherries
230 g water
20 g dried sour cherries
25 g sugar

Set aside eighteen of the Bing cherries to glaze. Combine the remaining Bing cherries with the rest of the ingredients in a saucepan over medium heat. Bring to a boil, crushing the cherries with the back of a spoon as they soften. Remove the mixture from the heat and let cool to room temperature. Strain the mixture through cheesecloth and discard the solids. Heat the liquid to a simmer in a saucepan over medium heat and reduce by half. Add the reserved cherries and stir to evenly coat. Remove the pan from the heat and let cool to room temperature. Halve six of the glazed cherries and keep the rest whole. Reserve the glazed cherries with their syrup in an airtight container, refrigerated, for up to 24 hours.

CONTINUED

PISTACHIO SPONGE CAKE

100 g flour, sifted
35 g potato starch, sifted
150 g Toasted Pistachios, coarsely chopped
9 egg yolks
210 g sugar
65 g trimoline
65 g Pistachio Paste
12 g vanilla extract
4 g salt
3 egg whites
100 g pistachio oil

Preheat the oven to 175°C/350°F. Line a 23 by 33-cm (9 by 13-inch) rimmed baking sheet with parchment paper. Combine the flour, potato starch, and the toasted pistachios in a mixing bowl and set aside. Using a stand mixer, whip the egg yolks, one-third of the sugar, trimoline, pistachio paste, vanilla, and salt on medium speed until the mixture is pale yellow and holds a ribbon, about 5 minutes. Remove the bowl from the mixer and set aside.

In a separate bowl, whip the egg whites on low speed until frothy, about 2 minutes. Slowly add the remaining 140 g sugar and turn to medium speed. Whip until it reaches soft peaks, about 4 minutes. Remove the bowl from the mixer and gently fold the whites into the yolk mixture using a rubber spatula. Alternating between the flour mixture and pistachio oil, gently fold into the batter in three separate additions. Transfer the batter to the prepared baking sheet and bake until a cake tester inserted in the center comes out clean, about 25 minutes. Let cool to room temperature. Invert the cake onto a cutting board. Trim off the outer edges. Tear the cake into 5-cm (2-inch) pieces.

TO FINISH

Cherry Sorbet (page 290)
Mascarpone Cherry Ice Cream (page 291)

Spread the smooth pistachio paste on each of four plates. Divide the pistachio brittle, pistachio sponge cake, candied pistachios, and glazed cherries among the plates. Scoop one quenelle of cherry sorbet and two quenelles of mascarpone cherry ice cream onto each plate.

BLACKBERRY
*Cobbler with Brioche
and Lime*

Serves 4

BLACKBERRY FILLING

335 g blackberries
85 g sugar
Grated zest of 2 lemons
85 g blackberry puree, 10 percent added sugar
20 g flour
25 g lemon juice

Heat the blackberries, sugar, and zest in a saucepan over low heat. Combine the blackberry puree and flour in a mixing bowl and whisk together until smooth. Set aside. Cook the berries, stirring occasionally to prevent burning, until the berries start to break down and release their liquid, about 5 minutes. Bring the liquid to a simmer, about 3 minutes more. Whisk the flour mixture into the pan. Continue to cook, stirring constantly, until the flour cooks out and thickens the mixture, about 3 minutes. Whisk in the lemon juice and remove the pan from the heat. Let cool to room temperature. Reserve the filling in an airtight container, refrigerated, for up to 1 week.

BROWN SUGAR CRUMBLE

90 g light brown sugar
90 g flour
45 g butter, cold
1 g salt

Combine the ingredients in a mixing bowl. Quickly work together by hand until the texture becomes coarse and crumbly. Make sure the butter stays cold. Refrigerate the crumble until ready to assemble the cobblers.

BLACKBERRY COBBLER

208 g bread flour
2 eggs
21 g water
13 g fresh yeast
30 g sugar
5 g salt
105 g butter, cold, cubed
Blackberry Filling
Brown Sugar Crumble

Place the flour, eggs, water, and yeast in the bowl of a stand mixer. Paddle on low speed until just combined, about 3 minutes. Switch to the dough hook attachment and mix on medium speed until the gluten has developed and the dough springs back when pressed, about 7 minutes. Add the sugar and salt and mix until fully incorporated, about 3 minutes. Turn the speed to low and add the butter all at once. Continue to mix until incorporated, about 5 minutes. Transfer the dough to a large mixing bowl lightly sprayed with nonstick cooking spray. Flip the dough over to evenly coat. Cover the bowl tightly with plastic wrap and refrigerate overnight to ferment.

Uncover the bowl and gently press down on the dough to degas. Portion and form the dough into 10-g balls. Divide the blackberry filling among four 9-cm (3 1/2-inch) cast-iron cocottes. Arrange six dough balls in each cocotte over the blackberry filling. Cover the cocottes with a damp towel and allow to proof at room temperature until doubled in size, about 1 1/2 hours. Preheat the oven to 175°C/350°F. Remove the towel and lightly spritz the proofed bread with water. Sprinkle each cobbler generously with the brown sugar crumble. Bake the cobblers in the oven until golden brown, about 20 minutes. Let the cobblers sit at room temperature for 10 minutes before serving.

BLACKBERRY DRUPELETS

2 blackberries

Place the blackberries in the freezer until frozen solid. Gently pull apart the pieces of the blackberries into individual drupelets. Keep frozen.

TO FINISH

Ricotta Ice Cream (page 292)
Lime Granita (page 290)

Serve the blackberry cobblers warm with ricotta ice cream, garnished with the lime granita and blackberry drupelets.

STRAWBERRY
Popsicles with Vanilla

Makes 4

———

VANILLA ICE

750 g cream
375 g milk
1 vanilla bean, split and scraped
180 g sugar
3 g salt

Prepare an ice bath. Heat the cream, milk, and vanilla bean in a saucepan over medium heat. Bring to a simmer and remove the pan from the heat. Cover and let steep at room temperature for 1 hour. Strain the infused cream through a chinois and transfer to a clean saucepan. Heat to a simmer over medium heat. Slowly whisk the sugar and salt into the simmering cream and stir until fully dissolved. Chill over the ice bath until cold.

Freeze in an ice cream machine and spread into a 23 by 33-cm (9 by 13-inch) baking dish in an even layer. Freeze the ice cream until firm, about 3 hours. Punch out four ice cream ovals using a 4.1-cm (1⅝ inch) oval cutter and transfer to a baking sheet lined with acetate. Freeze until firm.

———

TO FINISH

330 g strawberry puree, 10 percent added sugar
35 g Simple Syrup (page 300)

Whisk the puree and syrup together until fully incorporated. Fill the bottom of each of four 35-ml popsicle molds with 6 g of the strawberry mixture. Freeze until firm, about 1 hour. Place one oval of sweet cream ice cream in each mold and push a popsicle stick through. Cover with an additional 10 g of strawberry mixture to fill the molds and immediately return the molds to the freezer. Freeze until firm, about 2 hours.

PEACH
Roasted with Rosemary and Vanilla

Serves 4

———

ROASTING SYRUP

400 g dry white wine
60 g sugar
30 g orange blossom honey
2 sprigs rosemary

Heat the wine, sugar, and honey in a saucepan over high heat. Stir to dissolve the sugar. Bring to a boil and turn the heat to low. Simmer until the liquid is reduced by half. Add the rosemary to the pan and remove from the heat. Cover and let steep at room temperature for 30 minutes. Uncover and strain the syrup through a chinois. Reserve the syrup in an airtight container, refrigerated, for up to 3 days.

———

OVEN-ROASTED PEACHES

2 peaches, peeled
Roasting Syrup

Preheat the oven to 150°C/300°F. Halve and pit the peaches. Place in an oven-safe saucepan and cover halfway with the roasting syrup. Heat the pan over medium heat and bring the syrup to a simmer. Cook, gently basting the peaches to evenly cook, until they are slightly softened, about 5 minutes. Transfer the pan to the oven and roast the peaches until tender, about 25 minutes. Remove the pan from the oven and let cool to room temperature in the syrup.

———

CRÈME ANGLAISE

120 g cream
120 g milk
1/2 vanilla bean, split and scraped
6 egg yolks
40 g sugar
2 g salt

Prepare an ice bath. Heat the cream, milk, and vanilla in a saucepan. Bring to a simmer and remove the pan from the heat. Cover and let steep at room temperature for 30 minutes. Strain the cream through a chinois and set aside. Whisk the eggs and sugar together in a mixing bowl until smooth. Slowly whisk one-third of the warm cream into the egg mixture until fully incorporated. Pour the egg mixture into the rest of the warm cream, whisking. Cook over medium heat, whisking constantly, until heated to 84°C/183°F and thick enough to coat the back of a spoon. Strain the anglaise through a chinois and chill over the ice bath. Season with the salt. Reserve in an airtight container, refrigerated, for up to 3 days.

———

SHORTCAKE

2 eggs
255 g flour
100 g butter
60 g sugar
17 g baking powder
4 g salt
Grated zest of 1/2 lemon
190 g cream
5 g vanilla extract
Butter, softened, for brushing
Turbinado sugar, for dusting

Preheat the oven to 175°C/350°F. Prepare an ice bath. Heat a saucepan of water to a boil over high heat. Carefully submerge the eggs in the boiling water and cook until hard-boiled, about 10 minutes. Drain and shock the eggs in the ice bath until cold. Peel the eggs and discard the shells. Reserve the cooked whites for another use. Pass the yolks through a coarse-mesh tamis. Combine the cooked yolks, flour, butter, sugar, baking powder, salt, and lemon zest in a food processor. Pulse to a coarse crumble. Add the cream and vanilla, pulsing together until just combined. Turn the dough out onto a clean work surface and knead by hand to fully incorporate, about 1 minute. Roll the dough out on parchment paper to 1.3 cm (1/2 inch) thick. Transfer, along with the parchment, to a baking sheet. Lightly brush the dough with softened butter and dust with turbinado sugar. Bake until golden brown, about 10 minutes. Let cool to room temperature. Break into 2.5-cm (1-inch) pieces and reserve in a dry, airtight container.

CONTINUED

PEACH PUREE

2 peaches, pitted and diced 2.5 cm (1 inch)
75 g peach nectar
75 g dry white wine
25 g dried apricots, sliced
5 g crème de peche
2 g malic acid

Prepare an ice bath. Heat the peaches, nectar, wine, and dried apricots in a saucepan over medium heat. Bring the liquid to a simmer and turn the heat to low. Cook the peaches, stirring occasionally to prevent burning, until they are soft and the liquid reduces down to a glazelike consistency, about 25 minutes. Transfer the mixture to a blender and puree on high speed until smooth. Pass the puree through a chinois and chill over the ice bath. Season with the crème de peche and malic acid. Reserve the puree in an airtight container, refrigerated, for up to 3 days.

ROSEMARY POWDER

20 g rosemary leaves

Spread the rosemary leaves on a microwave safe plate. Microwave for 2 minutes. Turn the plate and continue microwaving the rosemary and turning the plate every 30 seconds until the rosemary is dried. Let cool to room temperature. When cool, grind the rosemary in the spice grinder to a fine powder. Keep the rosemary powder in a dry, airtight container.

TO FINISH

Rosemary Ice Cream (page 292)
Peach Ice Cream (page 292)

Spoon crème anglaise and peach puree onto each plate side by side. Place one warm peach on the crème anglaise on each plate. Divide the shortcake among the plates. Scoop one quenelle each of rosemary ice cream and peach ice cream onto each plate. Sprinkle a little rosemary powder on top of the rosemary ice cream to finish.

ORANGE
Creamsicle with Vanilla

Serves 4

——

ORANGE SAUCE

> *205 g orange juice*
> *0.5 g xanthan gum*
> *20 g sugar*
> *0.5 g citric acid*

Blend the orange juice and xanthan gum in a blender on medium speed for 1 minute to fully hydrate the gum. Blend in the sugar and citric acid until fully dissolved. Reserve the orange sauce in an airtight container, refrigerated, for up to 3 days.

——

ORANGE MERINGUE

> *Grated zest of ¹/₂ orange*
> *2 egg whites*
> *75 g sugar*

Preheat the oven to 95°C/200°F. Place the grated zest on a paper towel to blot. Line a baking sheet with a nonstick baking mat and set aside. Using a stand mixer, whip the egg whites on medium speed until foamy, about 2 minutes. Slowly add the sugar and continue to whip to form stiff peaks, about 5 minutes. Remove the bowl from the mixer and gently fold in the zest. Transfer the meringue to a piping bag fitted with a #802 piping tip. Pipe the meringue in straight lines onto the prepared baking sheet and dehydrate in the oven until crunchy, about 1 hour. Let the meringue cool to room temperature. Break the meringue into 1.3-cm (¹/₂-inch) pieces and reserve in a dry, airtight container.

——

VANILLA CREAM

> *2 sheets gelatin*
> *125 g milk*
> *¹/₂ vanilla bean, split and scraped*
> *45 g sugar*
> *13 g cornstarch*
> *2 egg yolks*
> *30 g butter*
> *2 g salt*
> *200 g cream*

Bloom the gelatin in ice water. Heat the milk and vanilla bean in a saucepan over medium heat. When the milk is at a simmer, remove the pan from the heat and let steep at room temperature for 30 minutes. Strain the infused milk through a chinois. Heat the strained milk in a saucepan over medium heat. Add half of the sugar and whisk to dissolve. Remove the pan from the heat and keep warm. Combine the cornstarch and the remaining half of the sugar in a mixing bowl, whisking to combine. Add the egg yolks and whisk until smooth. Slowly incorporate half of the warm milk into the yolk mixture, whisking constantly to combine. Place the remaining milk over medium heat, then slowly whisk the yolk mixture into the remaining milk, while heating to a boil. Continue to boil the mixture, whisking constantly, until the cornstarch cooks out and fully thickens the milk, about 1 minute. Remove the milk from the heat. Squeeze any excess water from the bloomed gelatin and stir it into the warm thickened milk until melted. Add the butter and salt, stirring until emulsified. Transfer the vanilla cream to a container and cover with a layer of plastic wrap directly on top of the cream. Refrigerate until chilled, about 2 hours. Using a stand mixer, paddle the custard until smooth on medium speed, about 1 minute. Slowly mix in the cream until incorporated. Reserve the cream in an airtight container, refrigerated, for up to 1 day. When ready to serve, place the cream in the bowl of a stand mixer and whip with the whisk attachment until thickened and aerated, about 3 minutes. Transfer to a piping bag.

——

VANILLA FINANCIERS

> *5 egg whites*
> *63 g almond flour*
> *180 g sugar*
> *3 g salt*
> *6 g vanilla extract*
> *85 g all-purpose flour*
> *125 g butter*
> *¹/₂ vanilla bean, split and scraped*

Preheat the oven to 180°C/350°F. Spray a mini muffin pan and a 23-cm (9-inch) loaf pan with nonstick baking spray. Put the egg whites, almond flour, sugar, salt, and vanilla extract in a mixing bowl. Whisk together until smooth and well combined. Put the flour in a separate large mixing bowl. Melt the butter in a saucepan over low heat and add the vanilla bean pod and seeds. Pour the warm butter over the flour and whisk together until smooth. Immediately fold in the egg white mixture until just

CONTINUED

ORANGE CREAMSICLE WITH VANILLA, CONTINUED

combined. Remove and discard the vanilla bean pod. Fill
eight of the prepared mini muffin molds three-quarters
full with the batter. Pour the remaining batter into the
loaf pan. Bake the financiers in the oven until a cake tester
inserted in the center of each comes out clean, about
15 minutes for the mini muffins and 30 minutes for the
loaf. Let cool to room temperature. Break each mini
muffin in half and reserve in a dry, airtight container.
Turn the oven temperature down to 105°C/225°F.
Unmold the financier loaf. Slice the loaf crosswise into
1.5-mm (1/16-inch) thick slices and arrange in a single
layer on a baking sheet lined with parchment paper.
Dehydrate the slices in the oven until crispy, about
1½ hours. Let cool to room temperature and reserve
in a dry, airtight container.

ORANGE FOAM

1 sheet gelatin
150 g tangerine juice
50 g sugar
3 egg whites
4 g citric acid

Bloom the gelatin in ice water and prepare an ice bath.
Heat the tangerine juice in a saucepan over medium heat.
Add the sugar, stirring to dissolve. When the juice is at a
simmer, remove the pan from the heat. Transfer the juice
to a blender and start to blend on low speed. Squeeze
any excess water from the bloomed gelatin and add it to
the blender while the juice is still warm. Slowly add the
egg whites and citric acid. Continue to blend on medium
speed for 1 minute. Strain through a chinois and chill
the mixture over the ice bath until cooled but not set.
Transfer to an iSi canister and charge with two charges
of N_2O. Refrigerate, shaking every 20 minutes, until the
foam is fully chilled, about 2 hours.

TO FINISH

Orange segments
Orange Oil (page 285)
Vanilla Ice Cream (page 293)
Orange Sorbet (page 291)

Pipe vanilla cream onto each of four plates. Spread the
vanilla cream slightly with a spoon. Divide the vanilla
financier mini muffin pieces, orange meringues, and
orange segments on each plate over the vanilla cream.
Sauce each plate with orange sauce and orange oil.
Scoop one quenelle each of vanilla ice cream and orange
sorbet over each arrangement. Expel orange foam onto
each plate in several places. Finish each plate with several
vanilla financier slices.

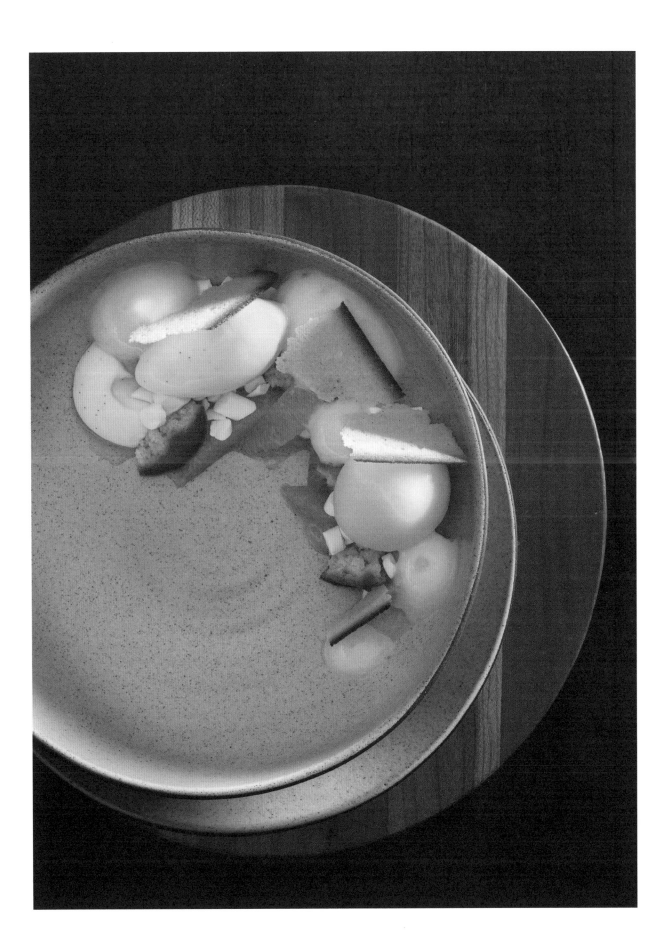

SWEET POTATO
with Chestnuts and Maple Syrup

Serves 4

———

CHESTNUT HONEY SHORTBREAD

30 g light brown sugar
75 g butter
100 g bread flour
35 g chestnut honey
1 g baking soda
1 g salt
1 g vanilla extract

Using a stand mixer with the paddle attachment, cream the brown sugar and butter together on medium speed until light and fluffy, about 5 minutes. Turn to low speed and add the bread flour, honey, baking soda, salt, and vanilla. Mix until incorporated, about 3 minutes. Roll the dough between two sheets of parchment paper to 1.5 mm (1/16 inch) thickness. Transfer the sandwiched dough to a baking sheet and refrigerate overnight. Preheat the oven to 175°C/350°F. Remove the top sheet of parchment paper and bake in the oven until set, about 15 minutes. Remove the shortbread from the oven and turn the temperature down to 95°C/200°F. Dehydrate the shortbread until crunchy throughout, about 1 hour. Remove from the oven and let cool to room temperature. Break into small pieces and reserve in a dry, airtight container.

———

GINGERBREAD CAKE

115 g flour
9 g ground cinnamon
8 g ground ginger
3 g baking soda
3 g salt
1 g ground cloves
75 g granulated sugar
65 g light brown sugar
1 egg
35 g grapeseed oil
5 g vanilla extract
13 g orange juice
200 g peeled sweet potato, coarsely grated

Preheat the oven to 175°C/350°F. Spray a 20-cm (8-inch) square cake pan with nonstick cooking spray and set aside. Combine the flour, cinnamon, ginger, baking soda, salt, and cloves in a mixing bowl and whisk to combine. Using a stand mixer, paddle together the sugars, egg, oil, and vanilla on medium speed until smooth and emulsified, about 3 minutes. Add the orange juice and mix to combine. Remove the bowl from the mixer and fold in the flour mixture until just combined. Fold in the sweet potato. Do not overmix. Transfer the batter to the prepared pan and place in the oven. Bake until a cake tester inserted in the center comes out clean, about 30 minutes. Remove from the oven and let cool to room temperature. Invert the cake onto a cutting board and trim the outer edges. Break the cake into 3.8-cm (1½-inch) pieces and reserve in a dry, airtight container.

———

CHESTNUT PUREE

200 g peeled chestnuts, coarsely chopped
110 g water
45 g sugar
½ vanilla bean, split and scraped
120 g cream
35 g chestnut honey

Preheat the oven to 150°C/325°F. Heat the chestnuts, water, sugar, and vanilla in a heatproof saucepan over medium heat. Bring to a boil, stirring to dissolve the sugar. Cover the pan and transfer the saucepan to the oven to cook the chestnuts until very tender, about 1 hour. Remove the pan from the oven. Remove and discard the vanilla bean.

Heat the pan over medium heat and bring the cooking liquid to a simmer. Reduce the liquid to a syruplike consistency, about 10 minutes. Combine the mixture in the blender with the cream and honey. Puree on high speed until smooth. Pass the puree through a fine-mesh tamis and reserve in an airtight container, refrigerated, for up to 3 days. When ready to serve, transfer the puree to a piping bag.

CONTINUED

SWEET POTATO CUSTARD

1 sweet potato, 125 g
3 sheets gelatin
90 g cream
90 g milk
1 vanilla bean, split and scraped
3 egg yolks
40 g granulated sugar
20 g light brown sugar
1 g salt
1 g ground ginger
1 g ground cinnamon

Preheat the oven to 175°C/375°F. Place the sweet potato on a baking sheet with a wire rack. Roast the sweet potato until tender, about 45 minutes. Remove from the oven and let rest at room temperature until cool enough to handle. Peel and discard the skins. Set aside the potato.

Bloom the gelatin in ice water. Heat the cream and milk in a saucepan over medium heat. Bring to a simmer and add the vanilla bean. Remove the pan from the heat. Cover and let steep at room temperature for 30 minutes. Uncover the pan and strain through a chinois. Transfer the cream to a clean saucepan and bring to a simmer over medium heat. Transfer the cream to a blender and start to blend on low speed. Add the yolks one at a time. Squeeze any excess water from the bloomed gelatin and blend into the mixture. Add the roasted and peeled sweet potato, sugars, salt, ginger, and cinnamon and puree on high speed until smooth. Strain the custard through a chinois and transfer to a mixing bowl. Place a layer of plastic wrap directly on top of the custard to cover and refrigerate until chilled, about 3 hours. Whip the custard smooth and reserve in an airtight container, refrigerated, for up to 3 days.

SWEET POTATO CHIPS

1 sweet potato
Canola oil, for frying
Sugar, for dusting

Using a mandoline, thinly slice the sweet potato into rounds. Heat 7.5 cm (3 inches) of oil in a heavy pot to 175°C/350°F. Fry the potato slices until golden brown and crispy, about 2 minutes. Place the chips on a paper towel to drain. Dust the chips with sugar on both sides while still warm.

TO FINISH

Aged maple syrup
Candied chestnuts (marrons glacés)
Maple Ice Cream (page 291)

Spread sweet potato custard onto each of four plates. Spoon chestnut puree onto each plate in a small circle. Using a spoon, create a well in the center of each circle of chestnut puree. Fill the well with maple syrup. Divide the gingerbread cake, chestnut honey shortbread, candied chestnuts, and sweet potato chips among the plates. Scoop quenelles of the maple ice cream onto each plate to finish.

APPLE
Variations with Buckwheat and Sage

Serves 4

APPLE PUREE

80 g butter
500 g peeled Macoun apples, thinly sliced
175 g dry Riesling
65 g sugar
40 g crème fraîche
1 g malic acid
1 g xanthan gum

Prepare an ice bath. Heat the butter in a saucepan over medium heat until foamy but not browned. Add the sliced apples to the pan. Turn the heat to low and cook, stirring frequently, until softened and without any color, about 15 minutes. Add the wine to the pan, bring to a simmer, and reduce the wine until almost dry. Remove the pan from the heat and transfer the cooked apples to a blender. Puree on high speed until smooth. Turn to low speed and slowly add the sugar, crème fraîche, malic acid, and xanthan gum. Turn to medium speed and blend for 1 minute to fully hydrate the gum. Pass the puree through a fine-mesh tamis and chill over the ice bath. Reserve the puree in an airtight container, refrigerated, for up to 3 days.

BUCKWHEAT CAKE

200 g apple cider
7 g baking soda
200 g Apple Puree, cold
240 g all-purpose flour
40 g buckwheat flour
7 g baking powder
90 g butter, softened
90 g sugar
80 g buckwheat honey
15 g vanilla extract
7 g salt
3 eggs

Preheat the oven to 175°C/350°F. Spray a 20-cm (8-inch) square cake pan with nonstick cooking spray and set aside. Heat the cider to a boil in a saucepan over medium heat. Whisk in the baking soda until fully dissolved and remove the pan from the heat. Whisk in the cold apple puree until incorporated and set aside. Combine both flours and the baking powder in a mixing bowl and set aside.

Using a stand mixer, cream together the butter, sugar, honey, vanilla, and salt on medium speed until light and fluffy, about 5 minutes. Turn to low speed and add the eggs one at a time. Mix on medium speed until smooth, about 3 minutes. Remove the bowl from the mixer and, using a rubber spatula, fold half of the flour mixture into the batter. Fold in the apple puree, followed by the remaining flour mixture, until just combined. Do not overmix. Transfer the batter to the prepared pan and bake until a cake tester inserted in the center comes out clean, about 45 minutes. Remove from the oven and let cool to room temperature. Invert the cake onto a cutting board and trim off the outer edges. Break into 5-cm (2-inch) pieces. Reserve the cake in a dry, airtight container for up to 3 days.

BUCKWHEAT BRITTLE CRUMBLE

85 g sugar
30 g butter
25 g water
20 g glucose syrup
17 g buckwheat honey
3 g salt
2 g baking soda
25 g Puffed Buckwheat (page 288)

Line a baking sheet with a nonstick baking mat. Heat the sugar, butter, water, glucose, and honey in a large saucepan over medium heat. Bring the mixture to a boil and cook, stirring constantly, until it becomes an amber colored caramel and reaches 146°C/295°F, about 15 minutes. Remove the pan from the heat. Using a rubber spatula, carefully stir in the salt, baking soda, and puffed buckwheat. Immediately pour the hot caramel out onto the prepared baking sheet. Using an offset spatula, spread the caramel out in a thin, even layer. Transfer the brittle to a food processor and pulse to a coarse crumble. Reserve the crumble in a dry, airtight container.

CONTINUED

GINGER PICKLED APPLES

125 g ginger juice
125 g water
75 g lemon juice
50 g sugar
1 Granny Smith apple

Combine the ginger juice, water, lemon juice, and sugar in a saucepan over medium heat and bring to a simmer, stirring to dissolve the sugar. Remove the pan from the heat and let cool to room temperature. Slice the cheeks off the apple and, using a mandoline, thinly slice into shaves. Immediately cover the apple shaves with the pickling liquid in an airtight container and refrigerate for 6 hours before serving.

APPLE TOFFEE GLAZE

480 g cream
120 g light brown sugar
70 g maple syrup
50 g Apple Cider Reduction (page 302)

Heat the ingredients in a heavy saucepan over medium heat and bring to a simmer. Cook, stirring occasionally, until dark brown in color and thick enough to coat the back of a spoon, about 20 minutes. Keep warm.

APPLE POACHING LIQUID

125 g apple cider
5 g buckwheat honey
Grated zest of 1/2 orange
1 cinnamon stick
1/2 vanilla bean, split and scraped
1 star anise pod
1 g cardamom pods
1 g Tellicherry peppercorns

Heat the ingredients in a saucepan over medium heat and bring to a boil. Remove the pan from the heat and cover. Let steep at room temperature for 30 minutes. Strain the liquid through a chinois and let cool to room temperature. Reserve the liquid in an airtight container, refrigerated, for up to 1 week.

POACHED APPLES

2 Honeycrisp apples
45 g Apple Poaching Liquid

Bring a large pot of water to a rolling boil and prepare an ice bath. Using a #25 melon baller, scoop out rounds from the apples. Seal the apple rounds and poaching liquid airtight in a sous vide bag. Submerge the bag in the water. Cook the apples until just tender, about 10 minutes. Shock the apples in the ice bath. When cold, remove the apples from the bag and reserve in the liquid in an airtight container, refrigerated.

APPLE COMPOTE

25 g butter
200 g peeled Macoun apples, diced 6 mm (1/4 inch)
1/2 vanilla bean, split and scraped
35 g dry Riesling
40 g sugar
30 g glucose syrup

Heat the butter in a saucepan over medium heat until foamy but not browned. Add the apples and vanilla. Cook, stirring occasionally, until the apples soften and release liquid, about 10 minutes. Add the wine, sugar, and glucose, stirring to incorporate, and bring to a simmer. Turn the heat to low and reduce until thick enough to coat the back of a spoon, about 5 minutes. Remove the pan from the heat and let cool to room temperature. Remove and discard the vanilla bean pod. Reserve the compote in an airtight container, refrigerated, for up to 3 days.

TO FINISH

Puffed Buckwheat (page 288)
Sage Ice Cream (page 293)

Freeze the cake until just firm, about 2 hours. Dip each piece in the apple toffee glaze to fully coat. Transfer the cake pieces to a wire rack set over a baking sheet to drain any excess glaze. Roll the cake pieces in puffed buckwheat to coat. Spoon the apple puree into the center of four plates. Spoon the buckwheat brittle crumble into the center, on top of the puree. Divide the glazed pieces of cake among the plates, along with the poached apples, apple compote, and pickled apples. Scoop quenelles of sage ice cream onto the buckwheat brittle crumble.

QUARK
Soufflé with Passion Fruit Sorbet

Serves 4

180 g quark
4 egg yolks
1/2 vanilla bean, split and scraped
115 g granulated sugar, plus more for dusting
14 g cornstarch
1 g salt
7 egg whites
3 g cream of tartar
Softened butter
Confectioners' sugar, for dusting
Passion Fruit Sorbet (page 291)

Preheat the oven to 175°C/350°F and prepare an ice bath. Combine the quark, egg yolks, and vanilla in a blender. Blend on medium speed until smooth, about 2 minutes. Slowly add one-third of the granulated sugar and the cornstarch and salt to the blender. Puree on high speed until smooth and warmed through, about 5 minutes. Transfer the mixture to a saucepan. Heat over medium heat and bring to a boil, whisking constantly. Cook the mixture, whisking to prevent burning, until thickened and the cornstarch is cooked out, about 5 minutes. Strain the mixture through a chinois and chill over the ice bath. Using a stand mixer, paddle the cold thickened quark mixture smooth on medium speed, about 3 minutes. Refrigerate. Whip the egg whites until foamy in a stand mixer on medium speed, about 3 minutes. Slowly add the remaining two-thirds of the granulated sugar and cream of tartar and continue to whip to stiff peaks, about 7 minutes. While whipping the egg whites, liberally brush the insides of four 9-cm (3 1/2-inch) cast-iron cocottes with butter and then dust with granulated sugar. Set aside. Transfer the cold quark cream to a large mixing bowl. Fold the whipped whites into the cream in three additions. Do not overmix. Fill each cocotte with the soufflé mixture. Using an offset spatula, scrape the tops to make level. Gently tap the sides to deflate any air pockets. Wipe the sides clean with a paper towel and place in the oven. Bake the soufflés until risen and golden brown, about 12 minutes. Remove the soufflés from the oven and dust the tops with confectioners' sugar. Serve immediately with passion fruit sorbet.

LEMON
Tart with Ricotta and Almond

Serves 4

TARTE CITRON FILLING

3 sheets gelatin
9 eggs
1 egg yolk
425 g sugar
1 g salt
275 g lemon juice
Grated zest of 3 lemons
20 g butter
4 g vanilla extract

Preheat the oven to 150°C/300°F. Line two 23 by 33-cm (9 by 13-inch) rimmed baking sheets with plastic wrap. Bloom the gelatin in ice water. Combine the eggs, egg yolk, sugar, salt, lemon juice, and zest in a mixing bowl and whisk thoroughly until smooth. Cook the mixture over a double boiler while whisking frequently, until the mixture is lightly thickened and pale yellow, about 15 minutes. Remove the bowl from heat. Squeeze any excess water from the bloomed gelatin and stir into the lemon mixture. Add the butter and vanilla, stirring until the mixture is fully emulsified. Strain the lemon filling through a chinois and pour onto one of the prepared baking sheets. Place the baking sheet in a baking dish and add warm water to the baking dish to just below the rim of the baking sheet. Bake the filling in the oven until just set, about 25 minutes. Remove the filling from the oven and let cool to room temperature. Cover with plastic wrap and transfer the filling to the freezer. Freeze the filling overnight. Using a 7-cm (2¾-inch) ring mold, punch out four rounds. Immediately transfer the lemon rounds onto the other prepared baking sheet. Cover with plastic wrap and reserve frozen until ready to assemble.

ALMOND SHORTBREAD

125 g butter, cold
60 g light brown sugar
175 g flour
50 g almonds, coarsely chopped
4 g salt

Preheat the oven to 160°C/325°F. Line a baking sheet with parchment paper. Using a stand mixer, paddle the ingredients together on low speed until just combined, keeping the dough in large chunks. Transfer the dough to the prepared baking sheet and bake until golden brown, about 30 minutes, stirring every 10 minutes to evenly brown the shortbread. Remove from the oven and let cool to room temperature. Reserve and set aside half of the shortbread for finishing. Transfer the remaining half to a food processor and pulse several times to a coarse crumble. Reserve the crumbled and whole shortbread separately in dry, airtight containers.

SHORTBREAD GLAZE

180 g all-purpose flour
110 g almond flour
110 g butter, cold
90 g confectioners' sugar
2 g salt
50 g grapeseed oil

Preheat the oven to 160°C/325°F. Line a baking sheet with parchment paper. Using a stand mixer, paddle both flours, butter, confectioners' sugar, and salt on low speed until the dough forms a crumbly texture. Transfer to the baking sheet and bake until golden brown, about 25 minutes, stirring every 10 minutes to evenly brown the shortbread. Let cool to room temperature. Transfer the mixture to a food processor and pulse to a fine crumble. Transfer the crumble to a blender and blend in the oil on low speed. Once fully incorporated, puree on high until the shortbread becomes liquefied. Reserve the shortbread glaze in an airtight container, refrigerated, for up to 1 week.

LEMON CONFIT

115 g sugar
60 g water
15 g glucose syrup
1 lemon, sliced 1.5 mm (¹/₁₆ inch) thick
Simple Syrup (page 300)

Heat the sugar, water, and glucose in a saucepan over medium heat. Cook, stirring, until the sugars dissolve. Remove the pan from the heat and set aside. Place the lemon slices in a clean saucepan with enough cold water to cover the bottom. Fill the pan with ice cubes. Heat over low heat until the ice completely melts and the water

CONTINUED

265

reaches 80°C/176°F. Carefully drain the lemons and refill the pan with the same amount of ice water. Return the heat to low and repeat the process four more times. After the fifth time, cover the lemon slices with the warm sugar mixture and heat over low heat until the mixture reaches 82°C/180°F. Remove the pan from the heat and let cool to room temperature. Repeat this process up to two more times until the pith appears nearly translucent. Remove the pan from the heat and let the lemons cool to room temperature in the syrup. Carefully drain the lemons from the syrup and cover with cold simple syrup. Store, refrigerated, for up to 2 days.

_____

LEMON MARMALADE

1 lemon, quartered and sliced 1.5 mm (¹/₁₆ inch) thick
250 g Simple Syrup (page 300)
15 g glucose syrup

Place the lemon slices in a saucepan with enough cold water to cover the bottom. Fill the pan with ice cubes. Heat over low heat until the ice completely melts and the water reaches 80°C/176°F. Carefully drain the lemons and refill the pan with the same amount of ice water. Return the heat to low. Repeat the process four more times. After the fifth time, cover the lemon slices with both syrups and heat over low heat. Bring to 107°C/225°F and cook until the pith appears nearly translucent, about 30 minutes. Remove the pan from the heat and let cool to room temperature in the syrup. Reserve the lemon marmalade in an airtight container, refrigerated, for up to 1 week. When ready to serve, let sit at room temperature for 30 minutes to temper.

_____

TO FINISH

4 Lemon Confit slices
Ricotta Ice Cream (page 292)
Lemon Oil (page 284)
Fleur de sel

Line a baking sheet with parchment paper. Place the almond shortbread crumble in a shallow baking dish. Gently rewarm the shortbread glaze in a saucepan over low heat until fluid. Using a fork, immediately dip each frozen round of tarte citron filling into the warm shortbread glaze and transfer these directly onto the almond shortbread crumble. Gently pick up each round, checking for an even bottom coating of crumble, and transfer to the baking sheet. Freeze until firm. When firm, cut each tart in half and place one cut tart on each of four plates. Divide the remaining almond shortbread crumble in a small pile next to each tart. Divide the lemon confit, lemon marmalade, and almond shortbread pieces among the plates. Scoop one quenelle of ricotta ice cream onto each plate, on the almond shortbread crumble. Finish each plate with lemon oil and fleur de sel.

MILK AND HONEY

Serves 4

HONEY BRITTLE

200 g sugar
50 g water
60 g butter
50 g honey
8 g salt
3 g baking soda

Line a baking sheet with a nonstick baking mat. Heat the sugar, water, butter, and honey in a heavy saucepan over medium heat. Bring to a boil, stirring with a rubber spatula, until the sugar is fully dissolved and turns amber colored, about 6 minutes. Stir in the salt and baking soda. Once fully incorporated, remove the pan from the heat and turn the caramel out onto the prepared baking sheet. Spread the brittle thinly and evenly and let cool to room temperature. Transfer to a food processor and pulse several times for a coarse crumble. Reserve the brittle in a dry, airtight container.

DEHYDRATED MILK FOAM

400 g milk
80 g glucose syrup

Preheat the oven to 65°C/150°F. Line a 23 by 33-cm (9 by 13-inch) rimmed baking sheet with acetate. Heat the milk and glucose in a saucepan over medium heat to 82°C/180°F. Remove the pan from the heat and froth using an immersion blender. Using a large spoon, scoop just the foam out onto the prepared baking sheet; avoid transferring any liquid. Scoop enough foam to fill the baking sheet, refrothing the milk as needed. Transfer the foam to the oven and dehydrate until crispy throughout, about 8 hours. Let the foam cool to room temperature. Break into small pieces and reserve in a dry, airtight container for up to 2 days.

HONEY-OATMEAL CRUMBLE

145 g butter, softened
65 g sugar
80 g honey
3 g salt
2 g vanilla extract
150 g flour
50 g rolled oats
1 g baking soda

Preheat the oven to 165°C/325°F. In a stand mixer, paddle together the butter, sugar, honey, salt, and vanilla. Add the flour, oats, and baking soda, mixing until just combined. Roll the dough out on a piece of parchment paper to 6 mm (¼ inch) thick, then transfer to a baking sheet and bake until golden brown, about 15 minutes. Turn the oven down to 65°C/150°F and continue to bake until crunchy throughout, about 30 minutes. Remove from the oven and let cool to room temperature. Break into small pieces and reserve in an airtight container for up to 2 days.

TO FINISH

Milk Ice (page 291)
Buckwheat honey

Divide the dehydrated milk foam, honey brittle, and honey-oatmeal crumble among four bowls. Scoop two quenelles of milk ice into each bowl. Drizzle lines of buckwheat honey across the top of one quenelle in each bowl.

ESPRESSO
Affogato with Cocoa Nibs

Serves 4

COCOA NIB BRITTLE

80 g cocoa nibs
Grated zest of ½ orange
135 g sugar
40 g butter
40 g water
30 g glucose syrup
2 g baking soda
2 g salt

Preheat the oven to 175°C/350°F. Line a baking sheet with a nonstick baking mat. Spread the cocoa nibs in an even layer on a baking sheet lined with parchment paper and toast in the oven until aromatic, about 8 minutes. Immediately place the toasted nibs in a mixing bowl with the orange zest, tossing together to combine. Heat the sugar, butter, water, and glucose in a heavy saucepan over medium heat. Cook, stirring frequently with a rubber spatula, until the sugar is fully dissolved and turns amber colored, about 6 minutes. Stir in the toasted nibs, baking soda, and salt. Once fully incorporated, remove the pan from the heat. Quickly turn the caramel out onto the prepared baking sheet and spread thinly and evenly. Let cool to room temperature. Transfer to a food processor and pulse several times for a coarse crumble. Reserve the brittle in a dry, airtight container.

ESPRESSO FOAM

4 sheets gelatin
185 g espresso
60 g sugar
½ vanilla bean, split and scraped
4 egg whites
2 g salt

Bloom the gelatin in ice water and set aside. Heat the espresso in a saucepan over low heat to 82°C/180°F. Remove the pan from the heat and whisk in the sugar until fully dissolved. Add the vanilla bean to the pan. Cover the pan and let steep at room temperature for 20 minutes. Squeeze any excess water from the bloomed gelatin and stir into the infused espresso until melted. Strain through a chinois and blend in the egg whites

using an immersion blender. Season with the salt and transfer to an iSi canister. Charge with 2 charges of N_2O and refrigerate, shaking every 20 minutes, until very cold, about 3 hours.

COCOA NIB TUILE

65 g cocoa nibs
4 g cocoa powder
115 g sugar
60 g butter
50 g glucose syrup
35 g milk
3 g salt

Place the nibs in a mixing bowl with the cocoa powder, tossing together to combine. Heat the sugar, butter, glucose, milk, and salt in a heavy saucepan over medium heat. Bring the mixture to a boil, stirring frequently with a rubber spatula. Continue to cook until the mixture reaches 106°C/223°F. Remove the pan from the heat and stir in the cocoa nibs. Pour the mixture out onto a work surface lined with parchment paper. Immediately place another sheet of parchment paper directly on top and roll out as thinly as possible. Keep the tuile sandwiched between parchment and transfer to a baking sheet. Freeze until set, about 3 hours. Preheat the oven to 175°C/350°F. Remove the top parchment and place in the oven. Bake the tuile until any large bubbles disappear, about 7 minutes. Let the tuile cool to room temperature and break into 2.5-cm (1-inch) pieces. Reserve the tuile in a dry, airtight container.

TO FINISH

Vanilla Ice Cream (page 293)
Espresso Granita (page 290)

Divide the brittle crumble among four bowls. Scoop three quenelles of vanilla ice cream into each bowl on the crumble. Spoon the espresso granita on and around the ice cream scoops. Expel the espresso foam in each bowl in several spots. Garnish each plate with several cocoa nib tuiles.

COOKIES AND CREAM

Makes 16 pieces

———

CHOCOLATE SHORTBREAD GLAZE

125 g flour
110 g butter, cold
90 g confectioners' sugar
25 g cocoa powder
2 g salt
50 g grapeseed oil

Preheat the oven to 175°C/350°F. Line a baking sheet with parchment paper. Using a stand mixer, paddle together the flour, butter, confectioners' sugar, cocoa, and salt on low speed to form a coarse crumble, about 4 minutes. Transfer the mixture onto the prepared baking sheet and spread in a thin layer. Bake until evenly browned, about 25 minutes. Remove from the oven and transfer the crumble to a blender. Blend on low speed until finely ground, about 2 minutes. Continue to blend and slowly add the oil. Puree on high speed until completely smooth. Reserve in an airtight container, refrigerated, for up to 1 week. When ready to assemble, gently rewarm the glaze in a saucepan over low heat until fluid.

———

CHOCOLATE COOKIE CRUMBLE

150 g sugar
90 g butter
67 g flour
46 g cocoa powder
1 egg
3 g salt

Using a stand mixer with the paddle attachment, cream the sugar and butter together on medium speed until combined, about 3 minutes. Turn to low speed and add the flour, cocoa, egg, and salt to the bowl. Mix on low speed just until incorporated, about 3 minutes. Roll the dough between two sheets of parchment paper to 1.5 mm (¹⁄₁₆ inch) thickness. Transfer the parchment-sandwiched dough to a baking sheet and refrigerate overnight.

Preheat the oven to 175°C/350°F. Remove the top sheet of parchment paper and bake in the oven until set, about 10 minutes. Remove the cookie from the oven and turn the oven down to 95°C/200°F. When the oven has come to temperature, return the cookie to the oven and dehydrate until crunchy throughout, about 45 minutes. Remove from the oven and let cool to room temperature.

Transfer the cookie sheet to a food processor and pulse several times to a coarse crumble. Reserve in a dry, airtight container.

———

TO FINISH

Vanilla Ice Cream (page 293)

Scoop sixteen quenelles of vanilla ice cream onto a baking sheet lined with acetate. Immediately freeze the scoops in the freezer until very firm, about 3 hours. Line a separate baking sheet with acetate and set aside in the freezer to keep cold. Working with the ice cream scoops one at a time, dip each scoop into the chocolate shortbread glaze and then immediately transfer the dipped scoop into the chocolate cookie crumble using a large fork. Roll each scoop around in the crumble to evenly coat and transfer to the frozen prepared baking sheet. Freeze until the glaze is completely set, about 1 hour. Reserve the cookies and cream scoops in an airtight container, frozen.

CHOCOLATE
Tart with Hazelnuts and Caramel

Serves 4

———

HAZELNUT SUCRÉE

110 g butter
75 g sugar
60 g hazelnut flour
1 egg
16 g water
185 g flour
2 g salt

Using a stand mixer with the paddle attachment, cream together the butter, sugar, and hazelnut flour on medium speed until light and fluffy, about 5 minutes. Add the egg and water and mix until incorporated, about 2 minutes. Add the flour and salt and mix until just combined. Roll the dough between two sheets of parchment paper to 1.5 mm (1/16 inch) thickness. Transfer the sandwiched dough to a baking sheet and refrigerate overnight.

———

PRALINE CARAMEL

150 g cream
60 g glucose syrup
95 g sugar
40 g butter
25 g praline paste
10 g 40 percent cacao chocolate, chopped
1/2 vanilla bean, split and scraped
3 g salt

Heat the cream and glucose in a saucepan over low heat to just under a simmer. Stir to incorporate and remove the pan from the heat. Keep warm. Heat the sugar in a large heavy pan over medium heat. As the sugar starts to brown around the edges, gently swirl the pan so that the sugar caramelizes evenly. When the sugar has completely melted and turned a deep brown color, about 15 minutes, carefully add the warm cream to the pan. Be careful; the mixture will bubble vigorously. Stir with a rubber spatula and continue to cook and stir occasionally, until the mixture reaches 118°C/244°F, about 25 minutes. Remove the pan from the heat and allow to cool to 80°C/176°F. Using an immersion blender, blend in the butter, praline paste, chocolate, vanilla, and salt until fully incorporated.

Strain the caramel through a chinois and reserve in an airtight container, refrigerated, for up to 1 week. When ready to assemble, gently rewarm the caramel in a saucepan over low heat until fluid.

———

PRALINE GANACHE

100 g 55 percent cacao chocolate, chopped
125 g cream
30 g praline paste

Place the chocolate in a heatproof bowl and set aside. Combine the cream and praline paste in a saucepan. Bring to just under a boil over medium heat, stirring to incorporate. Pour the hot cream over the chocolate and let stand at room temperature for 1 minute. Using an immersion blender, blend the ganache until fully emulsified. Keep warm.

———

CHOCOLATE TARTS

Hazelnut Sucrée
Praline Caramel
Praline Ganache
Fleur de sel

Preheat the oven to 160°C/325°F. Remove the top layer of parchment paper from the hazelnut sucrée. Using a fork, lightly prick the dough. This will help keep the dough from bubbling up as it bakes. Divide the dough into four equal-size portions. Using the parchment paper as an aid, line four 6-cm (2 3/8-inch) tart pans with the dough. Freeze the tart shells until firm, about 2 hours. Bake the tart shells in the oven until set, about 20 minutes. Allow to cool on a wire rack. Fill each tart shell halfway with the praline caramel. Refrigerate the tart shells until the caramel is firm, about 2 hours. Top off each tart shell with the praline ganache. Let stand at room temperature until set, about 1 hour. Finish each tart with fleur de sel just before serving.

———

TOASTED HAZELNUTS

130 g hazelnuts, peeled

Preheat the oven to 175°C/350°F. Spread the hazelnuts on a baking sheet lined with parchment paper. Toast in the oven until golden brown and aromatic, about 6 minutes. Remove from the oven and reserve in a dry, airtight container.

CONTINUED

HAZELNUT BRITTLE

100 g sugar
30 g butter
30 g water
22 g glucose syrup
2 g baking soda
4 g salt
85 g Toasted Hazelnuts

Line a baking sheet with a nonstick baking mat and set aside. Heat the sugar, butter, water, and glucose in a heavy saucepan over medium heat. Cook, stirring frequently with a rubber spatula, until the sugar is fully dissolved and turns amber colored, about 6 minutes. Stir in the baking soda and salt. Once fully incorporated, fold in the nuts and remove the pan from the heat. Quickly turn the caramel out onto the prepared sheet and spread thinly and evenly. Let cool to room temperature. Transfer to a food processor and pulse several times for a coarse crumble. Reserve the brittle in a dry, airtight container.

CANDIED HAZELNUTS

120 g honey
50 g sugar
Peeled zest of 1/2 lemon
5 g lemon juice
1/2 vanilla bean, split and scraped
45 g Toasted Hazelnuts

Heat the honey, sugar, zest, juice, and vanilla in a saucepan over medium heat. Bring the syrup to a boil, stirring occasionally. Remove the pan from the heat and let sit at room temperature for 20 minutes to steep. Strain the syrup through a chinois and transfer to a clean saucepan. Heat to a simmer over medium heat. Add the hazelnuts and turn the heat to low. Continue to simmer, stirring occasionally, until reduced to a glazelike consistency, about 30 minutes. Remove the pan from the heat and let cool to room temperature. Drain before serving.

PRALINE POWDER

20 g praline paste
7 g tapioca maltodextrin
Salt

Place the praline paste in a bowl and whisk in the tapioca maltodextrin. Thoroughly whisk together until the mixture turns into a powder. Season with salt.

COCOA SAUCE

60 g water
15 g cocoa powder

Pour the water into a mixing bowl and whisk in the cocoa powder until fully dissolved.

TO FINISH

Chocolate Praline Milk Ice (page 290)
Hazelnut oil

Place one chocolate tart on each of four plates. Spoon the hazelnut brittle next to each tart. Scoop one scoop of chocolate praline milk ice over the hazelnut brittle. Spoon the praline powder over the milk ice. Garnish each plate with candied hazelnuts and cocoa sauce. Break the sauce with hazelnut oil to finish.

CHOCOLATE
Malted Ganache with Malted Ice Cream

Serves 4

CHOCOLATE COOKIE SHARDS AND CRUMBLE

225 g sugar
130 g butter
5 g salt
1 egg
98 g flour
69 g cocoa powder

Using a stand mixer with the paddle attachment, cream the sugar and butter together on medium speed until combined, about 3 minutes. Turn to low speed and add the salt, egg, flour, and cocoa. Mix just until incorporated, about 3 minutes. Roll the dough between two sheets of parchment paper to 1.5 mm (1/16 inch) thickness. Transfer the parchment-sandwiched dough to a baking sheet and refrigerate overnight. Preheat the oven to 175°C/350°F. Remove the top sheet of parchment paper and bake until set, about 10 minutes. Remove the cookie from the oven and turn the oven down to 95°C/200°F. When the oven has come to temperature, return the cookie to the oven and dehydrate until crunchy throughout, about 45 minutes. Let cool to room temperature. Break half of the cookie into shards and transfer the remaining half to a food processor. Pulse several times to a coarse crumble. Reserve the shards and crumble separately in dry, airtight containers.

MALTED MILK GANACHE

100 g 40 percent cacao milk chocolate, chopped
200 g cream
30 g malted milk powder
1 g salt

Place the chocolate in a heatproof bowl and prepare an ice bath. Heat the cream to a boil in a saucepan over medium heat. Whisk in the malted milk powder and salt until fully dissolved. Pour over the chocolate. Let sit at room temperature for 1 minute. Blend the ganache using an immersion blender until fully emulsified. Chill over the ice bath. When cold, transfer to a piping bag and refrigerate until ready to serve.

CHOCOLATE CAKE

250 g sugar
190 g flour
95 g cocoa powder
4 g baking soda
3 g baking powder
2 g salt
100 g grapeseed oil
125 g milk
125 g brewed coffee
1 egg
8 g vanilla extract

Preheat the oven to 175°C/350°F. Spray a 20-cm (8-inch) square cake pan with nonstick cooking spray and set aside. Place the sugar, flour, cocoa powder, baking soda, baking powder, and salt in a mixing bowl. Stir to combine. In a separate mixing bowl, combine the oil, milk, coffee, egg, and vanilla extract and whisk to combine. Mix the milk mixture into the flour mixture and whisk together until just incorporated. Do not overmix. Transfer the batter to the prepared pan and bake in the oven until a cake tester inserted in the center comes out clean, about 35 minutes. Let the cake cool to room temperature. Invert the cake onto a cutting board. Trim the top and outer edges. Break the remaining cake into a coarse crumble and reserve in a dry, airtight container.

CHOCOLATE FONDANT

185 g 70 percent cacao chocolate, chopped
185 g 55 percent cacao chocolate, chopped
185 g butter
95 g sugar
7 eggs
Malted milk powder

Preheat the oven to 160°C/325°F. Line a 20-cm (8-inch) square cake pan with plastic wrap and place inside a large baking dish. Heat both chocolates over a double boiler, stirring together until fully melted. Add the butter and continue to stir until fully emulsified. Remove the bowl from the heat and set aside. Using a stand mixer, whip the sugar and eggs together on medium speed until smooth and pale yellow, about 5 minutes. Stir the egg mixture into the chocolate using a rubber spatula. Pour the mixture into the prepared pan. Carefully pour warm water into the baking dish so that the water level matches that of the fondant. Wrap the pan with aluminum foil. Place in the oven and bake in the water bath until set,

CONTINUED

about 1 hour. Remove the fondant from the water bath and refrigerate until cold, about 3 hours. Turn the fondant out onto a cutting board. Using a wet knife, slice into 2.5-cm (1-inch) pieces. Reserve the fondant in an airtight container, refrigerated, for up to 1 week. Just before serving, roll the fondant in malted milk powder to fully coat.

———

TO FINISH

Malted milk powder
Fleur de sel
Malted Milk Ice Cream (page 290)

Pipe the malted milk ganache onto each of four plates. Spread the ganache slightly with a spoon. Plate the cake crumble in a line over the ganache. Spoon the cookie crumble over the cake. Dust the cookie crumble lightly with malted milk powder and season with fleur de sel. Divide the chocolate fondant among the four plates, arranging them over the cookie crumble. Scoop a quenelle of the malted milk ice cream onto the center of the crumble on each plate. Finish with the chocolate cookie shards.

BISCOTTI

Makes about 24 pieces

155 g sugar
2 g salt
Grated zest of 1/2 orange
1 vanilla bean, split and scraped
3 g whole fennel seeds
1 g ground fennel seeds
1 egg
45 g butter, melted
40 g olive oil
200 g flour
75 g whole almonds, skin on
75 g shelled pistachios
40 g golden raisins
40 g Thompson raisins
5 g baking powder

Preheat the oven to 160°C/325°F. Combine the sugar, salt, orange zest, vanilla seeds, and whole and ground fennel seeds in the bowl of a stand mixer. Paddle on low speed for 3 minutes. Add the egg and mix until just combined. Add the melted butter and oil and mix just until emulsified. Add the flour, almonds, pistachios, both kinds of raisins, and baking powder and mix until just incorporated. Turn the dough out onto a baking sheet lined with parchment paper. Form the dough into two loaves, 30 by 15 cm (9 by 6 inches) each. Bake the loaves in the oven until lightly browned around the edges, about 45 minutes. Remove the loaves from the oven and let cool to room temperature. Turn the oven temperature to 120°C/250°F. Transfer the loaves to a cutting board and make crosswise slices 2 cm (3/4 inch) thick. Transfer the slices, cut side facing up, to another baking sheet lined with parchment paper. Bake in the oven until hardened, about 25 minutes. Remove the biscotti from the oven and transfer to a wire rack to let cool to room temperature. Reserve the biscotti in a dry, airtight container for up to 1 week.

BASICS

BUTTERS, OILS, AND DRESSINGS

BONE MARROW FAT

Makes about 100 g

6 beef marrow bones, about 1.4 kg

Place the marrow bones in a large mixing bowl. Pour enough hot water over the bones to cover and let sit at room temperature for 10 minutes. Drain the marrow bones and discard the water. Carefully extract the marrow by pushing it out through the wider ends of the bones. In an airtight container, combine the marrow pieces with enough ice water to generously cover. Refrigerate for 24 hours, changing out the ice water at least twice. Drain the marrow well and discard the soaking water.

Coarsely chop the marrow and place in a saucepan with a splash of water. Heat the marrow over low heat to begin rendering. Cook, stirring occasionally, until the water has completely evaporated and the rendered fat appears clear, about 10 minutes. Strain the fat through cheesecloth. Reserve the fat in an airtight container, refrigerated, for up to 1 week.

BROWN BUTTER

Makes about 680 g

1 kg butter, cubed

Heat the butter in a large saucepan over medium heat. As the butter melts and starts to foam, whisk occasionally to evenly cook. Turn the heat to low and continue to whisk occasionally to prevent burning. Cook until the butter turns dark brown and has a nutty aroma, about 30 minutes. Immediately strain the butter through a coffee filter, discarding the solids. Let cool to room temperature and reserve in an airtight container, refrigerated, for up to 1 week, or frozen for up to 1 month.

BUTTERMILK VINAIGRETTE

Makes about 260 g

100 g buttermilk
100 g crème fraîche
30 g olive oil
10 g white balsamic vinegar
5 g salt

Using an immersion blender, blend the buttermilk, crème fraîche, oil, and vinegar together until fully emulsified. Season with salt and reserve in an airtight container, refrigerated, for up to 5 days.

CHILE OIL

Makes about 185 g

200 g grapeseed oil
10 g dried red pepper flakes

Combine the oil and pepper flakes in a heatproof bowl. Cover tightly with plastic wrap and place over a double boiler. Heat the water to 91°C/195°F, just under a simmer, and cook the oil for 1½ hours. Remove the bowl from the double boiler and uncover. Strain the oil through cheesecloth and reserve in an airtight container, refrigerated, for up to 1 week.

CHIVE OIL

Makes about 200 g

200 g grapeseed oil
60 g chives, coarsely chopped

Prepare an ice bath. Combine the ingredients in a blender and pulse together until just blended, but not smooth. Transfer the mixture to a saucepan and heat over medium heat. Cook, whisking constantly, until heated to 71°C/160°F. Remove the pan from the heat and chill over the ice bath until cold. Strain the oil through a coffee filter refrigerated overnight. Discard the drained chives and reserve the oil in an airtight container, refrigerated, for up to 1 week.

LEMON OIL

Makes about 350 g

400 g grapeseed oil
45 g grated lemon zest (from about 15 lemons)

Prepare an ice bath. Combine the oil and zest in a bain-marie. Cover tightly with plastic wrap and place in a large pot filled halfway with water. Heat the pot over low heat and bring the water temperature to 91°C/195°F, just under a simmer. Cook the oil in the water bath for 1½ hours. Remove the bain-marie from the water bath and chill over the ice bath until cold. Cover and refrigerate overnight. Strain the oil through a chinois, discarding the zest. Reserve the lemon oil in an airtight container, refrigerated, for up to 1 week.

LEMON VINAIGRETTE

Makes about 150 g

50 g lemon juice
50 g Lemon Oil (page 284)
50 g olive oil
7 g salt

Whisk the ingredients together to combine. Refrigerate in an airtight container for up to 3 days.

ORANGE OIL

Makes about 150 g

180 g olive oil
Grated zest of 2 oranges

Combine the oil and orange zest in a heatproof bowl and cover with plastic wrap. Heat the orange oil in a double boiler over low heat and prepare an ice bath. Cook the oil for 1 hour to infuse. Strain the oil through a chinois. Chill the oil over the ice bath. Reserve the orange oil in an airtight container, refrigerated, for up to 1 week.

PARSLEY OIL

Makes about 100 g

50 g flat-leaf parsley leaves
120 g grapeseed oil

Prepare an ice bath. Combine the parsley and oil in a blender. Pulse together until just blended but not smooth. Transfer the parsley mixture to a saucepan and heat over low heat. Cook, whisking constantly, until the mixture heats to 71°C/160°F. Immediately chill over the ice bath until cold. Strain the oil through a coffee filter refrigerated overnight. Discard the strained parsley and reserve the oil in an airtight container, refrigerated, for up to 1 week.

SAVORY OIL

Makes about 100 g

40 g savory leaves
125 g olive oil

Prepare an ice bath. Place the savory in a heatproof bowl. Heat the oil to 82°C/180°F in a saucepan over low heat. Remove the oil from the heat and pour over the savory to completely cover. Let sit at room temperature for 15 minutes to steep. Strain the oil through a coffee filter. Discard the strained savory and let cool to room temperature. Reserve in an airtight container, refrigerated, for up to 1 week.

SMOKED BUTTER

Makes about 450 g

450 g butter, cubed

Preheat the broiler. Soak 35 g of applewood chips in cold water for 10 minutes. Drain. Line a roasting pan with aluminum foil. Arrange ten charcoal briquettes in a single layer in the pan and place under the broiler until lit, about 15 minutes. Remove the pan from the broiler and sprinkle enough wood chips on top to put out any live flames, but not so much that the embers are smothered. Turn the broiler off and let the oven cool. Place the cubed butter in single layer in a roasting pan. Fill two separate roasting pans with ice. Place the butter, charcoal, and ice in the oven that is shut off and tightly shut the oven door to smoke. Check to make sure the ice has not completely melted. After 15 minutes, remove the butter from the oven. The butter should be partially melted, but not completely. Immediately whisk the butter until smooth. Cover with plastic wrap and refrigerate until chilled. Reserve in an airtight container, frozen, for up to 1 month.

WHITE BALSAMIC VINAIGRETTE

Makes about 265 g

195 g olive oil
65 g white balsamic vinegar
8 g salt

Combine the ingredients in a mixing bowl and whisk until fully emulsified. Reserve the vinaigrette in an airtight container, refrigerated, for up to 1 week.

CRUMBLES, DOUGHS, AND GRAINS

BLACK TRUFFLE POTATO BREAD

Makes 1 (23-cm/9-inch) loaf

1 russet potato, about 500 g
75 g sugar
13 g salt
500 g bread flour
2 eggs, plus 1 egg lightly beaten for egg wash
120 g water
30 g fresh yeast
100 g butter, softened
100 g black truffle, finely chopped

Preheat the oven to 175°C/350°F. Prick the potato several times with a fork and place on a baking sheet lined with parchment paper. Roast the potato in the oven until completely tender, about 1½ hours. Remove the potato from the oven and let cool until it can be handled. Peel the potato and discard the peels. Pass the potato through a ricer or a food mill. Spread the riced potato out on a baking sheet lined with parchment paper and let cool to room temperature. Combine the sugar and salt in a mixing bowl and set aside. Place 450 g of the riced potatoes, flour, eggs, water, and yeast in the bowl of a stand mixer. Paddle on low speed until just combined, about 3 minutes. Switch to the dough hook attachment and mix on medium speed until the gluten has developed and the dough springs back when pressed, about 7 minutes. Mix in the sugar and salt in three additions, waiting for the previous addition to fully incorporate before adding the next. Once fully incorporated, turn to low speed and add the butter all at once. Continue to mix until incorporated, about 5 minutes. Turn the dough out into a large mixing bowl lightly sprayed with nonstick cooking spray. Flip the dough over to evenly coat. Cover the bowl tightly with plastic wrap and refrigerate overnight to ferment.

Preheat the oven to 175°C/350°F. Lightly spray a 23 by 13-cm (9 by 5-inch) loaf pan with nonstick cooking spray. Uncover the bowl and press down on the dough to release the gas. Turn the dough out onto a clean work surface and roll out into a 23-cm (9-inch) square. Brush the surface with the egg wash and sprinkle the black truffle evenly over the dough. Roll the dough into a log and place it in the loaf pan, seam side down. Cover

the dough with a damp kitchen towel and let sit at room temperature until nearly doubled in size, about 2 hours. Uncover the loaf and bake in the oven until golden brown, about 50 minutes. Turn the loaf out of the pan and let cool to room temperature before slicing to serve. The bread may be tightly wrapped and kept, frozen, for up to 1 week.

BONE MARROW CRUSTS

Makes about 20 crusts

12 g olive oil
½ shallot, finely chopped
135 g Brioche Bread Crumbs (page 287)
105 g butter, softened
1 g thyme leaves
2 g salt
20 g bone marrow, diced 6 mm (¼ inch)

Heat the olive oil in a sauté pan over low heat. Add the shallot and sweat until translucent without any color, about 5 minutes. Transfer the shallot to a paper towel to drain and let cool to room temperature. Combine the shallot, bread crumbs, butter, thyme, and salt in the bowl of a stand mixer. Paddle on medium speed until fully incorporated, about 5 minutes. Add the marrow and mix until just combined. Roll the dough between two sheets of parchment paper to 3 mm (⅛ inch) thick. Transfer the parchment-sandwiched dough to a baking sheet and refrigerate overnight. Using a 6.7-cm (2⅝-inch) ring cutter, punch the dough into rounds. Reserve the punches in an airtight container, refrigerated, for up to 1 week.

BRIOCHE

Makes 1 (23-cm/9-inch) loaf

70 g sugar
12 g salt
500 g bread flour
5 eggs, plus 1 egg lightly beaten, for egg wash
100 g water
30 g fresh yeast
250 g butter, softened

Combine the sugar and salt in a mixing bowl and set aside. Combine the flour, eggs, water, and yeast in the bowl of a stand mixer. Paddle on low speed until just combined, about 3 minutes. Switch to the dough hook attachment and mix on medium speed until the gluten has developed and the dough springs back when pressed, about 7 minutes. Mix in the sugar and salt in three additions, waiting for the previous addition to fully incorporate before adding the next. Once fully incorporated, turn to low speed and add the butter all at once. Continue to mix until incorporated, about 5 minutes. Turn the dough out into a large mixing bowl lightly sprayed with nonstick cooking spray. Flip the dough over to evenly coat. Cover the bowl tightly with plastic wrap and refrigerate overnight to ferment.

Preheat the oven to 175°C/350°F. Lightly spray a 23 by 13-cm (9 by 5-inch) loaf pan with nonstick cooking spray. Uncover the bowl and press down on the dough to release the gas. Turn the dough out onto a clean work surface and roll out into a 23-cm (9-inch) square. Roll the dough into a log. Place the log in the loaf pan seam side down. Cover the dough with a damp kitchen towel and let sit at room temperature until nearly doubled in size, about 2 hours. Uncover the loaf and bake in the oven until golden brown, about 50 minutes. Turn the brioche out of the pan and let cool to room temperature before slicing to serve. The bread may be tightly wrapped and kept, frozen, for up to 1 week.

——

BRIOCHE BREAD CRUMBS

Makes about 250 g

2 loaves Brioche (page 286)

Preheat the oven to 95°C/200°F. Trim the outer crusts from the loaf and discard. Cut the loaf into 5-cm (2-inch) cubes and spread on a baking sheet lined with parchment paper. Dry in the oven until dehydrated throughout, about 6 hours. Remove the brioche from the oven and let cool to room temperature. Transfer to a food processor and grind to a fine crumb. Reserve the bread crumbs in a dry, airtight container, frozen, for up to 1 month.

——

COOKED BULGUR WHEAT

Makes about 650 g

¹/₂ onion, diced 2.5 cm (1 inch)
1 carrot, peeled and diced 2.5 cm (1 inch)
1 celery stalk, diced 2.5 cm (1 inch)
3 sprigs thyme
1 bay leaf
5 kg water
200 g bulgur wheat
Salt

Line a baking sheet with parchment paper. Tie the vegetables and herbs together in a cheesecloth sachet. Combine with the water and bulgur wheat in a pot.

Bring to a simmer over medium heat. Season the water with salt. Turn the heat to low. Gently simmer until tender, about 20 minutes. Drain well and discard the sachet. Spread the bulgur on the baking sheet and let cool to room temperature. Reserve in an airtight container, refrigerated, for up to 3 days. Let temper to room temperature before serving.

——

COOKED QUINOA

Makes about 500 g

5 kg water
300 g red or yellow quinoa
Salt

Bring the water to a boil in a pot over high heat. Add the quinoa and lightly season the water with salt. Turn the heat to medium. Simmer and cook the quinoa until tender, about 20 minutes. Drain the quinoa well and spread on a baking sheet. Let cool to room temperature and reserve in an airtight container, refrigerated, for up to 3 days. Let temper to room temperature before serving.

——

COOKED WHEAT BERRIES

Makes about 700 g

¹/₂ onion, diced 2.5 cm (1 inch)
1 carrot, peeled and diced 2.5 cm (1 inch)
1 celery stalk, diced 2.5 cm (1 inch)
3 sprigs thyme
1 bay leaf
5 kg water
300 g wheat berries
Salt

Line a baking sheet with parchment paper. Tie the vegetables and herbs together in a cheesecloth sachet. Combine with the water and wheat berries in a pot. Bring to a simmer over medium heat. Season the water with salt and turn the heat to low. Gently simmer and cook until tender, about 3 hours. Drain the wheat berries well and discard the sachet. Spread out onto the baking sheet and let cool to room temperature. Reserve the wheat berries in an airtight container, refrigerated, for up to 3 days. Let temper to room temperature before serving.

OLIVE BRIOCHE CRUSTS

Makes about 10 crusts

40 g Taggiasca olives, finely chopped
65 g Brioche Bread Crumbs (page 287)
65 g butter, softened
1 g salt

Put the chopped olives on a microwave-safe plate in a single layer. Microwave the olives on high in 45-second intervals until the olives are crispy throughout, about 3 minutes. Let the olives cool to room temperature. Transfer to a mixing bowl and combine with the bread crumbs, butter, and salt. Mix well using a rubber spatula and place in between two sheets of parchment paper. Roll the crust out to 3 mm (1/8 inch) thickness still sandwiched between the parchment, then cover with plastic wrap and refrigerate until firm, about 3 hours. Unwrap the crust and punch out portions using a 4-cm (1 1/2-inch) ring cutter. Reserve in an airtight container, refrigerated, for up to 3 days.

PASTA DOUGH

Makes about 10 sheets

400 g tipo 00 flour
3 eggs
2 egg yolks
6 g salt
Semolina flour

Combine the 00 flour, eggs, egg yolks, and salt in the bowl of a stand mixer. Using the dough hook attachment, mix on low speed until just combined, about 5 minutes. The mixture should appear quite dry and just barely come together. Turn to medium speed and mix until the flour is fully hydrated, about 3 minutes. Turn the dough out onto a clean work surface and knead by hand several times to form into a ball. Cover the dough tightly with plastic wrap and refrigerate overnight.

Unwrap the dough. On a clean work surface, roll the dough out using a rolling pin, just so it can fit through the pasta machine. Set the machine to the widest setting and begin running the pasta through the machine. Lower the thickness by one notch with each roll, until it reaches setting #2. Fold the pasta over itself in thirds. Rotate the pasta 90 degrees so that the uncreased side will pass through the machine. Return the machine to the widest setting and repeat the rolling process two more times. After the third pass, do not fold the dough in thirds. Continue to roll the dough, lowering the setting by half

a notch with each pass to setting #0. Cut the sheet into 30-cm (11 3/4-inch) long sheets. Stack the sheets, with a light dusting of semolina flour in between each layer to prevent sticking, and cover with a lightly dampened paper towel to prevent from drying. Cut the dough to the desired shape or form and refrigerate in an airtight container for up to 24 hours.

PUFFED BUCKWHEAT

Makes about 240 g

3 kg water
200 g buckwheat kasha
Canola oil, for frying
Salt

Preheat the oven to 95°C/200°F. Line a baking sheet with parchment paper. Heat the water and buckwheat in a large saucepan over medium heat. Bring to a boil and turn the heat to low. Simmer and cook the buckwheat until tender, about 20 minutes. Drain and rinse under cold running water. Transfer to the baking sheet and dry in the oven until dehydrated throughout, about 5 hours.

Heat 7.5 cm (3 inches) of canola oil in a heavy pot to 246°C/475°F. Quickly fry the buckwheat in the oil in small batches until puffed and crispy, about 5 seconds. Immediately place on a paper towel to drain and season with salt. Let cool to room temperature and reserve in a dry, airtight container.

PUFFED BULGUR WHEAT

Makes about 75 g

200 g Cooked Bulgur Wheat (page 287)
Canola oil, for frying
Salt

Preheat the oven to 95°F/200°F. Transfer the bulgur wheat to a baking sheet lined with parchment paper. Place the tray in the oven and dry until dehydrated throughout, about 5 hours.

Heat 7.5 cm (3 inches) of canola oil in a heavy pot to 246°C/475°F. Quickly fry the bulgur wheat in the oil in small batches until puffed and crispy, about 5 seconds. Immediately place on a paper towel to drain and season with salt. Let cool to room temperature and reserve in a dry, airtight container.

PUFFED QUINOA

Makes about 125 g

150 g Cooked Quinoa (page 287)
Canola oil, for frying
Salt

Preheat the oven to 95°F/200°F. Transfer the quinoa to a baking sheet lined with parchment paper. Place the sheet in the oven and dry until dehydrated throughout, about 4 hours.

Heat 7.5 cm (3 inches) of canola oil in a heavy pot to 246°C/475°F. Quickly fry the quinoa in the oil in small batches until puffed and crispy, about 5 seconds. Immediately place on a paper towel to drain and season with salt. Let cool to room temperature and reserve in a dry, airtight container.

PUMPERNICKEL CRISPS

Makes 12 crisps

6 (3-mm/⅛-inch) slices pumpernickel bread
Salt
Olive oil

Preheat the oven to 160°C/325°F. Season the bread slices with salt. Cut parchment paper into twelve 10 by 8.5-cm (4 by 3¼-inch) pieces. Brush two pieces of parchment paper with olive oil and sandwich a bread slice between the oiled sides. Repeat with the remaining slices. Wrap each sandwiched slice around a copper tube 1.3 cm (½ inch) in diameter and at least 7.5 cm (3 inches) in length. The bread should form nearly a complete circle around the tube. Secure each sandwiched slice to the tube using a paper clip. Place the tubes on a baking sheet with a wire rack. Toast the bread in the oven until browned and crispy, about 15 minutes. Cool to room temperature before removing the paper clips. Carefully slide the toasts off the tubes and remove the parchment paper. Break each crisp in half.

RYE CRISPS

Makes 8 crisps

4 (3-mm/⅛-inch) slices rye bread
Salt
Olive oil

Preheat the oven to 160°C/325°F. Cut parchment paper into eight 10 by 8-cm (4 by 3¼-inch) pieces. Season the bread with salt on both sides. Brush two pieces of parchment paper with olive oil and sandwich a bread slice between the oiled sides. Repeat with the remaining slices. Wrap each sandwiched slice around a copper tube, 1.3 cm (½ inch) in diameter and at least 7.5 cm (3 inches) in length. The bread should nearly encircle the tube. Secure each sandwiched slice to the tube using a paper clip. Place the tubes on a wire rack set over a baking sheet. Toast the bread in the oven until browned and crispy, about 15 minutes. Let cool to room temperature before removing the paper clips. Carefully slide the toasts off the tubes and remove the parchment paper. Break each crisp in half lengthwise. Reserve the crisps in a dry, airtight container.

SOUR RYE CRISPS

Makes 24 crisps

24 (1.5-mm/¹⁄₁₆-inch) slices sour rye bread
Olive oil
Salt

Preheat the oven to 160°C/325°F. Spread the slices on a baking sheet lined with parchment paper in a single layer. Lightly brush the slices with olive oil and season with salt on both sides. Place in the oven and toast until crispy, but not browned, about 8 minutes. Remove from the oven and let cool to room temperature. Reserve the crisps in a dry, airtight container.

ICE CREAMS
AND SORBETS

CHERRY SORBET

Makes about 750 g

125 g water
45 g glucose powder
56 g sugar
5 g sorbet stabilizer
500 g cherry puree, 10 percent added sugar
31 g lime juice

Combine the water, glucose, sugar, and sorbet stabilizer in a small pot and whisk to combine. Cook the mixture over medium heat, whisking constantly, until the syrup comes to a simmer. Remove the syrup from the heat and chill in the refrigerator. Combine the cold syrup with the cherry puree and lime juice in a large mixing bowl and whisk to combine. Freeze in an ice cream machine and reserve in an airtight container, frozen.

CHOCOLATE PRALINE MILK ICE

Makes about 825 g

625 g milk
140 g cream
72 g trimoline
60 g 100 percent praline paste, no sugar added
Grated zest of 1 lemon
140 g sugar
25 g glucose powder
25 g nonfat milk powder
75 g 70 percent cacao chocolate, chopped
5 g salt

Prepare an ice bath. Heat the milk and cream in a saucepan over medium heat. Bring to a simmer. Stir in the trimoline, praline paste, and lemon zest. Continue to stir until fully incorporated. Slowly whisk in the sugar, glucose, and milk powder until fully dissolved. Bring the mixture back to a simmer, then remove the pan from the heat. Blend in the chocolate using an immersion blender, then strain through a chinois. Chill the mixture over the ice bath. Season with the salt. Freeze in an ice cream machine and reserve in an airtight container, frozen.

ESPRESSO GRANITA

Makes about 150 g

100 g brewed and cooled coffee
35 g Simple Syrup (page 300)
25 g brewed and cooled espresso

Pour the ingredients into a mixing bowl and whisk together until combined. Transfer to a shallow baking dish and place in the freezer. Whisk the mixture to break up any large chunks every 20 minutes, until the granita is frozen with a fluffed texture, about 2 hours total. Reserve in an airtight container, frozen.

LIME GRANITA

Makes about 175 g

115 g water
60 g lime juice
25 g sugar

Heat the water and juice in a saucepan over low heat until warmed through. Whisk in the sugar until fully dissolved. Transfer to a shallow baking dish and place in the freezer. Whisk the mixture to break up any large pieces every 20 minutes, until the granita is frozen with a fluffed texture, about 2 hours total. Reserve in an airtight container, frozen.

MALTED MILK ICE CREAM

Makes about 670 g

335 g milk
105 g cream
Grated zest of 1/2 orange
36 g glucose powder
35 g nonfat milk powder
17 g trimoline
4 egg yolks
60 g sugar
3 g salt
50 g malted milk powder

Prepare an ice bath. Heat the milk and cream to a simmer in a saucepan over medium heat. Add the orange zest to the pan and remove from the heat. Cover and let steep at room temperature for 30 minutes. Strain the infused milk through a chinois. Heat the infused milk in a clean saucepan over medium heat. Add the glucose and milk powders and trimoline to the pan, and whisk until fully dissolved. Bring the milk mixture to a simmer and remove the pan from the heat. Combine the eggs, sugar, and salt in a mixing bowl and whisk well. Whisk a third of the warm milk mixture into the eggs to temper. Whisk the egg mixture back into the milk mixture. Heat over medium heat. Whisk until heated to 84°C/183°F and thick enough to coat the back of a spoon. Remove the pan from the heat and, using an immersion blender, blend in the malt powder. Strain the mixture through a chinois and chill over the ice bath. Freeze in an ice cream machine and reserve in an airtight container, frozen.

MAPLE ICE CREAM

Makes about 500 g

430 g milk
15 g cornstarch
45 g butter
200 g maple syrup
1 g xanthan gum
6 g salt

Prepare an ice bath. Combine one-fourth of the milk in a bowl with the cornstarch and whisk to form a slurry. Heat the remaining milk and butter in a saucepan over medium heat. Slowly whisk the slurry into the simmering milk. Continue to simmer the milk, whisking constantly, until the starch cooks out and thickens the milk, about 5 minutes. Transfer the thickened mixture to a blender and blend on low speed. Slowly add the maple syrup and xanthan gum. Turn to medium speed and blend for 1 minute to fully hydrate the gum. Strain the mixture through a chinois and chill over the ice bath. Season with the salt. Freeze in an ice cream machine and reserve in an airtight container, frozen.

MASCARPONE CHERRY ICE CREAM

Makes about 750 g

425 g milk
95 g sugar
85 g trimoline
335 g mascarpone
85 g crème fraîche
100 g amarena cherries, drained and coarsely chopped

Prepare an ice bath. Heat the milk in a saucepan over medium heat to a simmer. Whisk in the sugar and trimoline until fully dissolved. Remove the pan from the heat and chill over the ice bath until cold. Blend the mascarpone and crème fraîche together using an immersion blender. Blend in the cold milk and strain through a chinois. Refrigerate until chilled, about 2 hours. Freeze in an ice cream machine and place in the freezer until chilled through, about 1 hour. Fold in the chopped cherries until evenly distributed. Return to the freezer and keep frozen in an airtight container.

MILK ICE

Makes 600 g

780 g milk
195 g cream
56 g nonfat milk powder
65 g sugar
40 g glucose syrup
3 g salt

Prepare an ice bath. Heat two-thirds of the milk in a saucepan over medium heat and bring to a simmer. Turn the heat to low and reduce the milk by half. Remove from the heat and transfer to a blender. Blend on low speed and add the rest of the milk and the cream, milk powder, sugar, glucose, and salt. Turn to high speed and blend until smooth, about 2 minutes. Strain through a chinois and chill over the ice bath. Freeze in an ice cream machine and reserve in an airtight container, frozen.

ORANGE SORBET

Makes about 650 g

105 g Sorbet Syrup (page 300)
600 g orange juice
1 g xanthan gum
7 g orange bitters
1 g citric acid

Gently warm the sorbet syrup in a saucepan over low heat until fluid. Start to blend the juice in a blender on low speed. Add the syrup and blend until incorporated. Slowly add the xanthan gum and blend on medium speed for 1 minute to fully hydrate the gum. Season the juice with the bitters and citric acid and strain through a chinois. Refrigerate overnight in an airtight container. Freeze in an ice cream machine and reserve in an airtight container, frozen.

PASSION FRUIT SORBET

Makes 750 g

185 g Sorbet Syrup (page 300)
230 g water
500 g 100 percent passion fruit juice

Gently warm the sorbet syrup in a saucepan over low heat until fluid. Combine the syrup, water, and juice in a blender and blend on medium speed until fully incorporated. Refrigerate overnight. Freeze in an ice cream machine and reserve in an airtight container, frozen.

PEACH ICE CREAM

Makes about 800 g

400 g milk
90 g cream
½ g vanilla bean, split and scraped
200 g sugar
30 g glucose powder
30 g dextrose
27 g nonfat milk powder
15 g trimoline
2 peaches, pitted and quartered
240 g peach nectar
2 g citric acid
2 g salt

Prepare an ice bath. Heat the milk and cream in a saucepan to a simmer over medium heat. Add the vanilla bean pod and seeds to the milk and remove from the heat. Cover and let steep at room temperature for 30 minutes. Combine the sugar, glucose powder, and dextrose in a mixing bowl. Strain the milk mixture through a chinois and transfer to a clean saucepan over medium heat. Bring to a simmer and slowly whisk in the sugar mixture, milk powder, and trimoline until fully dissolved. Remove the pan from the heat and set aside. Combine the peaches and nectar in a blender and puree on high until smooth. Pass the puree through a chinois and whisk into the milk mixture. Chill over the ice bath. Stir in the citric acid and salt. Freeze in an ice cream machine and reserve in an airtight container, frozen.

PINEAPPLE SORBET

Makes about 750 g

600 g pineapple juice (from about 1 pineapple)
1 g xanthan gum
185 g Sorbet Syrup (page 300)
2 g malic acid
3 g Star Anise Extract (page 300)

Start to blend the juice in a blender on low speed. Slowly add the xanthan gum and turn to medium speed. Blend for 1 minute to fully hydrate the gum. Blend in the sorbet syrup, malic acid, and star anise extract. Blend until fully incorporated. Refrigerate overnight. Freeze in an ice cream machine and reserve in an airtight container, frozen.

RICOTTA ICE CREAM

Makes about 900 g

415 g milk
135 g trimoline
100 g sugar
50 g glucose syrup
335 g Pressed Ricotta (page 299)
85 g crème fraîche
10 g lemon juice
6 g salt

Prepare an ice bath. Heat the milk to a simmer in a saucepan over medium heat. Whisk in the trimoline, sugar, and glucose until fully dissolved. Remove the pan from the heat. Transfer the milk mixture a blender and blend in the ricotta and crème fraîche until smooth. Strain through a chinois and chill over the ice bath. Season with the lemon juice and salt. Freeze in an ice cream machine and reserve in an airtight container, frozen.

ROSEMARY ICE CREAM

Makes about 750 g

500 g milk
160 g cream
8 g rosemary leaves
50 g nonfat milk powder
50 g glucose powder
25 g trimoline
5 egg yolks
105 g sugar
5 g salt

Prepare an ice bath. Heat the milk and cream in a saucepan over medium heat to a simmer. Add the rosemary leaves. Remove the pan from the heat and cover. Let steep at room temperature for 30 minutes. Strain the infused milk through a chinois. Transfer to a clean saucepan and bring to a simmer. Remove from the heat and keep warm. Slowly whisk in the milk powder, glucose, and trimoline until fully dissolved. Place the yolks in a mixing bowl. Slowly whisk in the sugar and salt until smooth. Pour one-third of the warm milk into the eggs while whisking constantly. Once fully incorporated, whisk the egg mixture back into the milk. Heat over medium heat, whisking constantly until heated to 84°C/183°F and thick enough to coat the back of a spoon. Remove from heat and strain through a chinois. Chill over the ice bath. Freeze in an ice cream machine and reserve in an airtight container, frozen.

SAGE ICE CREAM

Makes about 750 g

500 g milk
160 g cream
5 g sage leaves
50 g nonfat milk powder
50 g glucose powder
25 g trimoline
5 egg yolks
105 g sugar
5 g salt

Prepare an ice bath. Heat the milk and cream in a saucepan over medium heat to a simmer. Add the sage to the pan and remove from the heat. Cover and let steep at room temperature for 30 minutes. Strain the infused milk through a chinois. Transfer to a clean saucepan and bring to a simmer. Remove from the heat and keep warm. Slowly whisk in the milk powder, glucose, and trimoline until fully dissolved. Place the yolks in a mixing bowl. Slowly whisk in the sugar and salt until smooth. Pour one-third of the warm milk into the eggs while whisking constantly. Once fully incorporated, whisk the egg mixture back into the milk. Heat over medium heat, whisking constantly, until heated to 84°C/183°F and thick enough to coat the back of a spoon. Remove from heat and strain through a chinois. Chill over the ice bath. Freeze in an ice cream machine and reserve in an airtight container, frozen.

STRAWBERRY SORBET

Makes about 750 g

116 g water
16 g trimoline
100 g sugar
66 g glucose powder
4 g sorbet stabilizer
500 g strawberry puree, 10 percent added sugar

Combine the water and trimoline in a small pot and whisk to combine. Bring the trimoline mixture to a boil. Add the sugar, glucose, and sorbet stabilizer and return to a boil, whisking to dissolve the solids. Remove the syrup from the heat and chill in the refrigerator. Combine the cold syrup with the frozen strawberry puree. Freeze in an ice cream machine and reserve in an airtight container, frozen.

VANILLA ICE CREAM

Makes about 700 g

500 g milk
160 g cream
2 vanilla beans, split and scraped
50 g nonfat milk powder
20 g trimoline
5 egg yolks
115 g sugar
5 g salt

Prepare an ice bath. Heat the milk and cream in a saucepan over medium heat to a simmer. Add the vanilla pods and seeds, stirring to incorporate. Remove the pan from the heat and cover. Let steep at room temperature for 30 minutes. Strain the infused milk through a chinois. Transfer to a clean saucepan and bring to a simmer. Remove from the heat and keep warm. Slowly whisk in the milk powder and trimoline until fully dissolved. Place the yolks in a mixing bowl. Slowly whisk in the sugar and salt until smooth. Pour one-third of the warm milk into the eggs, whisking constantly. Once fully incorporated, whisk the egg mixture back into the milk. Heat over medium heat, whisking constantly, until heated to 84°C/183°F and thick enough to coat the back of a spoon. Remove from the heat and strain through a chinois. Chill over the ice bath. Freeze in an ice cream machine and reserve in an airtight container, frozen.

PICKLES

APRICOT PICKLING LIQUID

Makes about 800 g

230 g white port
230 g dry white wine
240 g white balsamic vinegar
100 g sugar
2 g fennel seeds
2 g whole coriander seeds
Salt
10 g white tea leaves

Combine the wines, vinegar, sugar, fennel, coriander, and salt in a saucepan and place over medium heat. Whisk to dissolve the sugar and bring to a simmer. Remove the pan from the heat and stir in the tea leaves. Cover the pan and let steep at room temperature for 5 minutes. Strain the liquid through a cheesecloth and reserve in an airtight container, refrigerated, for up to 3 days.

PICKLED APRICOT

Makes about 10 pieces

1 apricot
150 g White Balsamic Pickling Liquid (page 295)

Using a mandoline, thinly slice opposing sides of the apricot to form shaved rounds. Submerge the apricot shaves in the pickling liquid and refrigerate overnight.

PICKLED MUSTARD SEEDS

Makes about 300 g

100 g yellow or black mustard seeds
750 g White Balsamic Pickling Liquid (page 295)

Place the mustard seeds in a large heatproof container. Heat the pickling liquid to a boil in a saucepan over medium heat. Remove the pan from the heat and pour the liquid over the seeds to cover. Let cool to room temperature. Transfer the pickled mustard seeds to an airtight container. Refrigerate overnight before using and reserve for up to 2 weeks.

PICKLED RADISHES

Makes 12 pieces

6 Easter Egg radishes
45 g White Balsamic Pickling Liquid (page 295)

Bring a large pot of water to a boil and prepare an ice bath. Seal the radishes and pickling liquid airtight in a sous vide bag. Submerge the bag in the boiling water. Cook the radishes until tender, about 17 minutes. Shock in the ice bath until cold. Remove the radishes from the bag and keep covered in the liquid in an airtight container, refrigerated. When ready to serve, halve the radishes from the stem end.

PICKLED RED ONION RINGS

Makes about 30 rings

6 red pearl onions, peeled
8 g salt
8 g sugar
10 g grapeseed oil
90 g red wine vinegar

Prepare an ice bath. Slice the red onions into rings about 3 mm (1/8 inch) thick. Combine the rings with the salt and sugar, stirring to evenly season. Heat the oil in a sauté pan over high heat. When the oil just starts to smoke, wipe the pan with a paper towel to get rid of any excess oil. Turn the heat to medium and add the onion rings to the pan. Immediately stir to prevent color and add half of the red wine vinegar to the pan. Bring the vinegar to a boil and immediately transfer the onions to a metal dish set over the ice bath. Stir to chill quickly. Drain and discard the cooking liquid. Transfer to an airtight container. Cover with the remaining vinegar and reserve, refrigerated, for up to 2 days.

PLUM PICKLING LIQUID

Makes about 350 g

7 cloves
2 whole allspice berries
4 g black peppercorns
4 g juniper berries
2 g pink peppercorns
2 star anise pods
1 cinnamon stick
500 g dry red wine
50 g port
150 g red wine vinegar
100 g sugar
4 g Earl Grey tea leaves

Prepare an ice bath. Toast the spices in a sauté pan over low heat, stirring frequently, until fragrant, about 3 minutes. Combine the toasted spices, wines, vinegar, and sugar in a saucepan. Heat to a simmer over medium heat and reduce by half. Strain the liquid through a chinois. Add the tea leaves and cover. Let steep at room temperature for 10 minutes. Strain through a chinois and chill over the ice bath until cold. Reserve the pickling liquid in an airtight container, refrigerated, for up to 1 week.

WHITE BALSAMIC PICKLING LIQUID

Makes about 900 g

500 g white balsamic vinegar
200 g sugar
200 g water
50 g salt

Combine the ingredients in a large saucepan and bring to a simmer over high heat. Whisk to fully dissolve the sugar and salt and remove the pan from the heat. Let cool to room temperature and reserve in an airtight container, refrigerated, for up to 2 weeks.

PUREEWS, CONDIMENTS, ETCETERA

BACON MARMALADE

Makes about 150 g

200 g slab bacon, diced 6 mm (¼ inch)
20 g apple cider vinegar
25 g white distilled vinegar
25 g light brown sugar
15 g honey
25 g Pickled Mustard Seeds (page 294)
15 g Dijon mustard
Salt

Heat the bacon in a large sauté pan over low heat. Cook, stirring occasionally, until rendered but not completely crispy, about 8 minutes. Remove the bacon from the pan and place on a paper towel to drain. Drain and discard half of the rendered fat from the pan. Add both vinegars, brown sugar, and honey to the pan. Over medium heat, bring the mixture to a simmer and reduce until thickened to a syruplike consistency, about 4 minutes. Add the cooked bacon, pickled mustard seeds, and mustard. Season with salt. Stir until fully incorporated. Remove the pan from the heat and let cool to room temperature. Reserve in an airtight container, refrigerated, for up to 3 days. To serve, gently reheat in a saucepan over medium heat until warmed through.

BLACK TRUFFLE PUREE

Makes about 175 g

80 g butter
1 shallot, sliced
125 g black truffles, coarsely chopped
50 g Madeira
75 g black truffle juice
Water
15 g sherry vinegar
Salt

Prepare an ice bath. Heat half of the butter in a saucepan over medium heat until foamy but not browned. Add the shallot and sweat until tender but without any color, about 4 minutes. Add the truffles and cook until softened,

5 minutes. Add the wine and reduce until almost dry. Add the black truffle juice and simmer until reduced by half. Add just enough water to cover the truffles and bring to a simmer. Continue to cook, stirring occasionally, until the truffles are tender and the cooking liquid is nearly evaporated, about 20 minutes. Transfer the mixture to a blender and puree on high speed until smooth. Turn to low speed and slowly add the remaining butter. Blend until emulsified. Pass the puree through a fine-mesh tamis. Add the vinegar and season with salt. Chill the puree over the ice bath. Reserve in an airtight container, refrigerated, for up to 3 days.

CANDIED MEYER LEMON

Makes about 12 pieces

1 Meyer lemon
150 g water
100 g sugar

Trim the ends off the lemon and slice it into rounds 3 mm (⅛ inch) thick. Remove and discard any seeds. Transfer the sliced lemon to a saucepan and cover with cold water. Over low heat, bring the water to 82°C/180°F. Carefully drain the lemons, being careful to keep the rounds intact. Repeat this process two more times. After the third blanching, drain the lemons and set aside.

In a separate pan, combine the water and sugar and stir to dissolve the sugar. Place the blanched lemons in the sugar syrup and cook over low heat until the rinds become translucent and candied, about 1 hour. If, during the cooking process, the syrup starts to reduce by more than a quarter, add water to return it to the original volume so that the syrup does not get too sweet. Once cooked, remove the candied lemon slices from the syrup and let drain on a wire rack set over a baking sheet. Cut the slices in half before serving.

CHAMOMILE SIMPLE SYRUP

Makes about 125 g

140 g Simple Syrup (page 300)
3 g dried chamomile

Heat the syrup in a saucepan over medium heat and bring to a simmer. Remove the pan from the heat and stir in the chamomile. Cover and let steep at room temperature for 7 minutes. Strain the syrup through a coffee filter. Let cool to room temperature. Reserve the syrup in an airtight container, refrigerated, for up to 5 days.

COCO BEANS

Makes about 450 g, drained

200 g coco beans
1/2 onion, cut into 2.5-cm (1-inch) pieces
1 carrot, peeled and cut into 2.5-cm (1-inch) pieces
1 celery stalk, cut into 2.5-cm (1-inch) pieces
2 sprigs thyme
1 bay leaf
Salt

Cover the beans amply with water in an airtight container and refrigerate for 24 hours. Tie the vegetables and herbs in a cheesecloth sachet. Drain the beans of the soaking liquid and transfer to a large saucepan. Combine with the sachet and generously cover with cold water. Heat over medium heat and bring to a simmer. Turn the heat to low and continue to cook the beans until tender, about 1 1/2 hours. Season with salt and remove the pan from the heat. Let cool to room temperature in the cooking liquid. Remove and discard the sachet. Reserve the beans in an airtight container, covered in the cooking liquid, refrigerated, for up to 3 days.

DEMI-DEHYDRATED BEETS

Makes about 45 pieces

15 g water
45 g red wine vinegar
60 g olive oil
3 g salt
3 sprigs flat-leaf parsley
1 sprig chervil
2 sprigs dill
2 sprigs thyme
1 bay leaf
2 black peppercorns
2 red beets, top and bottom ends trimmed,
*   about 300 g each*

Bring a large pot of water to a rolling boil and prepare an ice bath. Combine the water, red wine vinegar, olive oil, and salt in a mixing bowl and whisk well to combine. Tie the parsley, chervil, dill, thyme, bay leaf, and peppercorns in a cheesecloth sachet. Seal the beets, sachet, and red wine mixture airtight in a sous vide bag. Submerge the bag in the boiling water and cook until the beets are tender, about 2 hours. Shock the beets in the ice bath. Preheat the oven to 95°C/200°F. When cold, remove the beets from the bag, reserving the cooking liquid for another use. With a clean kitchen towel, rub the skins away from the beets. Break the peeled beets by hand into

2.5-cm (1-inch) pieces. Arrange the beets in a single layer on a wire rack set over a baking sheet. Dehydrate the beets in the oven until they are chewy and appear wrinkled yet still retain some moisture, about 3 1/2 hours. Let the beets cool to room temperature. Reserve in an airtight container, refrigerated, for up to 1 week.

DEMI-DEHYDRATED TOMATOES

Makes 24 pieces

24 cherry tomatoes
20 g olive oil, plus more for storing
2 sprigs thyme
2 cloves garlic, crushed
Salt

Preheat the oven to 105°C/225°F. Line a baking sheet with parchment paper. Bring a large pot of salted water to a rolling boil and prepare an ice bath. Blanch the tomatoes in the water just long enough to loosen the skins, about 5 seconds. Shock the tomatoes in the ice bath. When cold, drain the tomatoes, peel and discard the tomato skins and combine with the oil, thyme, and garlic in a mixing bowl. Gently toss together and season with salt. Transfer the seasoned tomatoes to the lined baking sheet in a single layer and cook until nearly dehydrated, about 4 hours. The tomatoes should appear wrinkled but should still retain a bit of moisture. Let cool to room temperature. Reserve the tomatoes, covered in olive oil, in an airtight container, refrigerated, for up to 1 week.

DRIED SHAD ROE

Makes 1 piece

1 shad roe pair, about 170 g

Preheat the oven to 65°C/150°F. Place the shad roe on a wire rack set on a baking sheet. Dehydrate the shad roe in the oven until completely dried, about 6 hours. Reserve the dried shad roe in an airtight container, refrigerated, for up to 1 week.

GARLIC CONFIT

Makes about 450 g

15 cloves garlic, peeled
400 g olive oil
3 sprigs thyme
1 g salt

Cover the garlic with cold water in a saucepan. Over medium heat, bring the garlic to a simmer. Drain the garlic and return to the pan. Repeat this process two more times. After the third blanching, return the blanched garlic to the saucepan and cover with the oil. Add the thyme and heat over low heat to gently cook until tender, about 45 minutes. Remove the pan from the heat and let cool to room temperature. Remove and discard the thyme. Reserve the garlic, covered in the confit oil in an airtight container, refrigerated, for up to 1 week.

HORSERADISH GREMOLATA

Makes about 25 g

8 g finely chopped flat-leaf parsley
8 g finely chopped shallots
0.5 g grated horseradish
10 g olive oil
Salt

Combine the parsley, shallots, horseradish, and olive oil in a mixing bowl, season with salt, and mix well. Set aside.

KALE CHIPS

Makes 8 pieces

8 lacinato kale leaves
Canola oil, for frying
Salt

Cut the ribs from the kale leaves and discard. Heat 7.5 cm (3 inches) of canola oil to 175°C/350°F in a large heavy pot. Carefully fry the kale leaves in the hot oil until crispy, about 5 seconds. Be very careful, as the moisture in the kale leaves will cause the oil to pop quite violently. Remove the chips from the oil with a spider strainer and place them on a paper towel to drain. Season with salt.

LIVER MOUSSE

Makes about 300 g

150 g chicken or squab livers
Milk
150 g butter
1 shallot, thinly sliced
1/2 celery stalk, thinly sliced
2 cloves garlic, thinly sliced
35 g brandy
3 g pink curing salt #1
65 g cream
5 g Dijon mustard
10 g sherry vinegar
3 g salt

Cover the livers with milk in an airtight container and refrigerate overnight to soak. Drain the livers, discarding the soaking milk. Pat dry with a paper towel. Prepare an ice bath. Heat one-third of the butter in a large sauté pan over medium heat until foamy but not browned. Add the livers to the pan in a single layer. Cook, turning occasionally, until evenly seared and browned on all sides, about 3 minutes. Remove the livers from the pan and set aside. Add the shallot, celery, and garlic to the pan and turn the heat to low. Cook, stirring occasionally, until soft but without any color, about 8 minutes. Add the brandy and pink curing salt to the pan. Stir and bring the liquid to a simmer. Reduce the brandy by half. Add the cream and mustard to the pan, stirring to combine. Bring to a simmer and remove the pan from the heat. Combine the cooked vegetable mixture with the seared livers in a blender. Puree on high speed until smooth. Turn to low speed and slowly blend in the remaining butter until fully emulsified. Add the sherry vinegar and season with salt. Pass the mousse through a chinois while still warm and chill over the ice bath. Reserve the mousse in an airtight container, refrigerated, for up to 3 days.

MARINATED FOIE GRAS

Makes about 1 kg

2 lobes Hudson Valley foie gras, about 800 g each
15 g salt
2 g pink curing salt #1
2 g sugar
2 g white pepper
9 g Madeira
5 g brandy

Keep the foie gras in the original packaging and let sit at room temperature for 30 minutes to temper. Remove the foie from the packaging. Working with one lobe at a time, carefully push away the foie from the veins and lift the veins out of the foie. Repeat with the second lobe. Pass the deveined foie gras through a coarse-mesh tamis. Separate 1 kg of foie and place in a large mixing bowl. Reserve the rest for another use. Combine the salts, sugar, and white pepper in a spice grinder and grind to a fine powder. Season the foie with the powdered mix. Add the Madeira and brandy and mix until fully incorporated. Seal the seasoned foie gras airtight in a sous vide bag. Refrigerate overnight to marinate. Remove the marinated foie from the bag and transfer to the bowl of a stand mixer with the whisk attachment. Whip the foie on medium speed until smooth and emulsified, about 5 minutes. Immediately seal the foie airtight in a sous vide bag and reserve, refrigerated, for up to 1 week.

PRESERVED MEYER LEMONS

Makes 10 lemons

10 Meyer lemons
225 g salt
115 g sugar
9 g black peppercorns
3 g whole coriander seeds
1 g dried red pepper flakes
240 g Meyer lemon juice (from about 5 lemons)

Partially cut the lemons in quarters, leaving the stem end of each intact. Combine the salt and sugar in a bowl and stir to mix well. Season the lemons with the salt mixture, making sure to season both the interior and outsides of the lemons. Combine the lemons and spices in an airtight container. Pour the lemon juice over the lemons and place a weight on top. Seal the container and refrigerate for 1 month before using.

PRESSED RICOTTA

Makes about 500 g

550 g ricotta

Wrap the ricotta in cheesecloth and place in a colander set over a bowl. Cover the wrapped ricotta with another bowl and place a heavy object in the bowl to act as a weight. Refrigerate the ricotta as it presses overnight. Discard the liquid pressed out of the cheese. Reserve the pressed ricotta in an airtight container, refrigerated, for up to 3 days.

ROASTED GARLIC

Makes about 8 cloves

1 head garlic
30 g olive oil
Salt

Preheat the oven to 150°C/300°F. Place the head of garlic whole in a mixing bowl, add the oil, season with salt, and toss to evenly coat. Wrap the garlic in an aluminum foil packet and roast in a baking dish until tender and golden brown, about 1 hour. Remove the garlic from the oven and carefully separate the individual cloves. Keep warm.

ROASTED LADY APPLES

Makes 12 pieces

6 lady apples
20 g grapeseed oil
Brown Butter, melted (page 284)
Fleur de sel

Preheat the oven to 175°C/350°F. Cut the apples in half. Using a small melon baller, scoop the core out of each half and discard. Heat the oil in a sauté pan over medium heat. When the oil is hot, add the apples cut side down and sear until golden brown, about 3 minutes. Place the pan in the oven and roast the apples until tender, about 7 minutes. Remove the pan from the oven and place the apples on a paper towel to drain. Brush each half with brown butter and season with fleur de sel. Keep warm.

ROASTED TOMATOES

Makes 60 pieces

30 cherry tomatoes, halved
20 g olive oil
Salt

Preheat the oven to 95°C/200°F. Line a baking sheet with parchment paper. Combine the tomatoes with the olive oil in a mixing bowl and season with salt. Toss together to combine. Arrange the tomatoes in a single layer, cut side up, on the prepared baking sheet. Roast until shriveled on the outside, but still juicy, about 2 hours. Let cool to room temperature.

SIMPLE SYRUP

Makes about 400 g

200 g sugar
200 g water

Heat the water and sugar to a simmer in a saucepan over high heat, whisking to dissolve the sugar. Let the syrup cool to room temperature and reserve in an airtight container, refrigerated, for up to 1 month.

SLOW-POACHED QUAIL EGGS

Makes 12 eggs

12 quail eggs

Heat a water bath to 62°C/144°F and prepare an ice bath. Cook the eggs, still in the shells, in the hot water bath until soft poached, about 2 hours. Remove the eggs from the bath and shock in the ice bath until cold. Crack open the eggs into cold water and keep refrigerated until ready to plate.

SOFT-BOILED EGGS

Makes 4 eggs

4 eggs

Bring a large saucepan of water to a rolling boil over high heat and prepare an ice bath. Carefully place the eggs in the boiling water and cook until soft-boiled, about 8¹/₂ minutes. Immediately shock the eggs in the ice bath. When cold, peel the eggs and discard the shells.

SORBET SYRUP

Makes about 1 kg

240 g water
500 g sugar
320 g glucose powder
25 g sorbet stabilizer

Heat the water to a simmer in a saucepan over medium heat. Whisk together the sugar, glucose, and stabilizer in a mixing bowl. Slowly whisk the sugar mixture into the water in three additions, waiting for the previous addition to completely dissolve before adding the next. Continue to whisk the syrup until heated to 84°C/183°F. Reserve the syrup in an airtight container for up to 1 month, refrigerated. When ready to use, gently heat the syrup in a saucepan over low heat until fluid.

SQUASH ÉCRASER

Makes about 400 g

¹/₂ kabocha squash, halved and seeded, about 600 g
25 g olive oil
45 g butter
Salt

Preheat the oven to 160°C/325°F. In a mixing bowl, dress the squash with the oil and season with salt. Toss to evenly coat. Place the squash in a baking dish and cover with aluminum foil. Bake in the oven until tender, about 1 hour and 15 minutes. Remove the squash from the oven and scrape the flesh from the skin. Mash the squash thoroughly with a large fork. Add the butter and continue to mash the squash until the butter is completely melted in. Season the écraser with salt. Reserve in an airtight container, refrigerated, for up to 3 days. When ready to serve, gently heat in a saucepan over low heat until warmed through.

STAR ANISE EXTRACT

Makes about 200 g

250 g vodka
112 g star anise pods

Heat the vodka and star anise in a saucepan over low heat. Gently cook, without simmering, for 30 minutes. Strain through a chinois and let cool to room temperature. Reserve in an airtight container, refrigerated, for up to 1 month.

TOMATO RELISH

Makes about 220 g

7 roma tomatoes
60 g olive oil
3 g salt, plus more to season
2 cloves garlic, crushed
3 sprigs thyme
¹/₂ shallot, finely chopped
Grated zest of 1 lemon
8 g lemon juice

Preheat the oven to 105°C/225°F and prepare an ice bath. Bring a pot of salted water to a rolling boil over high heat. Blanch the tomatoes just until the skin loosens, about 10 seconds. Shock the tomatoes in the ice bath. When cold, drain the tomatoes and peel and discard the skins, leaving the flesh of the tomatoes intact and smooth. Halve each tomato from the stem end. Remove and discard the core and seeds. Pat dry with paper towels to remove any excess moisture. Place the tomatoes in a bowl and toss with half of the olive oil, the salt, garlic, and thyme. Gently toss to evenly coat. Line a baking sheet with parchment paper. Spread the tomatoes on the baking sheet in a single layer, cut sides down. Cook the tomatoes in the oven until nearly dehydrated, about 4 hours. The tomatoes should still retain a bit of moisture. Remove from the oven and let cool to room temperature. Finely chop the tomatoes. Transfer to a mixing bowl and combine with the remaining olive oil, shallot, lemon zest, and juice. Stir to combine. Season with salt and reserve in an airtight container, refrigerated, for up to 2 days.

––––

TOMATO WATER

Makes about 400 g

2 beefsteak tomatoes, cored and quartered
10 leaves basil
3 g salt

Line a colander with several layers of cheesecloth and fit over a large mixing bowl. Set aside. Combine the tomatoes, basil, and salt in a blender. Blend on high speed just until thoroughly crushed, but not smooth, about 15 seconds. Pour the mixture into the prepared colander. Refrigerate overnight to strain the liquid. Do not force or apply pressure. Discard the drained tomatoes and reserve the strained water in an airtight container, refrigerated, for up to 3 days, or frozen for up to 1 month.

––––

YOGURT GEL

Makes about 250 g

240 g sheep's milk yogurt
90 g water
4 g agar-agar
Salt

Heat the yogurt in a saucepan over low heat until warmed through. Remove the pan from the heat and keep warm. Combine the water and agar-agar in a saucepan. Heat over medium heat and bring to a boil, whisking constantly to dissolve the agar-agar. Continue to boil while whisking until the agar is fully hydrated and appears translucent, about 1 minute. Slowly whisk the agar-agar mixture into the warm yogurt. Whisk until thoroughly combined and remove the pan from the heat. Transfer to a shallow baking dish and refrigerate until fully set, about 3 hours. Break the gel into small pieces and transfer to a blender. Puree on high speed until smooth. Pass the gel through a fine-mesh tamis and season with salt. Reserve in an airtight container, refrigerated, for up to 3 days.

STOCKS AND SAUCES

APPLE CIDER REDUCTION

Makes about 120 g

800 g apple cider
1 vanilla bean, split and scraped
100 g peeled ginger, sliced
1 cinnamon stick
2 star anise pods
2 cardamom
Peeled zest of 1 orange

Heat the ingredients in a saucepan over medium heat.
Bring to a boil, then turn the heat to low. Continue to
simmer and reduce to a syruplike consistency, about
45 minutes. Strain the reduction through a chinois and
let cool to room temperature. Reserve in an airtight
container, refrigerated, for up to 1 week.

APRICOT GASTRIQUE

Makes about 300 g

125 g dry white wine
125 g white port
225 g dried apricots, finely chopped
225 g white balsamic vinegar
225 g sugar

Heat both wines in a saucepan over medium heat and
bring to a simmer. Continue to simmer the wines until
reduced by half. Add the apricots and vinegar to the pan,
stirring to combine. Remove the pan from the heat and
keep warm. Heat the sugar over medium heat in a wide,
heavy saucepan. As the sugar begins to brown around
the edges, gently swirl the pan around the heat to evenly
caramelize. Continue to cook the sugar until deep brown
and completely melted, about 10 minutes. Turn the heat
to low and add the reduced wine mixture. Stir to combine
using a rubber spatula. Continue to cook the mixture,
stirring, until reduced to a syruplike consistency, about
3 minutes. Strain the gastrique and discard the apricots.
Let cool to room temperature and reserve in an airtight
container, refrigerated, for up to 1 week.

BLACK TRUFFLE JUS

Makes about 150 g

12 g grapeseed oil
1 shallot, finely chopped
20 g black truffle, finely chopped
80 g Madeira
360 g Chicken Jus (page 303)
5 g sherry vinegar
Salt

Heat the oil in a saucepan over medium heat. Add the
shallot and black truffle. Cook, stirring occasionally,
until softened, about 7 minutes. Add the wine and bring
to a simmer. Reduce the wine until almost dry. Add the
chicken jus to the pan and bring to a simmer. Turn the
heat to low and gently reduce the jus until thick enough
to coat the back of a spoon. Add the sherry vinegar and
season the jus with salt. Reserve the jus in an airtight
container, refrigerated, for up to 1 week.

BROWN BUTTER SABAYON

Makes about 500 g

150 g Brown Butter (page 284)
50 g butter
240 g dry white wine
1 egg
3 egg yolks
30 g lemon juice
6 g salt

Heat a water bath to 62°C/145°F. Combine both butters
in a saucepan and heat over low heat until melted and
warmed through. Remove from the heat and keep warm.
Heat the wine to a simmer in a saucepan over medium
heat. Simmer and reduce the wine by three-quarters.
Remove the pan from the heat and keep warm. Combine
the egg and egg yolks in a mixing bowl and whisk to
combine. Using an immersion blender, slowly blend in the
warm reduced wine, lemon juice, and salt. Be careful not
to scramble the eggs. Once combined, slowly blend in the
warm butters, continuing to blend until fully emulsified.
Transfer the sabayon to an iSi canister and charge with
two charges of N_2O. Cook the sabayon in the water bath
for 45 minutes. Keep warm until ready to use.

CHICKEN JUS

Makes about 1 kg

24 g grapeseed oil
1¹/₂ carrots, peeled and chopped
1¹/₂ onions, chopped
2 celery stalks, chopped
30 g tomato paste
1.25 kg dry red wine
7 kg chicken wings
2 kg chicken legs
500 g chicken feet

Preheat the oven to 245°C/475°F. Heat the oil in a large pot over high heat. When the oil just starts to smoke, add the carrots, onions, and celery and cook, stirring occasionally, until the vegetables are softened and browned, about 12 minutes. Add the tomato paste and continue to cook, stirring frequently until well toasted, about 5 minutes. Add the wine and deglaze the pan, scraping up any bits that may have stuck to the bottom of the pot. Bring the wine to a simmer and reduce by half. Remove the pot from heat and set aside. Spread the chicken wings and legs in a single layer on four unlined baking sheets. Roast in the oven until caramelized and deep brown, about 45 minutes. Drain and discard any rendered fat. Scrape the wings and legs into a clean large pot. Add the chicken feet and enough cold water to generously cover. Heat over high heat and bring to a simmer. Skim and discard any impurities that may rise to the surface. Turn the heat to low and add the cooked vegetable mixture to the pot. Continue to simmer, skimming occasionally, for 8 hours. Strain the jus through a chinois and transfer to a clean large saucepan. Bring to a simmer over medium heat. Turn the heat to low and gently simmer until reduced to 1 kg. Reserve in an airtight container, refrigerated, for up to 1 week.

CHICKEN STOCK

Makes about 2.5 kg

3.5 kg chicken necks and backs
1 white onion, diced 5 cm (2 inches)
1 celery stalk, diced 5 cm (2 inches)
5 sprigs thyme

Put the chicken necks and backs in a large pot. Cover generously with cold water. Drain and discard the water. Repeat the rinsing process two times. After the third rinse, drain and cover with cold water. Heat over medium heat and bring to a simmer. Skim and discard any impurities that may rise to the surface. Add the onion, celery, and thyme to the pot and turn the heat to low. Continue to simmer the stock, skimming occasionally, for 6 hours. Strain the stock through a chinois. Reserve in an airtight container, refrigerated, for up to 3 days, or frozen for up to 1 month.

CHICKEN STOCK SLURRY

Makes about 200 g

180 g Chicken Stock (below left)
3 sprigs thyme
3 cloves garlic, crushed
13 g cornstarch
3 g salt

Heat two-thirds of the chicken stock, thyme, and garlic cloves in a saucepan over medium heat. Bring the stock to a boil. Whisk the cornstarch and remaining stock together in a bowl until the mixture forms a thick slurry, without any lumps. Slowly whisk the cornstarch slurry into the boiling stock. Continue to whisk until the simmering stock thickens and the starch cooks out, about 1 minute. Season the slurry with the salt and strain through a chinois. Reserve the slurry in an airtight container, refrigerated, for up to 3 days. When ready to use, gently heat the slurry in a saucepan over low heat until warmed through.

CITRUS BEURRE BLANC

Makes about 300 g

200 g dry white wine
92 g orange juice
50 g grapefruit juice
250 g butter, cubed
5 g lemon juice
2 g salt

Heat the wine to a simmer in a saucepan over medium heat. Turn the heat to low and simmer the wine until reduced by three-quarters. Add the orange and grapefruit juices to the pan. Return to a simmer and reduce to a syruplike consistency. Slowly whisk in the butter while maintaining the emulsion. Once fully incorporated, add the lemon juice and salt. Keep warm.

FISH FUMET

Makes about 2 kg

2.25 kg white fish bones, fins and bloodlines removed,
    cut into 7.5-cm (3-inch) pieces
25 g grapeseed oil
175 g leek, white and light green parts only, sliced
150 g button mushrooms, sliced
1 celery stalk, sliced
2 shallots, sliced
1 fennel bulb, sliced
400 g dry white wine
1 bay leaf
About 3 kg ice cubes

Cover the bones with ice water in an airtight container
and let purge overnight. Heat the oil in a large pot over
medium heat. Add the leek, mushrooms, celery, shallots,
and fennel and sweat until softened and without any
color, about 7 minutes. Add the wine to the pan and
bring to a simmer. Reduce until almost dry. Drain the fish
bones well from the soaking water and transfer to the
pan with the bay leaf. Place enough ice cubes in the pan
to generously cover the bones and vegetables. Continue
to cook until the ice melts, then bring the liquid to a
simmer. Skim and discard any impurities that rise to the
surface. Continue to simmer the stock for an additional
30 minutes, while skimming occasionally. Remove the
pan from the heat and let sit at room temperature for
10 minutes. Strain the stock through a chinois and again
through cheesecloth. Reserve in an airtight container,
refrigerated, for up to 3 days, or frozen for up to 1 month.

LEMON MAYONNAISE

Makes about 200 g

1 egg yolk
25 g lemon juice
5 g Dijon mustard
190 g Lemon Oil (page 284)
Salt

Combine the egg yolk, lemon juice, and mustard in
a food processor and start to blend. While blending,
slowly add the lemon oil to emulsify together. Season
the mayonnaise with salt. Reserve the mayonnaise in an
airtight container, refrigerated, for up to 1 week.

LOBSTER STOCK

Makes about 2 kg

4.5 kg lobster bodies
100 g grapeseed oil
2 onions, sliced
175 g leek, white and light green parts only, sliced
1 fennel bulb, sliced
1 carrot, peeled and sliced
2 celery stalks, sliced
200 g tomato paste
100 g brandy
400 g dry white wine
5 sprigs thyme
About 3 kg ice cubes

Remove and discard the outer top shells of the lobster
bodies with the antennae. Using a large spoon, scrape
and discard the gills from the sides of the bodies.
Remove and discard the entrails. Quarter the cleaned
bodies. Heat the oil in a large pot over high heat. When
the oil just starts to smoke, add the lobster bodies to
the pot. Roast the bodies, turning occasionally, until
deeply caramelized on all sides, about 7 minutes. Turn
the heat to medium and add the onions, leek, fennel,
carrot, and celery. Cook, stirring occasionally, until the
vegetables are soft, about 15 minutes. Add the tomato
paste and toast, stirring frequently, about 5 minutes.
Add the brandy and deglaze the pot. Bring the brandy
to a simmer and reduce until almost dry. Then add the
wine, bring it to a simmer, and reduce until almost dry.
Add enough ice cubes to generously cover. Bring the
stock to a simmer. Skim and discard any impurities that
may rise to the surface. Add the thyme and simmer the
stock for 30 minutes, skimming occasionally. Strain
the stock through a chinois and again through cheesecloth. Reserve in an airtight container, refrigerated, for
up to 3 days, or frozen for up to 1 month.

MAYONNAISE

Makes about 230 g

1 egg yolk
15 g lemon juice
200 g grapeseed oil
Salt

Combine the yolk and lemon juice in a food processor.
While blending, slowly add the oil and continue to blend
until fully emulsified. Season with salt. Reserve the
mayonnaise in an airtight container, refrigerated, for
up to 1 week.

MOREL CREAM

Makes about 325 g

25 g butter
125 g cremini mushrooms, sliced
350 g cream
5 g dried morels
2 sprigs thyme
Salt

Heat the butter in a saucepan over medium heat until foamy but not browned. Add the cremini mushrooms. Cook, stirring occasionally, until the mushrooms are softened and slightly caramelized, about 8 minutes. Add the cream, morels, and thyme. Heat to a simmer and remove the pan from the heat. Season with salt. Let the cream cool to room temperature and transfer to an airtight container. Refrigerate and infuse the cream overnight. Strain the cream through a chinois and reserve in an airtight container, refrigerated, for up to 5 days.

PARMESAN FOAM

Makes about 300 g

15 g butter
1 shallot, sliced
60 g dry white wine
120 g Chicken Stock (page 303)
125 g Parmesan, cubed 2.5 cm (1 inch),
  plus 20 g grated
200 g cream
Lime juice
Salt
Cayenne

Prepare an ice bath. Heat the butter in a saucepan over medium heat until foamy but not browned. Add the shallot and sweat, stirring occasionally, until translucent, about 5 minutes. Add the wine and bring to a simmer. Reduce the wine until almost dry. Add the stock and cubed Parmesan to the pan. Bring to a simmer and turn the heat to low. Continue to simmer, stirring occasionally to prevent the cheese from sticking to the bottom of the pan, until the cheese is softened, about 30 minutes. Add the heavy cream to the pan and turn the heat to medium, bringing the cream to a boil. Strain the mixture through cheesecloth. Using an immersion blender, blend in the grated cheese until melted and fully incorporated. Season with lime juice, salt, and cayenne. Chill the foam over the ice bath. Reserve in an airtight container, refrigerated, for up to 2 days. When ready to serve, gently heat in a saucepan over low heat until warmed through.

PARMESAN SAUCE

Makes about 200 g

1/2 shallot, sliced
2 anchovy fillets
1 clove garlic
2 egg yolks
15 g Parmesan, coarsely grated
15 g pecorino, coarsely grated
2 g Dijon mustard
2 g capers, drained and rinsed
1 g ground white pepper
40 g grapeseed oil
40 g olive oil
5 g lemon juice
7 g white balsamic vinegar
Salt

Combine the shallot, anchovies, garlic, egg yolks, Parmesan, pecorino, mustard, capers, and white pepper in a blender. Puree on high speed until smooth. Turn to low speed and slowly add both oils and blend until emulsified. Add the lemon juice and vinegar. Season with salt and blend until incorporated. Reserve the sauce in an airtight container, refrigerated, for up to 3 days. Before serving, let the sauce sit at room temperature for 30 minutes to temper.

PIG'S HEAD COOKING LIQUID

Makes about 7 kg

7 kg water
170 g dry white wine
1 celery stalk, cut into 5-cm (2-inch) pieces
1 carrot, peeled and cut into 5-cm (2-inch) pieces
1 onion, cut into 5-cm (2-inch) pieces
20 g pink curing salt #1
12 sprigs thyme
12 black peppercorns
2 bay leaves

Combine all of the ingredients for the cooking liquid and stir to dissolve the pink curing salt. Keep refrigerated until ready to use.

POMMERY MAYONNAISE

Makes about 310 g

170 g Mayonnaise (page 304)
70 g Dijon
70 g whole-grain mustard

Combine the mayonnaise and both mustards in a mixing bowl. Whisk to combine.

PORK BRINE

Makes about 5.5 kg

5 kg water
500 g salt
20 g pink curing salt #1

Heat the water in a pot over high heat and bring to a boil.
Remove the pot from the heat and whisk in both salts until
fully dissolved. Let cool to room temperature and reserve
in an airtight container, refrigerated, for up to 3 days.

ROASTED GARLIC CLAM STOCK

Makes about 250 g

50 g olive oil
50 g thinly sliced garlic
240 g clam juice

Prepare an ice bath. Heat the oil in a saucepan over
medium heat and prepare an ice bath. When the oil is
hot, add the garlic and immediately stir to separate the
individual slices. Fry the garlic, stirring occasionally, until
evenly golden brown, about 4 minutes. Immediately add
the clam juice to the pan and bring to a simmer. Once the
stock comes to a simmer, chill the stock over the ice bath.
Reserve in an airtight container, refrigerated, for up to
3 days.

SALSIFY COOKING LIQUID

Makes about 2 kg

2.3 kg water
3 carrots, peeled and chopped 2.5 cm (1 inch)
2 onions, chopped 2.5 cm (1 inch)
2 celery stalks, chopped 2.5 cm (1 inch)
175 g leek, pale white and green parts only, chopped
    2.5 cm (1 inch)
1 lemon, quartered
60 g chives, coarsely chopped
10 sprigs tarragon
10 sprigs flat-leaf parsley
8 g salt

Heat the water, carrots, onions, celery, and leek in a large
saucepan over medium heat. Combine the lemon and
herbs in a large heatproof container. When the water is
at a boil, pour the water and vegetables over the lemon
and herbs. Season the cooking liquid with the salt and
let cool to room temperature. Transfer the liquid to an
airtight container and refrigerate overnight or up to
3 days. Strain the cooking liquid through a chinois
before using.

SHEEP'S MILK YOGURT SAUCE

Makes about 170 g

170 g sheep's milk yogurt
Salt

In a mixing bowl, whisk the yogurt until completely
smooth. Season with salt. Let the yogurt sit at room
temperature for 30 minutes before serving.

YOGURT SAUCE

Makes about 180 g

60 g crème fraîche
60 g Greek yogurt
60 g whole milk yogurt
Salt

Combine the crème fraîche and the yogurts in a mixing
bowl and whisk together until fully incorporated. Season
with salt.

ACKNOWLEDGMENTS

Connie Chung, who leads our culinary research and development for both Eleven Madison Park and The NoMad, and her assistant Sarah Jo, were an essential part of the team behind this book. Testing and writing recipes for months on end, sourcing materials for our photo shoots, and so much more. . . . Their professionalism and skill made this cookbook a reality.

Aaron Ginsberg, our director of strategic development—who had the impossible task of herding together our incredible, yet sometimes dysfunctional family—motivated us to stay on schedule, inspired us to dig deep and put forward our best work, and made sure this book is truly a reflection of what the restaurant aspires to be each day

Amy Livingston, our exceedingly patient assistant, kept us organized at work and held us accountable in life.

James Kent, executive chef and one of the creative forces behind the food at The NoMad, spent endless hours deliberating and deciding which recipes to include in these pages and worked tirelessly each day to make sure the food was as delicious in the restaurant as it is beautiful in this book. He always makes certain we have a little bit of hip-hop in our lives.

Jeffrey Tascarella, our well-dressed general manager and arbiter of cool at The NoMad, brings a calm presence that makes our lively (and sometimes wild) restaurant work. His ability to embrace and embody the personality of The NoMad through the words he has written for this book is unmatched.

Mark Welker, our executive pastry chef and the greatest baker we've ever known, is responsible for all things sweet in this book. Along with his sous chef Bradley Ray, his commitment to excellence influences and inspires everyone in our company.

Our chef de cuisine, Brian Lockwood, and our executive sous chef, Ashley Abodeely, not only run our kitchens each night, but also do so with integrity and humility. They are two of the most gifted leaders we've ever worked with.

Laura Wagstaff, our events director, embodies the culture of our company more than any other, and reminds us that why and how we approach our work are more important than the work itself.

Thomas Pastuszak, our wine director, has passion and knowledge matched only by his love of hospitality and devotion to education.

Leo Robitschek, who runs the cocktail programs at Eleven Madison Park and The NoMad, has been working with us since the day we met back in 2006. In addition to being a member of our family, he is a truly brilliant bartender. What he has built on Twenty-Eighth and Broadway is nothing short of spectacular, so much so that we had to include a dedicated cocktail book as part of this one to fully tell the story of The NoMad.

David Black, our longtime book agent, provided the encouragement and love vital to bringing this book to life.

Aaron Wehner and Julie Bennett of Ten Speed Press embraced our idea for this book from the very beginning, acting as sounding boards, providing creative solutions, and collaborating with us every step of the way.

Reynald Philipe and Antoine Ricardou of be-pôles, brought playfulness and a clear understanding of our vision to the book's design.

Our incredibly talented team, past and present, that has impacted The NoMad since its opening, including: Abram Bissell, Alex Meyer, Alex Pfaffenbach, Anne Provost, Aubrey Hustead, Becky Quan, Benjy Leibowitz, Billy Peelle, Brandon Laterveer, Camilla Warner, Chris Flint, Chris Lowder, Christen Sturkie, Erin Carr, Jen Shuman, Jenna Robinson, Jill Edwards, John Taube III, Jonathan Lind, Joseph Cheuvront, Josh Harnden, Juan "Bautista" Taveras, Julian Sherman, Julianna Devlin, Kirk Kelewae, Kristen Millar, Leo Robitschek, Marcia Regen, Mark Bartley, Mary Helen Crafton, Mike Reilly, Mike Rellergert, Natasha McIrvin, Nicolas Mouchel, Nora McTwigan, Pietro Collina, Sandra DiCapua, Stacy Snyder, Toni Suppa, Vincent Chao, and Zach Schulz.

Our colleagues turned friends who run the hotel side of The NoMad: Meredith Morgan, Steve Rachmat, Mike Cashman, Brian Finkelman, and team.

Jake Lamstein, Jeremy Sillman, Blake Danner, Seth Dubner, Tanner Campbell, Joe Morales, and the rest of Andrew Zobler's team at Sydell . . . building The NoMad alongside them has been a true pleasure.

Our families, Frank and Juliette Guidara and Brigitte, Roland, Colette, Vivienne, and Justine Humm, who have always been by our sides, through good times and bad.

ABOUT THE AUTHORS

DANIEL HUMM is the chef/co-owner of Eleven Madison Park and The NoMad Hotel. His cuisine is focused on the locally sourced ingredients of New York, with an emphasis on simplicity, purity, and seasonal flavors. A native of Switzerland, he was exposed to food at a very young age and began working in kitchens at the age of fourteen. From there he spent time in some of the finest Swiss hotels and restaurants before earning his first Michelin star at the age of twenty-four. In 2003, Daniel moved to the United States to become the executive chef at Campton Place in San Francisco, where he received four stars from the *San Francisco Chronicle*. Three years later, he moved to New York to become the executive chef at Eleven Madison Park.

WILL GUIDARA is the restaurateur/co-owner of Eleven Madison Park and The NoMad Hotel. A native of Sleepy Hollow, New York, and the son of a lifelong restaurateur, he has been immersed in the restaurant industry since the age of thirteen. He is a graduate of the School of Hotel Administration at Cornell University, and an alumnus of Danny Meyer's Union Square Hospitality Group.

In 2006, Will became the general manager of Eleven Madison Park, where he spearheaded the transformation of the restaurant from a French brasserie to a fine dining destination. Will is also the co-founder of the Welcome Conference, an annual hospitality-driven event held in Manhattan that brings together the best minds from the world of hospitality for a day-long discussion.

Under Humm and Guidara's leadership, Eleven Madison Park received four stars from the *New York Times*, earned three Michelin stars, and was given a coveted spot on the San Pellegrino list of the World's 50 Best Restaurants. The restaurant has also received six James Beard Foundation awards, including Outstanding Chef and Outstanding Restaurant in America. In 2011, Humm and Guidara purchased Eleven Madison Park and, in early 2012, went on to open the food and beverage spaces at The NoMad Hotel. At The NoMad, they have received a three-star review from the *New York Times*, one Michelin star, a James Beard Foundation award, and landed on the San Pellegrino list of the World's 100 Best Restaurants. They are also the authors of *Eleven Madison Park: The Cookbook* and *I Love New York: Ingredients and Recipes*.

———

Born and raised in Italy, FRANCESCO TONELLI is a photographer and a food stylist based in New York City. He has worked as a chef in Europe, the United States, and Canada for more than twenty years and served as an associate professor in culinary arts at the Culinary Institute of America in Hyde Park, New York, before stepping behind the camera and taking full charge of the design, styling, and photography of food. Among his work, he was the photographer for *Eleven Madison Park: The Cookbook* and *I Love New York: Ingredients and Recipes*. Learn more at www.francescotonelli.com.

INDEX

Published in the United States by Ten Speed Press,
an imprint of the Crown Publishing Group, a division
of Penguin Random House LLC, New York.
www.crownpublishing.com
www.tenspeed.com

Ten Speed Press and the Ten Speed Press colophon are
registered trademarks of Penguin Random House LLC.

Library of Congress Cataloging-in-Publication Data
Humm, Daniel.
  The NoMad cookbook / Daniel Humm, Will Guidara,
and Leo Robitschek.–
First edition.
     pages cm
  Includes index.
1. Cooking. 2. NoMad Hotel (New York, N.Y.) I. Guidara,
Will. II.
Robitschek, Leo. III. Title.
  TX714.H8455 2015
  641.59747'1–dc23
                        2015007694

Hardcover ISBN: 978-1-60774-822-9
eBook ISBN: 978-1-60774-823-6

Printed in China

Design by be-pôles

10 9 8 7 6 5 4 3 2 1

First Edition